In the Roundest of Places

BY

RICK LYDON

ISBN: 1494977788
ISBN-13: 978-1494977788

DEDICATION

For Carol,
whose love and support
provides meaning and direction
for my life's journey.

CONTENTS

ACKNOWLEDGEMENTS

I would like to thank the following people
for their support and assistance on this project:

My amazing family, especially Carol and Jenna,
My incredible colleagues at the ALT School,
All of the inspiring young people with whom
I had the privilege to work with at the ALT School,
My friends and colleagues in the Nashua School District,
The staff at Dartmouth Hitchcock Hospital
and St. Joseph's Hospital Rehabilitation Unit,
My brilliant professors and classmates
at Antioch New England University,
My generous friends at SpringBrook Farm,
And my deepest gratitude to Wally Lamb
whose powerful words have changed lives, including mine.

This work would not have come into being
without all of you.

Except for my immediate family,
all the names in this story have been changed
to respect their privacy.

PART ONE

1

WHERE TO BEGIN . . .

"Come in and take a seat," I said, gesturing toward several empty chairs in the classroom. It seemed like a perfectly reasonable request.

Kimberly remained planted in the doorway, frozen, unable to decide what to do. She folded her arms tightly and gave me her *disgusted* look.

"Suck my dick," she replied flatly as she gazed past me, or should I say through me, trying to survey the reactions of her classmates in the room.

"Excuse me?" I asked, remaining calm, offering her a second chance. It was what I called a *do-over,* an opportunity for a wayward student to do the right thing.

"YOU HEARD ME!" Kimberly snarled. "I said, SUCK MY DICK!" Kimberly's eyes glared directly at me now, as defiant as her words.

I have to confess that she was not the first young lady to direct this particular obscenity at me. But I had learned to balance my outrage with a certain degree of amusement at her absurd misuse of language. In my world, it was not unusual for this vulgarity to spew from the mouth of an angry female adolescent, and I was now seasoned enough to know I had to carefully measure my response against the desired outcome.

I could never be absolutely sure if the student indeed suffered from a gender identity problem, or if it was just a penultimate expression of frustrated penis envy (pun intended.) Of course, a trained psychologist would most likely explain the incident as a desperate attempt by the perpetrator to use shock value as a method to regain a position of power. In Kimberly's case however, she might be merely repeating something she heard from one of her mother's many boyfriends. It could even have been suggestively directed at her as recently as last night. One never knew.

Standing near the doorway to my classroom in that particularly heated moment, there was certainly no way for me to know the source of her pain. Kimberly quite obviously had absolutely no interest in doing her schoolwork that day, so I wrote up the required red slip and spoke calmly into the intercom letting the office know she was coming.

The situation called for a simple and direct response.

"Go," was all I said to her as I walked over to the classroom door to facilitate her departure. She grabbed the red slip from my outstretched hand and I heard her muttering "Fucking asshole" as she stormed down the hall toward the school's main office.

No matter how many times it happened, I always hated to send someone to the office. It underscored my own failure to reach a student, to handle a situation the right way, or to provide whatever supports the student needed in that circumstance. But on some days, there was no other choice. I could lose the student, or I could lose the whole class. And so, on this particular day, when Kimberly apparently had no intention of doing any schoolwork and was determined to have the rest of the class join her, I chose the easy out: I sent her to the office.

Kimberly had been growing increasingly disruptive and inappropriate of late. It was obvious she was in a tough place and struggling to deal with something. It spilled over into the classroom regularly. I was not ready to give up on her though; we still had to somehow survive several months together until summer vacation. I had checked off a box on the red slip asking to have her parent called. I was hoping to elicit some support, clear the air, and come to some sort of truce, if not resolution.

I had gotten used to putting up with a lot of inappropriate language from my students at the ALT, our name for the alternative school, but I still tried to teach them how to be polite and respectful even in the face of a heated disagreement. My students knew there was a line that could not be crossed without serious consequences. Anything of graphic sexual nature, racial or ethnic slurs, swearing directly at teachers or adults, threatening violence – I had no tolerance for any of that.

"If you talk like that on the job, any job," I often told them, "you'll be fired on the spot and immediately escorted out the door." I tried to sound authoritative, but of course, I knew this particular fact was not entirely true.

Could it only have been a few years earlier? It felt like it happened in another lifetime. I was sitting at a long conference table in a clean and polished office building. I can't even remember the exact purpose for the meeting but it must have been important because all three shift managers were there, including myself. Our company had just recently lured a young man away from our chief competitor, and now suddenly, with the stroke of an internal memo, here he was, appointed by the powers that be, as our new boss. We were all still getting to know him as we dealt with this unexpected turn of events.

This newly hired superstar had been using the F-word frequently in his conversations around the office, but having been recently anointed king, everyone was willing to let him make his own bed and lay in it. "With a mouth like that, we'll see how long *this* guy lasts" was the word at the water bubbler. His aggressive personality was certainly not scoring any social points for him around the office.

Anyway, during this one particular meeting, in the middle of a conversation about customers and office politics, the new hotshot declared, "You might as well just cut off my dick and hand it to me on a plate!"

An uneasy silence descended upon the room. All three veteran managers looked at him, none of us knowing quite how to respond to his remark. In contrast to our recently acquired boss, each of us had over twenty years of experience at the respectable old company. We were all familiar with colorful language, but none of us had ever heard *that* expression before, in the office or elsewhere.

I was personally offended, not just by the graphic nature of this particular remark, but also by the thought that *this* was the kind of person that signaled success to the top executives who were running our company. From now on, F-bombs would not only be permitted; in fact, they might become required vocabulary for future management promotions. Swearing at work might not be grounds for dismissal after all. Indeed, it might even indicate a source of immeasurable political power around the office.

The memories drifting through my head were interrupted, as the classroom banter grew loud enough to regain my attention. Shifting back into teacher-mode, I began to move about the room calmly, confidently, helping students complete the day's assignment. With Kimberly gone, there was no more swearing. We had all moved on, and the class was getting some schoolwork accomplished. It was just another school day after all.

Near the end of the day, one of the classroom aides appeared in my doorway announcing she was there to take over the class for me. Kimberly's mother was in the office and the principal thought I might like to be present for the conversation. I jogged down to the office and joined a meeting already in progress. The guidance counselor and the vice-principal responsible for behavior were already speaking with her mom. The school nurse was present also to provide her input and professional insight into possible medication issues that may influence a student's behavior.

"She's a total bitch at home, too," Mom was shaking her head as she spoke. "We really haven't been getting along at all lately. She's always so nasty to me – I don't know what to do. I *hate* her, I just *hate* her!"

The four of us could not believe what we were hearing - mom publicly declaring her loathing for her own daughter. "And her father is a complete asshole," Mom continued. "Him and his bimbo girlfriend let her get away with everything. I'm the only one who ever tries to set any limits. That's why she hates me and says she wants to run away or die."

"She's been saying she wants to die?" asked the nurse. We all had concerned looks on our faces now at this mention of a suicidal threat.

"Well, she's so moody and explosive. She says things like that all the time for attention, you know how she is." Mom's body language became defensive, as if she thought we might slap her. "I don't think she really means it," she finally concluded, glancing down at the cell phone in her lap.

"Why not?" I thought to myself. You just told us you *hate* her.

I decided to venture in. "Before we can deal with her language and her inappropriate behavior, we need to be sure Kimberly is safe. She needs to be evaluated by professionals as to whether or not she really is suicidal," I offered. "Everything else takes second place next to that." Everyone, and eventually even mom, agreed.

So it was decided that mom would bring her to the hospital and have her daughter evaluated by the crisis team. As professional educators, we were relieved to know that the official protocol for a suicidal threat would be followed. It would have to be sometime later in the week though, Kimberley's mom insisted. Tonight was not a good time; there was supposedly something already on her calendar.

"Are they open on weekends?" she asked innocently.

In response to our protests, mom finally agreed to keep her home from school the next day and promised to bring her to the emergency room the following morning. She would tell Kimberly they were going clothes shopping together at the mall, but she would bring her to the hospital instead. Kimberly never missed out on an opportunity to get something new to wear, mom cleverly informed us.

"Why don't we offer classes for parents?" I wondered to myself.

Kimberly began meeting with a counselor on a regular basis after that, and she was put on one of the anti-depressant medications. Her mood, her behavior and her schoolwork all improved, and she could occasionally be seen smiling, not as much as we would like, but more than before. She and

I eventually eased into a place of coexistence in the classroom, and somehow we managed to get through the rest of the school year.

A few months later, at the end-of-the-year awards ceremony, I noticed Kimberly's mom standing off to the side of the crowded room. When the ceremony concluded I went up to her and shook her hand.

"Congratulations!" I said.

She stared blankly at me as if she had absolutely no clue why I was congratulating her.

"Hang in there," I told her. "Life with teenagers is never easy." She just smiled and nodded. We looked over across the room and saw Kimberly bawling her eyes out like a little baby among the small group of students.

"She doesn't want the school year to end," said mom. "She LOVES it here."

"Nobody would ever believe this," I thought. And for the hundredth time, I said to myself, "I really should be writing all this down."

And so eventually, I did just that: I wrote it all down, as best as I could remember, every bit of it. The truth is, I've known I had a story to tell for quite some time, I just didn't know exactly who the story was *for* until now. I needed time and people and events to come together in a certain way to bring it into focus and make it happen.

But I have to warn you: this is not just one story – it's a bunch of stories that are somehow all intertwined and rolled into one. It's more of a journey than a story, except that it doesn't have a beginning, middle or end. It weaves in and out of itself so that you don't always know where one part leaves off and another begins. My story is messy, just like real life.

And that's OK with me. It's how I know you are going to understand what I'm about to tell you. I know your life is messy: all of our lives get messy from time to time. Without the messiness, I may have never been able to tell my story, let alone grasp some of its significance.

Now, I say I am finally ready to *TELL* you my story, but the truth is I really need to *GIVE* you my story, although it's not at all clear why I should give you anything at all. I certainly don't owe you anything. But forces deep inside me are trying to make sense of the last few years, searching for order amidst the chaos. If I can organize what I have been living into words, it may help clarify the big picture, for myself, for others, and perhaps most importantly, even for you.

My story is really all I have to give you right now. It's all I can do. I hope it will be enough.

2

NOT JUST FLIPPING HAMBURGERS

I have not always been a teacher.

Like so many others, I have lived another life. My driver's license would still identify me as Rick Lydon and my DNA was undeniably the same, but I was a totally different person. Once upon a time, I had a title, a place in the organizational chart. I had my own desk, a parking spot, and employees who reported directly to me. I wore ties every day: bright pink power ties, no less.

I had spent many years learning the printing trade: busting my hump, working long hours, rising up the corporate ladder to a position of customer service manager for a large, international corporation. It was a 24-hour, 7-day operation. Our business was financial printing, and I had become one of the bosses, the Night Manager, to be exact.

No, we did not print money, although I often told people we did because it was easier to explain. We brought companies public, which meant helping them to issue stock and raise huge sums of money. We also assisted with their regulatory filings with the Securities and Exchange Commission, their quarterly and annual reports, mergers, acquisitions, and communications with their stockholders, stuff like that. It was pretty intense work. I spent most of my waking hours in that mysterious and exciting world where insider trading could, and sometimes did, take place.

It was not like this was part of some childhood dream or anything. I had applied for the job on a lark. We had been living and working in New Hampshire for a few years since our wedding, and Carol had just given birth to our fourth child in five-and-a-half years. I needed to make more money, but I told myself there was no way I was going to commute 60 miles every day into Boston. Nothing was worth the aggravation of fighting the nightmare of daily rush hour traffic. I convinced myself to go to the interview just for the heck of it. Job interviews were always good experience to improve one's communication skills.

I met with both the vice-president and president of the Boston office in one of their impressive conference rooms. I must have come across as extremely nervous because they told me to relax and spoke about how tense job interviews tend to be. I told them I was not the least bit nervous about the job interview, but that I had a vasectomy scheduled for the next day. I was much more nervous about that. By the end of the interview, they offered me the job, along with plenty of free fatherly advice.

Financial printing can be an intense business to work in. After a few months into the job, my boss took me aside when I had mixed up some documents during an all-night stock deal. He looked me sternly in the eye as he spelled out to me the huge sums of money that were involved if I screwed up the filing and the package missed its flight to Washington. The stock market could open without the documents being on file at the Securities and Exchange Commission, and the parties involved could lose millions and millions of dollars. His shoulders tensed and he clutched his fists as he told me it would all be *my fault*, just because I messed up copying some documents or accidentally left something out.

"DO YOU GET THE PICTURE?" he glared at me. I got the picture - no mistakes allowed here, not even little ones, or I'll be out on the street looking for a new job in no time. Did I tell you it was intense?

Over the course of twenty years, I worked hard, received promotions and increased responsibilities, and acquired a good deal of recognition and satisfaction for my achievements. I was averaging 50 to 60 hours a week, not including my commute time. The paycheck and benefits were good, too. I was able to provide comfortably for my wife and four children and put a little aside for retirement. We didn't live a lavish lifestyle, but money was definitely not a problem. I felt proud of my accomplishments and the respect I was earning as a leader within the company. I had *arrived.*

Now, this company I worked for was one of the oldest and most stable and respected corporations in America. When you got a job there, you pictured yourself retiring there. (And many did.) Every once in a while, someone would get laid off or even fired, and there were always rumors about affairs or other goings on. Some of the rumors were even true, like the one about the messenger who was caught trafficking a little cocaine along with our printed documents. But that was unusual. Most people there were good people, hard workers, 'in it for life'.

Even me. After a few years I thought I was a 'lifer'. I'd never be able to make this kind of money elsewhere and I was pretty good at what I was doing, so it became comfortable. So what if the stress was overwhelming at times? So what if I had to pull all-nighters when a big deal was going on? So what if I had a 60-mile commute each way and I was burning through cars and gasoline? And so what if I was working the crazy nightshift, only seeing my family on weekends? What's a little stress when you're financially comfortable? It was just part of the job description.

Looking back on it, I am surprised at what my family and I endured to avoid upsetting the applecart. But then again, as I gained experience and seniority, I was also starting to get some perks. I got to manage people. I went to workshops in Chicago, Dallas and New York. Eventually, I became a workshop presenter in addition to my regular job. It kept things interesting, and the paychecks kept coming. Time passed, years in fact, without me even noticing the person I had become. With two kids in college and two more expected to go in the next few years, I was firmly on the hook. What could I do? I was the Dad, the provider. I had to suck it up and take care of my family. That's what Dads do.

I can still vividly remember my first visit to New York City, the location of our corporate headquarters. My hotel room looked out at the famous World Trade Center across the street. I went to the window of my room on the 54th floor and I still had to strain my neck to peer up to the top of the twin towers across the street. I tried to describe the impressive sight to my young son over the phone. It's amazing how some simple little moments like that can come back to haunt us for the rest of our lives.

I had been summoned to New York to teach a class to newly recruited customer service representatives: they were mostly young and had no idea what they were doing. I had become the expert, the old pro. At the end of class one day, I casually asked them if they knew what it was that our company actually did? Did any of them know? There were the usual answers: SEC filings, printing and dissemination of financial documents, communicating with customers.

"Yes, yes, yes, but what is it that we *REALLY* do?" I pressed on. They looked at me, confused.

Finally with a bit of prompting, I got one of them to admit that we helped companies raise money.

"Yes, that's right, *money*, a lot of money. And what do our customers *DO* with all that money?" I pressed on.

They expand their businesses, someone said.

"Yes, they do. And what kind of businesses do we help?" At this point my words were on fire and I had gained everybody's attention.

"All kinds of businesses" was their response.

"Right. All kinds of businesses. We are helping drug and biotech companies find cures for diseases like cancer, Alzheimer's and AIDS. We are helping to create millions of jobs all around the world. We are helping to build universities, hospitals and schools. We are helping develop new technology that will change the way our world works and communicates. *WE* are the ones at the very forefront of all the changes that are occurring in our culture. *DON'T YOU GET IT?*"

All eyes were upon me now as my voice cracked with passion.

"We are not just flipping hamburgers here, people. We are doing important, important work! *You* are doing important work. And you're being well compensated and taken care of besides. *You* are one of the lucky people! *You* can actually have it all! There are not many people who can say that about their jobs." There was a dramatic pause as everyone stared at me. "And don't ever forget that when you are dealing with our customers!"

There was silence for a few seconds. Then they started looking around the room at each other. I'm not sure if they thought I was crazy or that all of a sudden they were feeling pretty good about what they were doing. Maybe it was a little of both. But everybody in that room knew that something special had just happened, including me. It was another one of those moments I will never forget.

In that instant, I knew I was meant to teach. I wasn't sure where my path was going to take me, but I knew I had just taken a turn. And it felt good inside, *real* good. Whatever my future held in store, somehow it would involve me teaching somebody something.

3

HATCHING A PLAN

You can lie to yourself sometimes. Little lies. Sometimes even big lies. We all do it. Some people are naturals; they get so good at lying to themselves they can even forget what the truth really is.

People lie about their relationships and affairs; they lie about money; they lie about what they have done and what they think they can do. They are especially sneaky and deceitful when it comes to how they really feel about other people, or even how they feel about themselves. Ask any psychologist.

It turns out that in business, especially in corporate America, there is a lot of lying going on. I know because I got sucked into some of it too.

For quite a while, I almost believed that running training programs in the corporate world would be enough to keep me satisfied. It was fun and challenging. I told myself I could do this indefinitely. Of course that attractive paycheck still held a lot of power over me too. I tried to see myself as a 'lifer', working for the company until I was ready to retire.

In the corporate environment, opportunities for promotions arise on a regular basis, and when they did, I would think, yeah, I could do that job easily with all my experience. I had a record that included a strong work ethic and dedication to the company, not to mention my excellent people skills. I was the perfect candidate for the position, I thought, and I wasn't even lying all that much. Why not throw my hat into the ring along with the others for an even bigger paycheck with a private office. So I did.

Then I would drive into work, be called into the vice-president's office, and find out they were offering the job to one of the young guys I had trained. I should consider it a compliment, I was told, because I trained people so well. This happened not once, but several times. I began to notice how other "older" employees were also getting the shaft. Experience didn't matter; kissing up did. Playing golf mattered. Who you had lunch with mattered. The company said we were all like family, but it sure didn't feel like family, at least not any family I wanted to belong to.

I hated feeling bitter about the company that had been so good to me when I was younger. I had enjoyed job security and financial stability for years. I had been successful coordinating stock offerings and mergers and acquisitions. The future had seemed promising. But for some reason, I was no longer on the rise. I had unwittingly somehow become dead wood.

It finally got to me. One Friday before I was scheduled to go on vacation, I was once again called in to the VP's office to be told that I was not going to be offered a high-level management position, which I felt I deserved and was well qualified for. Instead, they were offering it to one of my former assistants. It became crystal clear to me: I was stuck in my current position with no hope for promotion. Some invisible force was blocking me from moving any higher up the corporate ladder. This was it; I had indeed arrived at my final corporate destination.

For me, the most frustrating part of my predicament was that I did not know what obstacle was blocking my path. Was it an individual who disliked me or felt threatened by me? Had I not gained some critical training along the way that I didn't even know I lacked? Had I misread all the cues about my stellar performance over the years? Had I become totally paranoid and were all of my coworkers lying to me? I was a mess, totally devastated. I felt like a trapped animal with no way out.

I went on vacation the next day as planned, camping with my wife, Carol. We sat by a lake in the North Woods for days. Very, very long days. Some vacation! I had never felt so low in my life. I kept thinking, what could I have done differently? Why was life so unfair? What was I going to do with the rest of my life? How could I go back to work after the vacation? Carol became my lifejacket, the only thing I could cling to as I drowned in my river of despair.

Looking back on this time is still painful for me today. But now I also know it was probably one of the best things to ever happen to me. I guess that's the thing about life-changing events. You just don't know how it is all going to play out. It could turn out awful. It could turn out great. Or it could just turn out unlike anything you ever imagined.

Together, Carol and I came up with a plan – and this is where the lying really starts to come in. I would go back to work. I had to. We still had the kids' tuition bills and we badly needed the paycheck. But we decided I needed more from my job than security and a good paycheck. I needed to become a new person, to re-make myself. I would begin to live a secret life unknown to any of my coworkers. I would go back to school in September and begin working toward a Masters degree in Education. I knew it would take some time, but I would become a teacher, and there was nothing the company would be able to do to stop me. I would take back the power, control my own destiny.

The plan was perfect! With me as a teacher, Carol and I would have all our vacations together since she was already a kindergarten teacher. I wouldn't have to work nights anymore. No more long commutes into Boston. We could enjoy long summer vacations traveling across the country. And I would be teaching instead of bearing witness to the bloodbath of corporate backstabbing at endless meetings.

I figured it would take me a few years to get my degree and teaching certification while working and going to school part time. And by the time I was ready to make the move, the kids should all be through with college and I wouldn't be so dependent on the paycheck. Carol and I fantasized about the places we would visit and how we could both live comfortably (if not lavishly) on two teachers' salaries. Hope was not lost.

I had a plan. I had a plan. Thank God, Almighty, I had a plan!

4

TO SIR, WITH …

I couldn't believe how nervous I was. What was I doing? Did I look old? Did I have everything I needed? Was I in the right classroom? Would I actually be able to do this?

On the inside, I was an absolute train wreck.

On the outside, I was a hip 47-year-old dude who had decided it was never too late to go back to school. I was a veritable fountain of youth, even if I was sprouting a few grey hairs. Pretty cool, huh? Yeah, right.

The school happened to be the local extension branch of the state university. The course was World Geography. Apparently, teachers had to know where everything in the world was; that meant we all had to study world geography to become certified. Thankfully, the professor was still old enough to be my father, a very "old school" kind of guy. The other students in the class, however, were all in their early twenties at best.

I was a diligent student. If I could bring a company public, surely I could "do" geography. As the class progressed across the globe, the professor would quiz us on naming all the countries, rivers, mountains and major cities in each continent. I found myself practicing my memorization skills on the commute to work each day. Could I name all the countries in Africa before I got off the highway? At work I was drawing maps at my desk and labeling them as I was speaking on the telephone with customers. I was getting 'A's on all my tests and some of my young classmates would ask to copy my notes when they missed a class. I was feeling proud of my smart old self. I can do this, I kept telling myself.

One day in class, I noticed a cute girl across the room was watching me. In fact, she seemed to be staring at me. She definitely was; it was not some middle-aged fantasy thing I was having. Oh my God, she's checking me out, I thought. This was definitely not part of the plan! The next thing I knew, class had ended and she was coming over to me. She was heading straight towards me. I couldn't believe this was happening. Now don't make a fool of yourself, I told myself.

"Excuse me", she began.

I smiled and stammered a "Yes?"

"Did I hear the professor say your last name was 'Lydon'?"

"Uh, yes, that's right," I said, wondering where this was going.

"Do you have a son named Scott?" she asked.

"Why, yes, I do" I sputtered.

"Wow!" she exclaimed. "I graduated high school with him!"

"Oh, really", I replied. Ouch, I thought.

"Tell him Sarah says 'Hi'. Nice to meet you, sir," she said as she scooted out the door.

I felt like an old fool at that moment, that was for sure. But did she have to rub it in and call me *SIR*? That really hurt!

In the end, I passed my first class with flying colors. I was on my way to becoming a teacher. I wasn't too old to think and learn after all. My back-to-school plan had begun. Now I would just need to find a graduate school with a good education program that would fit into my schedule.

And I'm particularly proud to say that, even today, I can still probably name most of the countries in Africa. Yes, sir!

5

MORE THAN A NECKTIE

I was beginning to enjoy the idea that I had a "secret life" away from the office. Sure, I put on the tie, went to meetings, managed my people and continued being the good employee that I had been before. I was still the same old me on the outside. But I knew I had changed and become an imposter. I was not really one of *them* anymore. I had *other* plans.

I had come to terms with the fact that this re-tooling of my professional self was going to be a long, tedious, and expensive process. I searched for courses that would lead to teaching certification that were offered at a time and a place I would be able to take without calling any undue attention to myself. Since I was managing the night shift, I needed to take classes during the day. Sounds simple, right?

I never realized how many colleges offered courses for "older students" who were balancing both jobs and families along with their schooling. But, of course, all *those* programs were offered in the evening while I was working. Not going to work for this undercover career changer.

Then I heard about the Masters of Education program offered at Antioch New England University (ANE). Not only did they offer classes during the day, most of their students were a little more *experienced* than recent college grads. On top of that, Antioch took pride in their "creative" approach to education, which really appealed to my undergrad degree in Fine Art. The down side was their location: it was over an hour out of my way, actually going the opposite direction from work.

Everything worthwhile in life involves some sort of sacrifice. I decided to give it a try. I would enroll as a "special" student and take a couple of courses to see if it would work for me.

My first course at Antioch was called *Conceptual Development and the Child*. As I walked into the classroom, I felt all eyes on me, all female eyes. Not only was I old, I was the only male. I can do this, I told myself. At least there were several women close to my age so I wasn't the only *old* one.

The instructor was a space shot, and I loved her immediately. She wore lots of colorful layers of clothing and scarves and usually a hat from which her long blonde ringlets hung down. And there were boots, always boots, no matter what the rest of the outfit was. Definitely a hippie throwback. She had left New York City to live on a mountaintop in Vermont. She fit into my plan perfectly.

I will always remember that first class. We all sat in a large circle telling our name and what kind of car we drove. Sue drove a VW, Ellen drove a Ford escort. The first Beth drove something large, I think, but the second Beth had a jeep. I can't remember what the third Beth drove. I was having a hard time remembering names since there were over 30 women in the class with me. They all knew I was Rick and I drove a Mazda.

I stuck with it though. I found the content material for the course absolutely fascinating, and the instructor surprisingly brilliant and inspiring. At work I snuck my textbook out whenever I could to read about how the mind works when learning is taking place. I completed writing assignments and reflection essays on my computer at my desk, e-mailing them to myself at home without anyone knowing what I was doing. I told my co-workers I was working on a project for the computer-training program and no one suspected a thing. I was so proud of my covert status.

For one class assignment we each had to teach the class some new skill. I decided to put all the corporate neckties in my closet to some good use. I brought a huge bag of them into class, distributed them to the women, and proceeded to teach them how to tie a tie, a Half-Windsor to be exact. I demonstrated the method taught me by my father and his father before him. I then asked them to follow my instructions to tie their own ties. Some did a fair job considering they had never worn a tie before. Then the professor instructed them to disregard my instructions and tie them any way they wished. In my life, I have never seen so many different ways to wear a necktie. There were headbands and waistbands and bows and ornaments the likes of which I had never seen. And I had to admit, some were wearing their ties in ways that were quite stylish and interesting and totally appropriate for the business world.

I chuckled as I drove to work that night. Never had I, or any of my male coworkers, ever considered wearing our ties in such an unconventional manner. Why not? What had smothered our creativity? Why was it so easy for this group of future teachers to turn the world of conservative neckties upside down? And why did it feel so good, so right? I loosened my necktie a little bit that night and discovered a new bounce in my step as I masqueraded around the office and smiled through the motions of my usual nightly routines.

6

IN GOOD HANDS

My first few courses as a part-time "special" student at Antioch convinced me that the program they offered was a perfect fit for me. The only problem was that it was a full time program, and there was no way I was going to be able to attend school full time while holding down my job in Boston. What was I going to do? Give up the dream? Quit my job? How could I provide for my family with two kids still in college?

So far I had been successful hiding my student status at work, secretly reading the latest articles on educational philosophy, researching and writing papers, even collaborating with students online – all while my coworkers thought I was diligently working on quality assurance plans and corporate training materials on harassment in the workplace. Sure, I felt some guilt, but I also knew I had to take care of myself first. Too often I had seen how the company held no allegiance to its employees, especially the older ones.

I explained my predicament to the admission people at Antioch and the head of the Education department. By this time, I was pretty well known in my classes as hard working, creative and an active contributor in the ANE learning community. We came up with a plan that would spread my studies out for an extra year, I would take all the required courses and I would pay the same costs in tuition that everyone else was paying. It would mean hard work on my part and a grueling schedule. I would have to plan my summer vacation so I could take weeklong summer classes. I would have to put a million miles on my old Mazda. It would be hell for my wife and family. But it was feasible: I could do it.

And that is exactly what I did for the next two years. My typical day would start at 7am, grab a banana and coffee to eat in the car, and drive and hour and a half west to Keene for a 9am class. Another class from noon to 2:00. Drive 2 hours to Boston to be at work by 4:00. Work from 4:00 to midnight (or later). Drive an hour-and-a-half home. Get to bed around 2am. Get up at 7am. Etcetera, etc. Fortunately, I did not have classes every day. That gave me a chance to do some reading and homework. It also gave me a chance to take out the garbage or pay some bills.

I suppose, looking back on it, it was a dangerous gamble. I had to fight off sleep many times as I drove home from work. I would slap myself in the face, blast loud music, and ride with the window open in the middle of winter. I didn't want to drink coffee because I knew I had to get to sleep when I got home.

One night as I drove home, I realized I was gripping the steering wheel very tightly, holding on so I would not fall asleep. I came upon an exit for Lowell, Massachusetts and gripped that steering wheel as tight as I could so I would not miss that exit. I was so happy I hadn't fallen asleep and proud of my ability to get on the road to Lowell. The only problem was, I didn't live in Lowell and had no idea why I was going there. The mind does weird things when it starts to shut down. Somehow, I was able to turn around and make it home that night. (Carol is going to kill me when she reads this.)

Another night I got off at the wrong exit so I could take a shortcut home. Trouble was, there was no shortcut. I found myself sitting at a green traffic light and I had no idea how long I had been there. These were scary times, and I was definitely a danger on the road to others and myself. Somehow I survived. But I knew I could not continue this way much longer without doing some serious damage.

My classes, on the other hand, were a blast. I was thriving in the stimulating climate of the university. My brain had been intellectually dead for far too long. My creativity was being tapped again as it had been when I was an art student in my early twenties. Of course, I was over-achieving in all my classes and my experience in the business world provided a unique perspective for my classmates. I found learning about learning was absolutely fascinating and I dove into every class with excitement and enthusiasm.

Now, you should know that classes at Antioch were not always your usual run of the mill classes like at any other college. The course catalog offered classes on outdoor education, vernal pools and even something called *Sheep to Shawls* where students learned the process of growing, gathering, carding and knitting wool products. Of course there were academic courses offered on child development, educational philosophy and special education. But the fun ones were really out there!

I especially remember one class that was mostly about children's play. We were doing a unit on outdoor play and the professor took us to an area nearby that had a hillside of small rock caves to explore and play in. We each had to choose a spot somewhere between the boulders and fix it up, build a fort, hang out, meditate, whatever. Then we discovered a fairly large cave and we all crammed into it, smelling the pungent moist odor of mold and feeling like kids again. This was not the typical classroom learning experience and certainly one that I will never forget.

After a few hours exploring the hillside and climbing up to see the view, we were all feeling the heat as well as the exhilaration. The professor knew of a nearby swimming hole we could go to if we wished to cool off.

We headed back to our cars and he led us to a parking area up the road a little bit. As we got out of the cars, we could see there was a fairly large river squeezing its way through a deep, narrow gorge about 100 feet below. There were a few other parked cars and it was obvious this was a favorite hangout for the locals wishing to take a dip.

We scampered, stumbled and climbed down the embankment to the rushing river below. It was beautiful. The water was refreshingly cool. We took off our shoes and waded into the river's edge in our shorts. Some local kids were diving off a huge rock nearby and we thought they were crazy. A few of my classmates began floating around the rock, and we realized that the water in the middle was actually quite deep, at least deep enough to dive. We certainly couldn't touch bottom.

I was somewhat cautious, being the old guy from corporate America, the father of four kids. But the water felt great, like a whirlpool bath with the jets on full force. The rocks were slippery with moss and slime. I lost my footing and suddenly found myself floating out into the river, laughing and enjoying myself, appreciating the total immersion in Mother Nature.

The current was pulling me softly around the rock and I was relaxing, floating on my back, deeply lost in my personal experience of the afternoon's events.

Somewhere in the distance I could hear people on the riverbank calling "Feet first, feet first", but I had no idea they were calling to me. I felt the current picking up now, pulling me faster, stronger down into the gorge. By the time I came to my senses, it was way too late to have any control over where I was going. I was bumping into rocks, being thrown this way and that; wherever the river wanted to take me was where I was going to go. "Holy shit!" I said to myself, what have I done now?

I was bouncing and banging down the river headfirst when suddenly there was a huge boulder in the middle of the river and I wrapped myself around it and clung on for dear life. In the clarity of the moment I could hear the roar of the river ahead as it seemed to disappear from view. Great! There's a waterfall in front of me. The river kept pounding my back with its relentless pressure making it hard for my lungs to expand enough to take in air. I didn't know how long I would be able to hang on. But I knew if I let go, I was going over the waterfall and I couldn't see how far down it was. At the very least, I was going to lose my glasses and not be able to drive anywhere. And then there was the very real possibility that I was going to die or break a bunch of bones. How was I going to explain this to my wife and kids? How was I going to explain why I was so late for work?

In the darkest of times, there are always people you can count on. Very often, they turn out to be teachers. My professor had realized I was in deep trouble and he had climbed and worked his way down the riverbank to try to help me. He probably had come to the realization that it would not look good if he killed one of his students during class that day. He perched himself on some rocks a few feet from me along the edge. He could not quite reach me and there was no way I was letting go of the boulder I was clinging to. He spoke calmly and with assurance. He told me to reach out and grab hold of his arm. He would pull me in. I looked down the river at the water tumbling over the waterfall. I looked over at him, at the space that separated us. The river continued to beat its chaotic rhythm on my back. I had a choice: I could trust my teacher or I could be on the front page of the newspaper in the morning.

My heart racing, I reached out and slipped from the rock, the water pulling me down the gorge. Then I felt his hand taking hold of my arm, pulling me toward the edge of the river. In a minute we were both gasping on the rocks at the water's edge; disaster had been averted. I had never been in such awe at the power of nature as I was at that moment.

I learned some powerful lessons that day, not only about the force of gravity and its effect on water. It is true though, that since that day, I have a profound respect for water safety. But more importantly, I learned that it is hard to let go of the things we cling to, especially when the outcome is unknown. I learned that sometimes, you just have to trust someone. And if that someone happens to be a teacher, then you're probably in pretty good hands.

7

RECRUITED

I loved my classes at Antioch. I loved my professors; I loved the intellectual stimulation; I loved the personal growth I was experiencing. Most of all, I loved the idea that I was not only going to become a teacher, but I was showing potential to become a *great* teacher. I don't mean to be bragging here; that's really not my style. It's just that everything seemed to be coming together for me regarding my second career. I was definitely in a good place.

Now, I already told you how an education at Antioch is not exactly the same as what takes place at many other teacher-training programs. The classes are different, the people are different, and ultimately, the outcome is different. ANE is a very earth-friendly, people-friendly, art-friendly program. There are vegetarians everywhere and the level of social consciousness is truly inspiring.

Of course, any good teacher education program includes a mandatory semester of student teaching as part of its program. If you're going to teach, you had better spend some time with kids to make sure you're cut out for the job. And true to Antioch's overachieving nature, there were *two* required semesters of student teaching, not just one, along with classes to take at the same time so that one could share and process the experience thoroughly.

I was so tempted to quit my job for this phase of my re-tooling. The office politics were sickening, the meetings seemed pointless, and the bureaucratic red tape was strangling me. The highlight of each evening at the office had become the ordering of dinner from a take-out restaurant. Would it be Italian, Chinese, or maybe some of Boston's famous chowdah?

How was I going to student-teach and work at the same time? I tried to convince myself I should just quit the job. *Then* they'd be sorry. *Then* they'd miss me. I was so looking forward to the day I could tell my bosses what they could do with their job. I was ready to be done with the boredom and routine and I found myself having to talk myself into going to work each night. The thrill was long since gone. At work I was definitely *not* in a good place.

On the other hand, reality still provided a steady supply of monthly bills, the tuition payments, and a taste for the comfortable quality of life we had become accustomed to. What's a grown man to do?

I thought if I could find a nice elementary school that was on the way to my office, I could teach during the day and still make it to work in time for my shift. Let's face it, it was just student teaching; it wasn't like I was really being the teacher. It couldn't be that hard to do. After all I had been through already, I should be able to pull this off. So I looked for a school that would fit the bill.

Now it just so happened that my wife Carol had a friend who had just become principal for a new alternative middle-high school that was right off the highway on my way to work. I had designed a project for one of my classes and needed some real-live students to work with. Carol's friend said I could come in any time and work with the kids, as long as I passed the criminal check and had my fingerprints on file.

Talk about getting real. Don't get me wrong; I knew I would have to do these things eventually, somewhere down the road, at some point in the distant future. But now? Already? There was an unmistakable sense of commitment involved in the taking of fingerprints and criminal background checks. The plan in my head was becoming very, very real.

It's not like I was afraid some dark secret from my past would turn up and everyone would find out that I was a secret child murderer or anything. At worst, I guess I could be accused of being a bad parent for abandoning my family while I worked the night shift. I fantasized on what interesting tidbits might turn up in my 'experience with children' file.

My mind flashed back to a scene many years earlier when my youngest son accused me of being the worst parent ever because I wouldn't let him sleep over at friend's house. Would that be in my permanent file, I wondered? It should be if I'm going to work with children, I reasoned.

Milford, NH, May, 1994 – Worst Parent Ever – Richard Lydon

How would my parenting record hold up to close scrutiny? In that heated moment Jared actually told me he *hated* me and I'll never forget that, fingerprints or not. As the mature adult, I knew the incident would pass and our relationship would heal in time. And it did. But I won't deny that it was an ugly parental moment. I worried that I had turned into my own father, despite my efforts to overcompensate for some of the emotional starvation I had suffered as a child.

Don't get me wrong: my dad was a good provider, a *great* provider actually, when it came to a home, food, clothing. We were not rich but we did not have to worry about the next meal or having clothes or a place to sleep. He worked a lot. All the time, actually. That was who he was: he worked. But our relationship always left me hungry. I couldn't talk to him – and still can't to this day – at least not the way I felt a son should be able to talk to his father. Maybe it was the social culture of the times, maybe it was a clash in our personalities or our politics, maybe it was just some hunger I could not satisfy and he could not meet. I still don't know.

I warned you my story would get messy and you might not always know where one leaves off and another begins.

Anyway, I took care of the criminal check and the fingerprints and the talk with my son to see if he still hated me now that he was in high school. And yes, my record was clear. Before I knew it, I was heading to the ALT school to work with some middle school kids on an assignment for one of my classes. This experience would also help me decide if I wanted to student-teach at the school in the spring for my first internship.

The ALT school had just opened in September, the first alternative school in the district to serve "at-risk" youth. The students there had all been identified as 'likely' to drop out of school for a variety of reasons. They had all been unsuccessful in a traditional school setting; they needed something *different.*

It sounded exciting to me. If I was going to leave corporate America and all that it entailed, I might as well go where the action was. I had always wanted to join the Peace Corps when I was younger. This would be a similar form of service, but I wouldn't have to leave the country. How convenient.

And besides, I had now raised four kids of my own, so I figured teaching at-risk kids couldn't be much harder than that. The principal was very enthusiastic about the alternative program, the kids, and her teaching staff. In fact, she told me there were two teachers in particular that were outstanding educators. She thought I would greatly benefit from spending some time in their classrooms observing them in action.

The first class I went into seemed a bit wild and chaotic. A group of sixth grade students were all sitting with their desks in a circle and the teacher was trying desperately to get their attention. Their chatting continued as she asked a question and then proceeded to pass a "talking object" around the circle. From my classes at ANE, I knew that this was a strategy to empower one person to talk while everyone else was supposed to listen. You could only speak if the talking object was passed to you. At least that's how it was supposed to work in theory.

The teacher's talking object happened to be a wooden frog that had a bumpy back, and you could run a stick along the back to make different sounds or bang on it certain ways to make various noises. Very clever, I thought, if somewhat bizarre. The students did in fact pass it around the circle, making various noises and vulgar comments to the frog and to each other. The teacher meanwhile struggled to elicit appropriate responses to the questions she was asking. This was definitely unlike any other classroom experience I had ever been in myself, or with any of my own children.

For the record, I did have considerable experience as a volunteer in all of my children's classrooms over the years: a fringe benefit of working the night shift. I had also spent a few years coaching my kids' Odyssey of the Mind team, a creative competition. It's not like I didn't have anything to compare this to.

I can't remember if the students ever really accomplished any schoolwork during that whole class period or what we actually did. I just remember leaving at the end of the class and shaking my head wondering what had I gotten myself into?

The principal led me to the other teacher's class that she wanted me to consider. As soon as I walked into Eleanor's classroom, I could see things were different in here. First of all, the legs to all the chairs and tables had fuzzy yellow tennis balls attached to them. This made the whole classroom quieter, she explained. She asked one student to come up and tell me about the prepositions he was studying. He broke into a rap song naming all the prepositions, and the class began chiming in with him. It was astonishing, and I thought, WOW! This teacher can teach! Even these tough kids.

Eleanor immediately set me up with a small reading group of four boys. We were reading the story *HOLES* out loud together. I was enjoying reading aloud to the boys, feeling very 'teachery.' They might be at-risk sixth-graders, but they seemed like a good bunch of kids, ones you could find in any school. After a few minutes of my reading out loud, I noticed one boy, Tommy, was eyeing me intently as I read, not following along in the book, as he should have been. I silently pointed to the place in his book where he should be reading, hoping to get him to follow along with us. Instead, he continued to look me straight in the eye. I realized he was actually reading *me.*

"You're going to walk out on us, just like all the rest," he finally said, unemotional, as if he were commenting on the weather.

Taken off guard, I stammered "No, no I'm not."

He just nodded with a little knowing smile. "Yeah, you will," he said.

"No, I won't" I said with more conviction.

Tommy pretended to follow along with us as we read, but his darting eyes showed his mind was elsewhere, searching for god knows what.

For the second time that day, at the end of class, I found myself shaking my head and asking, "What have I gotten myself into?"

As I drove to the office that night, thinking about the day's events, I recalled a discussion topic from one of my classes at Antioch. I can't recall if it was in a child development class, a teaching methods class or a philosophy of education class – and it really doesn't matter. I do know it emphasized the primary importance that *relationship* plays between a teacher and a student. And I clearly remember the warning: beware of the ever-present danger of being recruited by your students.

Low and behold: I had been recruited.

8

A SENSE OF COMMUNITY

I was becoming increasingly intrigued by these troubled, at-risk kids I was secretly working with. Each one had a story of his or her own. They were rude and hyperactive and honest to the point of brutality. They were liars and thieves, and yet the most innocent of victims - the product of generations of messed-up adults reincarnated in a kid's body. I always liked a challenge, and now I had certainly found one, conveniently located just off the highway on the way to the office.

One of my classes at ANE was exploring the role of community in a classroom. We were assigned to develop a community-building classroom activity, deliver it to a group of students, and report back any findings. I thought this assignment was a perfect opportunity to investigate whatever sense of community existed within this group of at-risk kids.

The lesson I had designed involved having the kids share a skill they were good at, and then having students build small trophies for another student in the class and present it to them. It sounded very positive and affirming to me, a way for the kids to feel good about themselves. I called it my "heroes" lesson and got permission to try it out on Eleanor's class.

My first mistake was thinking I had any control over how the lesson would turn out. It got off to a slow start when the students didn't seem the least bit interested in participating. I had not taken into account that kids who have been beaten down by so many forces have difficulty sharing things, especially in a public setting, and with someone they hardly knew, no less. They didn't trust people, and certainly not adults. At first, I couldn't get them to respond at all. Maybe this wasn't going to work, I thought.

But then, thank God, I discovered the "alpha" male of the group. It turned out that he was so good at everything he could fill in for anybody who did not have something to share with the class. CJ sang an original rap song, successfully chucked crumpled paper across the room into a waste basket several times, demonstrated the fine art of tagging (on some paper), and proceeded to walk around the room several times on his hands.

That got things going. I found out that several kids claimed to be able to cook quite well and, in fact, did much of the cooking at home. I discovered a twelve-year-old who was driving his mom's car when she was too drunk to drive home. I learned that a few were good at skateboarding and one was good at video games. One of the girls said she could braid hair really well. (Actually she said, "real good", but as a budding teacher, I have difficulty writing that without correcting their grammar.)

We managed to get through the sharing, and the kids had fun making the trophies. We used all kinds of art scraps and odd things glued together. They really enjoyed taking them outside and spray-painting them gold. I had to keep my eye on the cans of paint though – some of the students wanted to borrow them for projects they were supposedly working on at home, although the details seemed fuzzy.

When we presented our trophies to each other, the kids smiled as we said nice things to each other. I could tell that they felt very good about the whole thing, but I also sensed this was an experience they were not used to, and certainly not one they were very comfortable with. When students were receiving compliments from their classmates, they often had a suspicious look in their eyes, as if they were waiting for the other shoe to drop.

I did discover an unmistakable sense of community in Eleanor's classroom that day, although it was oddly different from anything I was familiar with. The kids obviously recognized a distinct hierarchy of power that was crystal clear to them, and yet I had trouble figuring out where the power came from and what determined the pecking order. Was it size and physical strength? Or was it something else? And psychologically speaking, I found the process of observing these kids in action totally fascinating.

I later learned that my class leader CJ was not just dealing with the typical issues of a young adolescent. He lived with his mother, who happened to be lesbian and a drug addict. She had delivered him when she was only 14. Mom was considered to be of borderline intelligence and CJ pretty much ran the show at home. At age 12, he was already well known to the local police. CJ was as at-risk as a kid could be. But I tell you, that boy sure knew how to work a crowd. He was learning something every day, that was for sure, even if it had nothing to do with the school district's established curriculum.

That night at work, I went through the motions, took care of business, met deadlines and presided over meetings. I took care of all my usual managerial duties. But CJ was heavy on my mind that night. And so were the other kids. Did they have any dinner? Were they safe? What did the future hold in store for them? And what did the future hold in store for me? What *was* I getting myself into?

9

WEAVING IN AND OUT

It was time to make a decision. Should I do my student-teaching internship at the alternative school or should I just go into a regular classroom with your typical middle class kids? I had a lot on my plate with school, the job, and the family: my stress level was off the chart. A traditional classroom would probably be a whole lot easier.

To help with my decision I did try working with a "gifted" student in another school for one of my Math methods courses, mostly to see what it would be like to teach a kid that was destined for college and beyond. He was a great kid and it was an interesting experience, but it just didn't have the "draw" for me that the at-risk kids had. Besides, I had given Tommy my word – I told him I wouldn't walk out on him. I should at least give it a try.

At first, my advisor at the university thought I was crazy. Teaching is hard enough without asking for trouble, he told me. But he could tell I was already hooked. And he knew if anybody could do this, I could. I will remain forever grateful for his unwavering support and belief in my teaching potential.

So after the holidays, I started working in the sixth grade class I had done my "Heroes" lesson in. My cooperating teacher, Eleanor, was absolutely thrilled. She was a short, loving, grandmotherly lady who had been teaching in the district forever. She had mostly taught first grade, but decided to come to the alternative school for a change. She knew the kids desperately needed help with their reading so she thought it would be a great fit. Everybody at the school loved her.

Right from the start she put me to good use. It seemed that the class had something called "advisory" where they were supposed to do team building exercises, practice study skills, share what was going on in their lives, that sort of thing. It was not the structured type of reading activity Eleanor was typically used to and she had some unique ideas about how to control the energy of the young hooligans.

For one thing, she kept a small basketball hoop up on the wall of her classroom at all times. This was very popular during advisory - and at every other time of day. I personally found it very distracting and a nuisance, but it was *her* classroom and who was I, just a student teacher, to say anything about her methods. She had been a teacher forever. So, on my first full day, the advisory period was suddenly upon us and she confessed to me that she had nothing planned for the class, nothing to keep them out of trouble. She waved me over near her desk so she could tell me something in private.

"Would you mind running out to the convenient store and picking up a case of soda?" she asked. "I'll pay for it of course," she added.

I was somewhat taken aback, but easy-going me, I said "Sure, no problem."

"They like Coca-Cola," she whispered as I headed out the door.

Little did I know at the time, that this would soon become a regular pattern and one of my assumed classroom duties. It wasn't always soda, of course. Some days she asked me to run and get a dozen donuts or some cookies. And of course I often would refuse the money since I was making much more than she was at my corporate job. It's funny how people settle into their roles once expectations are established. I even started making brownies and cookies at home in my spare time to bring in on the days I was student teaching. My family didn't mind too much as long as I left a few samples home for them.

I became very much aware of the role that food and rewards play in the classroom when working with children of low socio-economic means. Food was a powerful motivational tool; it provided emotional as well as physical nourishment. It also provided a familiar social structure that everyone could relate to. Eating brought a sense of normalcy despite our disparate backgrounds. Everyone eats.

When I first started working in the classroom, I was often asked to run off copies in the office, to walk an angry young man around the building to cool him down, and various other errands. They were chores almost anybody could do – I was just a warm body. But I also began to work with the kids in reading and math, and eventually I was given responsibility to plan and execute a whole social studies unit. I was on a steep learning curve figuring out what worked with these kids both educationally and behaviorally.

One day, a teacher down the hall was absent, and there was a substitute teacher brought in to cover for her. Now, we all know it is common practice in every school for students to act up and give subs a hard time in class; with at-risk kids the acting up becomes exponential. Apparently the kids gave this particular substitute teacher such a hard time, he said to them, "Life is too short to spend another minute of my time here with you kids!" and he walked out of the building. That was a first: substitutes were usually able to make it through the day before they decided never to return again.

Since I had been doing so well in Eleanor's class and the kids seemed to be responding to me, I was asked if I would consider becoming a substitute. That way I could even earn a little money while I was working at the school. It made sense to me, so I filled out the paperwork and was all set. The experience working in different classrooms at the school would be good for me, I told myself. I began subbing to cover absent teachers (including my cooperating teacher Eleanor) quite regularly after that.

One day I was subbing for the teacher across the hall and everything was going great. The teacher had left complete lesson plans ready for me, and the day was sailing along smoothly. I felt I was making some real progress with a particularly difficult street-smart girl named Bianca. I had been getting her to teach me a little Spanish as a way to make a connection with her while we worked on her assignment. It was fun for both of us.

Suddenly another girl from a different class burst into the room, screaming and carrying on with Bianca. Now, Bianca was not the type of girl to back down, and the girls began yelling back and forth at each other. I couldn't tell if they were fighting over a boy, or possibly their Mom's boyfriend, or if they were just plain trash-talking. All I know is that they went after each other, grabbing clothes, fists flying, clutching each other's hair and pulling. The scene in front of me exploded in horror.

Oddly enough, I could not recall specific training from any of my education classes to quickly put into practice in this situation. I had no experience diffusing fighting students, especially young ladies. I did what came natural: I went into "Dad" role. I put myself in between the tussling girls while I called out for immediate assistance. All I knew was I had to separate them. The crowd of classmates gathering around us chanting "FIGHT, FIGHT, FIGHT!" was not much help, either.

Somehow I managed to get the aggressor girl to back up a bit just as the principal entered the room and she ushered her into the hallway. Bianca, who a few minutes earlier had been sweetly teaching me a few words in Spanish, was now unable to calm herself down. Suddenly, I became the target of all her rage and emotion. She screamed at me and kept poking her finger into my forehead as she shouted. I felt that I had somehow been transported onto the *Jerry Springer Show* where these types of confrontations were the norm. I expected the kids to start chanting:

R-I-C-K-Y, R-I-C-K-Y, R-I-C-K-Y. (The ALT school policy allowed students to call teachers by their first names, an attempt to break down the student-teacher barrier.)

By now the school psychologist had also arrived on the scene, a big guy who was well trained in methods of physical restraint. He was able to muscle Bianca out the door and down the hall to the principal's office. The police were called, Bianca was arrested and charged with assaulting a teacher. I felt awful. What could I have done differently?

Sadly, there really isn't an ending to this part of the story – at least not one that provided any sort of closure. I received a summons to appear on the appointed court date, but thankfully I didn't have to testify. I learned that Bianca's family was pretty messed up, no stranger to the court system; anger issues erupted at her house on a regular basis.

Sitting in the courtroom I couldn't pry my eyes off of her family. Mom, Dad, Grandma all sat with her siblings, seven of them, ranging in age from Bianca at fourteen down to a squirming two-year-old. They may be crazy and violent and poor, but they were a family nonetheless. And they were there to support Bianca as best they knew how.

I didn't know it at the time, but six years later I would have Bianca's little sister in my class and she would be asking me if it hurt to have a baby because she really wanted to have one (at 15 years old). And somehow I would muddle through an answer.

But that's how it was with these kids: just another story connected to, and weaving in and out of another story.

10

THE LITTLE THINGS

Somehow, with all this craziness in my life, I had still not blown my cover at work. I was student teaching at the ALT school Mondays, Tuesdays and Wednesdays and attending my classes at Antioch on Thursdays, Fridays and some weekends. I still dutifully worked from 4pm to midnight (or later) coordinating financial transactions. No one at my night job had any idea I was taking classes at Antioch, let alone working at the alternative school during the day.

My university classes became richer in the context of working so closely with at-risk kids. The abstract concepts of sound educational theory took on new meaning as I attempted to connect them to my students in crisis. I had become very popular in my class discussions at Antioch because my practical experience was so drastically different from any of my classmates. They could not wait to hear my stories each week.

I readily admit that being assaulted by my students was more interesting to discuss than the argument between phonics versus whole language. The fact that so many of my students were extremely poor and victims of so many unfortunate circumstances gave a deep social context to our discussions about the process of learning. Did equality exist in education? Or was society consciously and intentionally choosing which children would be left behind? These were tough questions that always led to great discussions, but not a lot of answers.

I was the first graduate student at Antioch to choose an internship working in an alternative school environment and my advisor was anxious to come and visit me for a classroom observation. I warned him not to expect much because you never knew what was going to happen next. We set up a date for him to come and observe me in action, and I set to work planning a lesson that would knock his socks off! Or at least I would try.

My cooperating teacher Eleanor had asked me to take over the science and social studies curriculum for her class so she could focus on language arts and math. That was fine with me since it gave me some freedom to do some planning and teaching on my own under her supervision. We were covering the colonial period in America and I wanted to share a story about Benjamin Franklin, planning to integrate science with the historical aspects.

It is commonly accepted that students who have struggled in traditional classrooms usually have difficulty reading. In fact many of my sixth graders were reading two or more grade levels below their chronological age. This caused them great frustration and embarrassment. It was easier for them to act out than to appear stupid to their classmates. At-risk kids also have a high percentage of attention deficit, hyperactivity, or both.

I asked myself, "How am I going to teach these kids the story of Ben Franklin, in front of my advisor, without all hell breaking loose?" They can't read, they can't sit still, and they really don't give a damn about some dude that lived over two hundred years ago.

I thought long and hard. I put all my brainpower into what I had been learning in my classes about the needs of adolescent children. They need to be doing something while I read them the story, I thought, and it should be something that they can feel proud of. Somehow I came up with this idea of braided rugs. It was very colonial, very hands-on, not too complicated, and relatively cheap.

My advisor, Don showed up on the appointed day and was very polite at morning meeting. He was taking it all in and enjoying every minute of the experience. He came with me to class and I proceeded through my lesson plan, talking about how the people had to make their own rugs back in those days, demonstrating the braiding process, getting each student started on braiding a long strand of ripped cloth. So far, so good.

Once they were all working on their braids, I began to read them the book about Ben Franklin, holding the book up to show the pictures from time to time, just the way teachers often do in the younger grades. I finished the story, we had some discussion about life in colonial times, and I showed them how their individual braids would be put together to make a big rug (or at least a large placemat.)

I could not have asked for a better class to be observed in. At-risk or not, this had been a great learning experience for all, myself included. Needless to say, Don was quite impressed. Eleanor had been sitting at the back of the room correcting papers the whole time I was teaching and seemed to be stunned by the whole thing. She encouraged me to walk Don out so we would have a chance to talk.

Don and I sat down in the cafeteria and chatted for a while. I told him that it did not always go like that, today's class was quite unusual, but I was always grateful when a lesson plan went well. He kept pouring praise on me, saying how hard these kids were, how great I was doing, how I was a "natural", and how lucky these kids were to have me.

I had to admit, I was feeling pretty good. Just then, a student from another class came walking through the cafeteria and passed near Don and I. Even though I did not have this particular student in class, I knew his name, so I gave him a friendly greeting, "Hey, Justin, how ya doin?"

"Fuck off," came the reply.

I looked at Don who was doing all he could to keep from busting his gut.

"See?" I said. "That's just how it is around here."

When the student was out of sight we both broke out laughing long and hard. I decided it's the little things you appreciate most working with these kids.

11

DISCOVERING LIFE

The topic for one of my elective courses at Antioch that spring was vernal pools. In case you don't know, a vernal pool is actually a big puddle in the middle of the woods caused by melting snow and spring rains. It dries up in the summer, but in the spring, it is virtually teeming with life. Without vernal pools, the entire ecological balance of the northern forest would be upset. The survival of many species depends on them.

So my Antioch class would often tramp out into the woods to look for vernal pools and observe the habitat. We would dig down into the mud and leaves to examine insect larvae. We would take samples of water to observe under a microscope. We would shriek with joy should we discover some evidence of salamander eggs or a live spring peeper. I know, it sounds a little geeky, but it really *was* exciting. And besides, it gave us an excuse to be outdoors for class.

This was a relatively new experience for me, working like a scientist in the field, and I was coming to the conclusion that most learning actually takes place outside of the classroom anyway, not inside it. The classroom's role is more of a check-in, a place to share ideas or maybe commiserate. There could be no substitute for the hands-on learning that takes place when you actually experience it first-hand.

I wanted to find a way to share my excitement for this feeling of being actively involved in science with my students back at the ALT school, but I was definitely not yet brave enough to take my little cherubs out into the woods. My crew would be gone in a minute, off to find a safe place to smoke (or worse). They would trample a tranquil vernal pool in seconds and impact the local ecological balance for decades to come. I had to find a way to share this experience with them that was safe for the environment, safe for them, and safe for me.

In my basement was a large aquarium that had not been used for a few years. My wife had given it to me as a gift, and for several years I had kept a number of saltwater fish and invertebrates in it. I truly enjoyed the marine ecology and found it very relaxing to watch the fish and corals, to maintain the chemical balance of the water and listen to the gurgling of the water filter as it spilled clean saltwater into the tank. The fish were beautiful and also quite expensive. But that was during my heyday of corporate status where $50 or $100 for a fish was still considered disposable income. Eventually, some of the bigger fish ate the smaller fish, I grew tired of checking the pH levels, and a good deal of algae was covering the coral. When the last fish died, I decided to give the tank a break, stuck it in the basement, and forgot about it.

Now the tank held a new interest for me. If I couldn't bring the kids to the vernal pool, then I would bring the vernal pool to them. Why not? I thought it was brilliant. I could manage their access to the tank and the wildlife it contained and they could still experience the wonder of science first-hand. All I needed to do was find a local pool and gather the water in containers, and viola! The ALT vernal pool would be open for business.

Between my own graduate classes, teaching, working, and being a dad, I was a pretty busy guy. So one night I asked my youngest son, (who was in high school at the time and no longer hated me) if he would accompany me into the woods to gather pond water so I could bring it to school the next day. I knew of a place in a nearby conservation area that had some promising vernal pools we could check out. It just so happened he did not have any plans with his friends that night and could squeeze me into his busy schedule, so he agreed to help out.

Now, I can't speak for every father, but it is often difficult for fathers and sons to share positive bonding experiences, especially when the son is a typical, active teenager. There seems to be some natural force pushing the two apart and friction can be generated by even the slightest interaction. It may be an instinctual process where the oldest male has to kick the male offspring out of the den, or it may be the young offspring's need to express his independence, I don't really know. What I do know is that I was always looking for ways to stay close to my son even as we struggled to understand each other.

So there we were one night carrying a bunch of empty milk jugs and plastic containers down a dark path into the woods. We could barely see where we were going even though there was supposed to be a full moon. I assured Jared that it should eventually get brighter when the moon rose high enough to cast some light. We were chatting and making a lot of noise as we walked, but neither of us would admit that we were trying to scare away anything that might be lurking in the bushes. The chirping of the tree frogs was both beautiful and haunting in the murkiness of the evening. It was one of those situations where your senses are heightened. We felt totally alive in the experience of the moment.

After a short but exhilarating hike, we arrived at the vernal pool. I took out a couple of small flashlights and we carefully worked our way around the edges looking for any signs of eggs or larvae or anything else of interest. We filled our containers with mud and water and leaves and sticks. We really couldn't see what we were gathering but we figured it probably didn't matter anyway.

We had to work hard lugging those heavy containers back down the trail through the darkness to the car. We sweated, we tripped, we soaked ourselves, and we laughed. We still didn't say anything about how scary the woods were at night. By the time we got back to the trailhead and the car, the moon still had not risen. We loaded what remained of the muddy water into the back of the car cursing the darkness. As we were driving back home, the moon finally appeared as promised, huge and round and as bright as it could possibly be, a commitment finally kept.

All in all, it was a good night, one I will always cherish in my heart.

The next morning I emptied all the contents of the containers into the tank in my classroom filling it about three-quarters of the way. I placed an assortment of magnifying glasses, nets and collection jars around the tank, along with field guides to local insects, frogs and other creatures they might hopefully discover. I would give them all the tools of a scientist and see what they could come up with. I even prepared an "observation" sheet the students could fill out if they saw anything interesting and record their observations in either words or pictures.

When the kids came into class, I had all I could do to keep them from climbing into the tank. I patiently showed them how to pour small samples into containers and look for "stuff". I had gathered some plastic trays in which they could spread out the mud and leaves to look for things, and I demonstrated how to do that. I showed them how to look in the field guides if they found anything so they could figure out what the specimen was.

I was in teacher heaven, moving about the room, monitoring all the kids and helping them, when suddenly I heard Teddie shouting from across the room.

"THERE'S LIFE, THERE'S LIFE! I DISCOVERED LIFE!" Teddie was screaming out at the top of his lungs. A bunch of kids gathered around him to see what it was he was screaming about. They were all pushing in to get a good look.

I instructed Teddie to draw what he saw on the observation sheet. He grabbed a pencil and started sketching furiously, but with great detail. I brought the field guide over to him and asked him to try to find a picture of his "life" in the field guide. Then I went back to helping some other students sort through some mud and leaves.

After a few minutes I heard Teddie yelling again.

"I FOUND IT! I FOUND IT!" he shouted. Again the crowd gathered around him.

"IT'S A MOSQUINTO! IT'S A MOSQUINTO!" declared Teddie.

"What's a mosquinto?" asked one of the other kids.

"I don't know," said Teddie.

"It's pronounced "mosquito" I said quietly.

"Wow!" said Teddie. "A real mosquito. A baby mosquito." He proudly studied his find.

From the speechless crowd gathered around Teddie I heard someone say, "So. It's still *LIFE*".

"Yes, it is." I agreed. "It certainly is." Who would have ever thought I'd discover life in my first year of teaching?

12

NOTHIN'S EVER GONNA CHANGE

As I was nearing the end of my internship at the ALT school, my cooperating teacher Eleanor had some personal family illness and needed to take several weeks off from school. I had already filled in for her on a few occasions and was no longer petrified of being left on my own in the classroom. The kids were still giving me a run for my money, for sure, but I was able to take whatever came up in stride. I agreed to cover for her until she could return.

Now I was getting exposure to teaching Math and Language Arts in addition to the Science and Social Studies I had already been teaching. I had to plan my own lessons and modify them to account for the "unknown" factor. The "unknown" factor included things like the kids might be unusually hungry or tired on a given day. Or somebody may have had a violent break-up with a boyfriend the night before. Or Mom may have had a friend over last night and the kid had to sleep at a Dad's place on the couch in the living room with the TV on. Or someone was arrested. You could never predict how the "unknown factor" might present itself.

Most of the kids in the class seemed to like me, but I was certain that some were projecting their anger about their Dads onto me. For example, the boy who had first recruited me to the ALT school by challenging me not to walk out, Tommy, seemed to hate me with a passion. But only sometimes. Other times I could tell he really wanted me to be a surrogate Dad and a big brother all rolled into one. He was unpredictably vicious with his classmates and me and had a very hard time socializing. It sounds strange, but Tommy prided himself on being a "fast hider". He could dart out a door, down the hall, into another classroom, and hide in a closet faster than anyone I ever knew. Tommy felt very proud of this skill.

There were a number of behavior referrals about Tommy on file and I was puzzled about his explosive temper. He was certainly very bright and an excellent artist, but there was always this deep pool of anger ready to overflow and fill the room. As Mother's Day approached Tommy was working intensely on a card for his mom. He had created some very elaborate artwork with a red rose that was truly quite remarkable. The card showed a sensitive side of Tommy that I had not seen before. I tried to be very supportive, complimenting him on his card and how much his mother was going to love it. He told me to go fuck myself.

I was extremely upset by his unexpected venom. For the life of me, I could not understand why he hated me so much. My analytic side argued that I was going to have to toughen myself up if I was going to continue to work with these kids. But my emotional side felt their pain so deeply, so totally, so helplessly. I instinctively understood that my empathy or lack of it would also make or break my connection to them as a teacher.

One day I asked the guidance counselor if she could give me some clues how to deal with Tommy. I learned that his bio dad was presently in jail, and that as a youngster, Tommy had frequently witnessed his dad beating up his mom. Perhaps that had something to do with it, suggested the counselor. Yah think?

Then there was another kid in the class, Michael, who was a real comedian. His quick wit indicated he was very smart intellectually, but somehow had never really learned to read. I found out his dad couldn't read either. His family was very poor. Even though Michael was also a great artist, whenever there was real "academic" work to be done, he would shut down and refuse to do it, even if it was easy. I would try to encourage him and cajole him into making an attempt at the task, but he would always refuse, burying his head in his arms on the table, another form of hiding.

One day after one of those sessions of me prodding and pushing Michael to get some work out of him, he looked at me and said "What difference does it make? Nothin's ever gonna change!" He buried his head back into his arms, retreating back into a world I could not even imagine.

I thought about Michael the whole drive into the office that night and the whole time I was working. When I got home, I couldn't sleep well because I was thinking about what he had said, about what his life must be like. I could feel his helplessness, trying to fight the overwhelming current of circumstances and events that were pounding on him, drowning him. I remembered clinging to a rock once myself to keep from drowning, and having a teacher to help pull me through.

The next day I took Michael aside to talk to him. I told him I listened to what he had said about nothing ever changing, and that I had thought about it all night. I told him that, in a way, he was absolutely right. That there *were* a lot of things that he could not change. He couldn't change who his family was, or where they lived, or that they didn't have a lot of money. But there was one thing that he *could* change: *himself*. Little by little, *HE* could change, and slowly but surely, things would start to change around him. And the way he could start to change was by learning new things. The more he can learn, I assured him, the more control he would have over where he lived as a young man and what he could do. He might start small, but eventually he could change his whole life. His future didn't always have to be like this. *He* was the thing he could change.

Michael didn't say much, but his eyes seemed to be listening to me. We had a pretty good day that day. I came to the realization that even if he *was* listening, I would never know if he really *heard* me. How could I?

Tommy and Michael and all the rest of the kids at the ALT school taught me some important lessons during that springtime of my student teaching. There was a limit to what I was going to be able to do for them. I could never ever make things right for Tommy or Michael, or for any of the other kids I was dealing with. I had to be OK with that if I was going to survive emotionally in this environment. I might make a difference or I might not. And even if I did, I would probably never know.

I must confess that, from time to time, I do wonder where those boys are now, and what they are doing. But I'm OK with not knowing. Maybe it's *better* if I don't know.

13

A CHAPTER CLOSED

My student-teaching internship was rapidly coming to an end and I was full of mixed emotions. My daily schedule was physically exhausting and the kids were emotionally draining. Eleanor, who had been absent about three weeks, was coming back to school. I knew the kids would be in good hands for the remainder of the school year after I left. I needed some time to think about the last few months, to let things sink in. Life not only existed inside our vernal pool; it existed outside of the ALT school, too.

There was also a part of me that found it hard to leave the kids. Each day with them challenged me to be my best, to work a little harder, to try new approaches. I felt needed by them. And I had to admit, as difficult as they were, they were still a whole lot more fun and interesting than the folks at the office every night.

It's not that all my co-workers at the office were dull or bad people, or anything like that. Some were great to work with and fun to be around too. But there was no way to avoid having to work with some obnoxious, self-centered jerks who were a constant annoyance. It was one thing to be a dysfunctional kid and be a jerk, but adults should be held to a higher standard, especially when they were getting paid for it.

I felt guilty about not confiding my secret life with my closest staff. They had no idea what I had been doing the past few months. I wanted to share the richness of the kids' stories and I desperately wanted them to know that there was life – rich, fulfilling life - outside the 'Company'. But I managed to keep quiet. It wasn't time to spill the beans – yet.

The financial printing industry had undergone significant changes over the past year as well, and not exactly changes for the better. When economic times were good, a lot of money was raised in the financial markets to finance amazing work: creating jobs, expanding industry, discovering new medicines and technology, all sorts of breakthroughs and advances. You felt like you were driving the engine that moved all of mankind forward, one deal at a time.

When financial times turn sour, however, financial printing companies serve a different purpose. For the past year, with the economy in a downturn, most of the deals had been about "restructuring debt", which is financial doublespeak for how the top executives in a company hide their money. I had access to a lot of 'insider' information about corporate payouts and golden parachutes to the executive officers of many publicly held companies. I did not like what I was seeing nor did I want to be a party to it. The financial reorganizations that I was helping to facilitate may have been technically legal, but they certainly seemed unethical at best.

During the day I was working with the kids of the poorest of the poor. At night I got to assist the wealthiest of the wealthy find ways to hold onto their money. The gap between the two was hard to comprehend and even harder to justify. Wasn't there some way to equitably distribute the wealth of our great nation? Where was Robin Hood when we needed him?

I was more convinced than ever that my decision to re-make myself and switch careers was the right one. I looked forward to the day I would give notice and move on to my new career, but that day was still in the distant future. I had six more months of classes, and another internship to complete, not to mention I would still have to land a teaching job. But even with that timetable, my plan was right on track because my youngest kids would be in college for a few more years. The plan called for me to switch jobs in two or three years when they completed college. At that point Carol and I should be able to absorb the drastic pay cut I would take as a teacher.

My final day as a student teacher at the ALT school started like every other school day. The students all gathered in the cafeteria for morning meeting, and I suspected that the principal would recognize my last day in some way. As always, I was prepared. I had written a rap-song about the school and how great the kids and staff had been to me. My hip-hop rhythm grabbed everyone's attention as I rapped about how the ALT was a special place. My song pointed out some of the things that made it so special. The kids were quite surprised that I could actually be so *snap*.

Later in Eleanor's classroom, I was presented with a huge card and a poster that included mementos from many of the lessons I had done over the course of the past few months. It was quite touching – my first 'teacher gift'. I know that most of the kids did not want me to go, so I gave the usual perfunctory comments about "coming back to visit".

"Oh, sure you'll see me," I said, not knowing if I really *would* ever see them again. Eleanor had picked up donuts and coke for the celebration.

But it was done. Another chapter closed. I still had plenty to do before becoming a teacher. I would keep moving forward with "my plan."

14

GOING FOR IT

A week later I got a call from Pam, the principal at the ALT school. There were definitely going to be a few openings at the ALT school for September and she was hoping I might be interested in applying for a bona fide teaching position. I could come in for an interview any time that was convenient.

Hmmm… Not exactly part of the plan.

Hmmm… A huge pay cut in the immediate future, not years away.

Hmmm… Do I really want to teach these tough kids?

"But I'm not certified yet," I told her.

"Not a problem," she was ready with her answer. "As an alternative school we have some flexibility as long as you're working toward certification, which you are."

"I don't know, I wasn't thinking about switching careers so soon." I said. "I'll have to think about it and talk it over with Carol."

"Of course," she said "But I know you would be a fabulous addition to our staff."

"I still have some classes to take at Antioch so it might impact my schedule." I was surprised to hear myself thinking in terms of practical logistics. Could I actually do this?

"Whatever time you need for your classes, we'll build it into your schedule" was her reply.

Hmmm… It *was* tempting. And it was pretty obvious she really wanted me. I told her I was flattered, and that I would seriously consider it and get back to her.

I had a lot to think about, and I had a lot to talk about with my family. If I did this, it would have an immediate impact on everybody in my family. I also had to see if Antioch would approve. I still had to do another internship in the fall. Would a paid teaching position count as an internship?

First, Carol and I sat down with our budget. I calculated I was going to take about a $50,000 cut in pay annually. I would be paid the salary of a first-year teacher with no experience. Ouch! Big time Ouch! Everyone always talks about how important teachers are, but apparently their pay scale is not commensurate with their importance. Hollywood celebrities and professional ball players, on the other hand, must be far more critical to the future of mankind.

On the plus side of our balance sheet, both of our cars were paid off, our credit cards were in good shape, and the kids were out of the house so our living expenses were low. I also had a hefty 401K investment plan and I was fully vested in my pension. Our eventual retirement seemed secure. Carol's position was solidly established so we could count on that as well. We had a nice, affordable house, a camper, relatively new bicycles and kayaks. What more did we need?

On the negative side of the balance sheet lurked those college tuition bills for my youngest two kids. But, back to the plus side, we would most likely qualify for more financial aid at the colleges with my new (swallow hard) salary adjustment.

It would be tight for a few years until my salary level increased, but on paper it looked like we could squeak by. We would not have any discretionary income for vacations or eating out, and we would not be wearing the latest fashions, that was sure. But we should be able to survive the hit financially.

Emotionally, there was really no question. I was miserable in my job. The stress was affecting my health. I was spending a minimum of three hours a day driving back and forth to work, piling the mileage on my car. My company continued to treat people like they were expendable commodities. And at this point, I was so capable at my job I found it extremely boring and unfulfilling. Maybe it *was* time for a change. With ten weeks off in the summer, weeks off at Christmas, winter and spring vacations, snow days and holidays – one could almost say that I was semi-retired, I rationalized.

Carol and I knew it would be extremely painful financially, but everything else pointed to "GO FOR IT!" At this point in our lives, it was not about the money. Carol's unwavering support and courage to make such a drastic change in our lives deserves a story all its own.

With her blessing, I called Pam back and set up the interview.

I remember interviewing for the position in the principal's office with three of the teachers from the ALT school. The room was only about six feet by six feet, a little larger than a closet. Our knees were practically touching as I sat facing the three of them. I'm sure they asked me a number of questions about how I would handle behavior, how I handle stress, things like that. But there is only one question I recall from the interview.

"If you could only choose three words to describe your teaching, what would they be?"

I thought for a moment and answered, "The three C's" I said. "Creative, Committed, and Caring."

I told them how creativity was a central aspect of my being, whether through my artwork, cooking, or solving any problem. I spoke about my sense of commitment to any challenge I take on. I told them I have the stamina and persistence to see something through to its resolution no matter how difficult the journey. I described the importance of the relationship between a teacher and student based on trust, respect and a willingness to accept each other for who we are. You had to care about these kids if you were going to be able to teach them. It seemed pretty simple to me.

The next day Pam called and said my next step was to be interviewed by the assistant superintendent. I was scheduled to meet with her later that week. I breezed through that one. Then I had to have my name placed before the Board of Education for their approval. They were meeting the following week. If all went well, I would be offered a contract by the beginning of June. To sum it up, the whole process only took about three weeks, and I was in. I would start the last week in August. I would be teaching middle school Math and Science.

My head was spinning. I had already scheduled my vacation weeks for June so that I could take a number of courses at Antioch during their summer semester. I worked out the schedule of classes remaining that I would need to take to complete my Masters degree, and I received approval that my teaching position would count as my fall internship. Everything was falling into place.

I had to keep telling myself, "Yes, this is really happening!" It seemed like a dream.

I still had fantasies about not showing up for work one day and just saying "Oh, I guess I forgot to tell you. I QUIT." But that was not my style. I knew there was going to be a shifting of power in the office when I left and I wanted to enjoy the show, to see what people would do to get my job. I also wanted to take the high road and leave the company with respect and my good reputation intact. I was never one to burn my bridges behind me.

When I got back from vacation, which consisted of two more courses and six more credits towards my Masters, I walked into the plant manager's office and politely told him I would be leaving. As a courtesy, I was giving six weeks notice but would not say anything until the company wished to break the news. I told him how I had gone back to school and was being offered a teaching position for the fall. He was surprised, but I could also tell he was impressed. Few people at the company had ever accomplished what I was about to do: I was about to walk away. It was going to be *MY* choice, not an executive decision made by the company and handed down as a memo to the appropriate managers.

I was fully prepared to continue to perform my job duties with no one knowing what I was about to do, but the next day word had spread throughout the building like wildfire. There were claps on the back, handshakes, and admiring looks everywhere I went. I was the one who was going to get out. "This must be what it feels like when you are getting out of prison," I thought.

My final six weeks in corporate America flew by. Surprisingly, I was even consulted on who I thought would be a good candidate for my replacement. Once again, and for the final time, my assistant got the job. This time I was happy for him.

My last night was marked by a small celebration with a lot of reminiscing. My coworkers presented me with a collection of things every new teacher would need, including a huge bottle of aspirin. It was a sweet ending to a bittersweet journey.

15

GIDDY

I had two weeks off in August to complete my total makeover from a corporate manager to a classroom teacher. And being the over-achiever that I am, I wanted everything to be perfect. I must have been difficult to live with at the time, but Carol did not complain. I smiled constantly, humming through my last-minute preparations. I was happier than I had been in many years, almost giddy with excitement.

In contrast, Carol was a seasoned veteran in the business of education. Unbelievably, she actually knew she was going to be a teacher ever since she was six years old (unlike mid-life me). We met in college where she majored in education and she has been teaching ever since. Even when Carol was home with our young children for a few years, she was still a teacher at heart. She initially taught middle school reading, but the adolescent drama almost did her in. She switched and taught younger grades after that, and it became her forte. She had been teaching kindergarten for about 15 years when I made my career change.

Now, I have to tell you, Carol is not just a teacher; she is an outstanding kindergarten teacher, probably one of the best ever. I spent a lot of time in her classroom, helping her in a variety of ways. Her class is warm, inviting, organized and fun. She is a thoughtful, prepared educator constantly striving to challenge students to learn in fun, engaging ways. I have probably learned more from her about being an educator than all my college courses combined. Let's just say the bar was set pretty high for my latest career challenge.

In my new position at the alternative school, I was going to teach math and science. I would be teaming with another teacher, Brenda, who would be responsible for language arts and social studies. She had been teaching special education for many years but would also be new to the ALT school. Brenda was a sweetheart who must have thought I was an absolute psycho case.

I invited Brenda over to our house before school began so we could meet and exchange philosophies and "collaborate". I had already prepared class lists and a proposed schedule. I had assembled all kinds of ideas how to manage the classroom the way a "responsive" classroom should be run. I had designed some *get-to-know-you* activities we could do in our classes the first week of school. My brain was overflowing with ideas.

Brenda smiled and took it all in. She was very positive and encouraging in her remarks. She was enjoying my enthusiasm, she claimed. At one point I had to leave the room to get something and I heard Carol say something to her about my being very excited to be finally becoming a teacher. Carol also explained how I work very hard at everything I do. When I came back into the room they both looked at me and smiled, an amused look in their eyes.

"Just wait…" is what they were probably thinking. "Just wait…"

I visited the ALT school to check out my new digs. My classroom was only about 12 feet deep by 16 feet wide. As far as classrooms go, this was a small classroom. One might say extremely small. And I was expecting to have twelve or so adolescents in the room during classes. There were no windows. None. So, with twelve smelly teenagers and no windows, this *was* going to be quite a challenge, I thought. "How am I going to make this work?" I wondered.

The first thing I decided to do was to paint a mural on the back wall: mountains in the distance and a large open sky. It would open up the room and create the illusion of virtual space where none existed. The principal granted me permission to paint the mural, and then I got the brainstorm to involve some of my soon-to-be students in the painting process. I contacted three students and brought them in to work on the wall a few days before school was supposed to start. Painting the mural would help them take some ownership for the classroom, and I would be able to build some connections with a few kids right from the get-go.

The mural turned out amazingly well. The kids would paint a section under my direction, I would buy a pizza for lunch and they would go home. I would then spend a few hours fixing it and touching it up. The next day they would come in and comment on how good it looked; they didn't know "they could paint so good." When it was done, I placed a green carpet on the floor in front of it so it looked like grass. Add a few beanbag chairs and some painted shelves and the room looked like something from *Home Make-Over.* The room might be small but it looked like it was sitting in the middle of the White Mountains.

A few days before school was scheduled to begin, I attended the mandatory workshops for new teachers that the district provided. I was pleased to know I was not the only "older" person who was a new teacher that year. There was actually one who looked older than me.

I found it interesting that whenever anyone asked where I was teaching and I told them the ALT school, they would always make a face and say things like "Wow! You're brave!" or "I could never do that!"

I didn't care. I was walking on clouds. I had a classroom; I had students; I had my whole second career ahead of me. I couldn't wait for the open house and my first day of school. I couldn't wait to begin teaching in my very own classroom. I was prepared. I was as ready as I could possibly be. "Bring them on," I thought, "Bring them on!"

16

OPEN HOUSE

The night before the first day of school, the ALT held an open house and ice cream social for staff to meet the students and their families. The teachers were all supposed to hang out in their rooms and talk a little about their program, small talk with the families, let the kids feel comfortable. We wanted to believe that our students' families were truly excited about the value of a good education, but we all knew the ice cream sundaes were the real "draw".

The kids came with their parents, their siblings, their mothers' and fathers' boyfriends and girlfriends. There were close friends of the family, cousins, aunts and uncles. There were a few people we couldn't figure out who they were with. That's one thing I learned early on: if you want a good turnout, offer food.

I was in my room greeting people, proud of how I had turned a large windowless closet into an inviting space for advanced learning. A family came parading into the room with young kids, middle-aged kids, young adults and an older woman I assumed was a grandmother. I went up to one of the kids and introduced myself and asked what his name was.

"Oh, I'm not going to school here," he answered. "My sister is."

"Can you introduce me to your sister?" I asked, trying out my best *teacher* voice.

"That's her right there," he said pointing to a young woman standing at the rear of the crowd.

I'd say I did a double take, but it was more like a triple or quintuple-take. The young lady was not only quite attractive; she was the most developed eighth-grader I had ever seen in my life. She had the body of a 22-year-old. Somehow I smiled and introduced myself and exchange pleasantries with the family. But I could not help thinking, number one, how the boys in the class were going to *love* this classmate, and number two, the image I had established in my head of these sweet, innocent youths was forever shattered.

I had planned to take a photograph of each of my students that night as part of my introduction. It would help me remember who was who, plus I had this idea of using their photos as part of a class display on the mural. I planned to have each kid's photo flying in a hot air balloon over the mountains on the wall. The students would write their hopes and dreams for the upcoming school year on the hot air balloons. It was all so inspiring, so organized, so optimistic.

When I asked the gorgeous eighth grader, Jerrica, if I could take her picture, she looked at me with suspicion. So did the rest of her family, including grandma. Their eyes and body language regarded me suspiciously as if I were a crazy pervert. I carefully explained that I was going to use the photo as part of a class project and their concerned faces all relaxed a little. You could tell that this was a very close family.

Ah, yes, I thought. This is going to be a memorable year.

That night, as we stood in my tiny classroom, little did any of us know that, in about five years, this large family would again be gathered for Jerrica. But this time they would be celebrating her graduation from high school, the first person to do so in her family. I am certain they would not have believed me if I told them they would get to hear Jerrica speak at the graduation ceremony as valedictorian of the night school program. They would have again looked at me as if I were crazy, if not a pervert.

As the evening wore on, people kept pouring into my classroom and I was busy greeting everyone and taking pictures of my students. The students who had helped me paint the mural proudly displayed "their work" to their moms and I was glad I had included them in the project.

One family came in with a very tough-looking young man, Karlos, obviously very street-smart, probably already involved in a gang, I thought. His dad was very friendly, had a bandana tied around his head and wore skater shorts. Mom did not speak much English and several young children clutched her leg as she walked. I had strategically placed a few small puzzles on a table and Karlos made a point to show me how smart he was by solving one of them. I knew I was going to like this kid. Sometime later that night, I noticed that one of the puzzles was missing. Just a coincidence, I suspected.

All in all, the night was a great success. I had met many of my new students and I was prepared to take them on. Seeing their families was very powerful too. It's remarkable how much of our families we unconsciously carry around with us every day, I thought. I went home to embrace my own family, to share my stories of the night and to try to get a little sleep before my first real day of school.

17

MY SECOND FIRST DAY OF SCHOOL

Believe it or not, I can still vividly remember my own first day of kindergarten 50 some-odd years ago. Standing at the bus stop, clutching my mother's legs as I cried, the smell of those huge crayons, even Mrs. Paretti's kind face. One would think after years of planning and preparation, all the hard work and sacrifice, that my first day of school as a teacher in my very own classroom would be indelibly etched upon my brain. I know I should be able to remember every minute detail. The truth is, however, most of the day was a blur.

I do vaguely remember a few small successes. Jan, an elective mute, actually spoke during one of the community-building activities I had designed for the class to get to know one another. I recall that Michael's behavior all day was very good, which stood in stark contrast to his typical day the previous year when I was student teaching. And I remember Adrian was not overly hyper that first day; perhaps he was on a new medication.

There were, however, two distinct poignant moments I clearly remember from that first day. The first occurred near the end of the day as the kids were dismissed. I was proud that I had survived my first day intact. I was smiling, as my students got ready to leave, and the next thing I knew they were all running out the door heading for the busses. My smile turned into a chuckle, then a laugh and a series of long, hard belly laughs. If anyone had come into my room at that moment, they would have wondered what could possibly be so funny. And, strangely, I would not have been able to put it into words. It was just an uncontrollable physical reaction that my body was experiencing – a moment of feeling purely alive.

I stuck my head in the principal's office to let Pam know I had survived the day. She told me she was just about to head out for a couple of home visits. She wanted to follow up on a couple of kids who had not come to school that first day and invited me to join her if I was so inclined.

"Sure," I said. "Why not?" I was feeling confident, and I had always wanted to see where some of our students lived. I was in no hurry to see this momentous day end.

We tracked down the apartment of the first kid. It was not in the best of neighborhoods, and I was glad I was accompanying the principal. Safety in numbers, you know. We climbed some dingy stairs to a second story apartment and knocked on the door. A young child opened the door and went running back inside the darkened room shouting something in Spanish. Eventually the mother of our student came to the door. Pam was fluent in Spanish and was able to explain who we were, and that we were wondering why her son had not come to school today.

The woman explained to us that her son did not have clothes for school, and he was embarrassed to wear what he had. She told us she was going to take him shopping to get some clothes and he would be there tomorrow. We told her that she did not have to buy him clothes, he could just wear jeans and a tee shirt; whatever he wore was OK. In Spanish, Mom argued that he was very particular about his clothes and would not just wear anything. As the conversation went on she began crying. It seemed that she had no food in the house and she was afraid they were going to be evicted from the apartment.

Suddenly, the visit was not just about a truant young man. It was about survival of a family. We told her we would put her in touch with some social agencies that might be able to help her, and that we were looking forward to seeing her son in school tomorrow.

When we got back to the car Pam said to me, "See? This is why it is so important to make home visits."

I was speechless.

The next stop was a few blocks away. Again, it was an old apartment building with a stairway around the side. There were some kids hanging around the porch, and I detected a faint smell of cigarettes. One of the kids went in to get the mother. The girl who had not been in school was hanging out on the porch with her cousins. Mom came to the door with a cigarette in her mouth. Her make-up was grotesquely overdone and there was way too much cleavage exposed for my comfort. Pam's message was friendly and welcoming, but down to business. Get her to school; you don't want to deal with truancy petitions, end of discussion. I suspected that mom's idea of "business" was quite different from our idea of "business". Sometimes it's best not to know too much.

Our third stop was across town in another poor section of the city. We drove up and down the street but could not find the house. It was like the street numbers jumped and the house we were looking for didn't exist. Then we realized that there was a small house tucked in behind the apartment building. We walked down the alley that served as a driveway and saw a man raking some weeds. Pam spoke to him in Spanish and he indicated the mother of the child was inside; he would get her. The little grey bungalow seemed to be in pretty good repair from the outside, but it was dwarfed by the large run-down apartment buildings surrounding it.

We waited outside a few moments until the senora opened the door for us. "Venga, venga" she said as she beckoned us inside. Once inside I was flabbergasted at how meticulous the interior of this small house was. You could literally eat off the polished wood floors. There was a couch and a chair and a very large TV set. Not much else for furniture. No books. As we sat down on the couch, she offered to get us something to eat or drink. We politely declined even though my gut told me "I bet this woman can really cook!"

The woman's daughter came out from another room and she sat with us. We told them both how she really needed to be in school, and we were wondering why she didn't come that first day. Mom explained that the daughter was afraid of school, afraid of the kids; she had not done well in school before.

We assured her the ALT school was different, we would help her, she would be safe, and she should come the next day. We left smiling and shaking hands. They promised she would be in school the following morning. In our hearts, we wondered if she would actually show up.

Which brings me to the second thought I clearly remember about my first day of school: I should never make the mistake of thinking that I really know what my students are dealing with. I might know a little, and they might even tell me a little. But their worlds may be very different from the world in which I live each and every day. I might be ready to teach, but that doesn't mean that they are ready to learn.

I was exhilarated after my first day as a real teacher, but as I headed home, I was also truly humbled by the responsibilities it entailed.

18

WHO'S THE STUDENT?

The beanbag chairs were the first things to go. It's funny how some things that seem so right, that appear to be such an obvious solution to a problem, can be so totally wrong.

Here I was trying to make my room comfortable for my students, trying to create an atmosphere where they would feel safe enough to take the risk of learning. We *were* an alternative school, after all. Whoever decided students have to sit at desks in order to learn? Why couldn't they read and write and think in bean bag chairs?

On paper, my innocent (dare I say naïve?) idea seemed perfect. The beanbags could be stored away nicely under a table in my tiny room when not in use. They could be used as incentives for students who completed an assignment. They were portable and could be placed flexibly anywhere around the room depending on what was going on. They even matched the color scheme of the mountain mural on the back wall: blue and green and purple. They looked great!

Correction: they looked great when they were on the floor, or when a student was reading in one. They did not look as great when students lifted them over their heads to throw them at each other. They lost much of their appeal with two students making out on them. They were even less attractive when they got punctured and the tiny, white foam beads began appearing all over the carpet.

The bean bags made a trip to the dumpster after about the first week. We would sit on regular, hard, non-descript school chairs after all. I chalked it up to another lesson learned. With at-risk kids, the rules were all changed. This was a concept I would continue to work on and refine during the first few weeks (no, make that months or even years) of school.

The ALT school had purchased a wonderful piece of technology called a 'smart board'. It was a huge, portable whiteboard on wheels that you could bring into your classroom and hook up to a laptop computer. There was an LCD projector that would project the image from the computer screen onto the smart board, and the neat thing about it was that the board itself became interactive. You could touch the board and the computer would respond as if it were a touch-sensitive screen. I was so excited about the potential for this state-of-the-art piece of technology in the class. I could not wait to try it out!

I already knew that my students' math skills were very low. Many could barely add and subtract; a few could attempt simple multiplication, but none could perform long division. They didn't even seem to grasp the concept. My work was cut out for me, so I figured I better start the year off by brushing them up on the basics.

I had found a wonderful online game to practice basic math skills set up like a virtual baseball game. This was perfect for the smart board, I thought. I can get the kids to do math exercises while they are playing the baseball game. And there was football and basketball we could eventually play, too. We could follow all the seasonal sports as we develop our math skills and have fun at the same time. I was all about making learning fun!

After learning the technology to set up the board, I practiced with it to make sure it worked. That was something my instructors emphasized in college: try everything out first to troubleshoot your lessons. You don't want to make a fool of yourself in front of your students. Understand your technology. I rearranged the classroom to get the best exposure for all my students and felt like I was all set to go 'live'.

The next day in class, I enthusiastically explained the activity to my students. My instructions were very specific about what we would be doing, how to play the game, and I demonstrated how the smart board worked. I tried my best to make this Math lesson sound exciting and fun. We divided the class into teams and started to play the game.

Dusty was up first and he got the first addition problem correct. A virtual baseball player jogged down to first base. Let the games begin, I thought. Karlos had been sitting on the floor up front near the smart board, taking everything in. As the next batter was getting up, he touched the board where home plate was and the virtual runner circled the bases. Johnny got upset with this so he reached up and touched the pitcher three times fast so that the next batter had struck out before anyone really knew what was going on. Tommy kept poking the scoreboard when he realized he could change the score by touching it.

I watched in horror as my well thought out math lesson disintegrated before my very eyes. As I tried to block one student from getting to the smart board, another would poke at it from another direction. I could not be in enough places at the same time to manage the situation. So I did what any quick-thinking teacher would have done: I pulled the electric cord out from the wall socket. I could only pray that my failure to follow the correct protocol for shutting down the computer would not adversely affect this expensive piece of technology. Standing there with the cord dangling from my hand, all eyes were upon me as they awaited my next brilliant idea.

In retrospect, I should have suspected something was up when the smart board was sitting unused in the back of the teacher's lounge. It had seemed odd none of the other teachers were using this amazing piece of technology. Now I knew why.

At first I was angry and annoyed at my students. Didn't they understand I was trying to help them? Didn't they want learning to be fun? They obviously didn't know how important math skills were for success. Most of all, I was upset that I didn't get to call all the shots about what happened in my classroom. After all, I *was* the teacher, wasn't I?

As it turned out that first year, I ended up being more of the *student* than the teacher. Oh, I had the position of authority all right, and I was the one who entered the grades on the report cards. That much was true. But my students actually taught *me* a lot more that first year than I taught *them*.

In time, I learned to appreciate all the learning experiences they were giving me every day, even when it seemed like a fiasco. I had so much to learn about this teaching business. I carefully observed their reactions and their interactions. I examined and recorded their ideas about the chaotic world that surrounded them. I took notes on what worked and what didn't. I studied how they solved problems and what they were truly interested in. And the more I learned about my students, the more they earned my deepest respect.

19

THE ISLAND OF MISFITS

Students came to the ALT school for a variety of reasons, but they all had difficulty in a traditional school setting for one reason or another. Their stories were all different, yet eerily very much the same. None of them EVER wanted to be called a '*SPED*' student; that label would somehow be *proof* that they were not normal, defective in some way. To put it in their terms, it was everyone *else* that was fucked up, not them.

The group of students in my class that first year represented the wide variety of reasons why there is such an increasing need for alternative educational programs in American society today. I affectionately thought of us as the '*island of misfits*', lifting the phrase from a TV cartoon about Rudolph the Reindeer who, similarly, had trouble fitting in.

Take Dusty, for example. Dusty lived with his dad in a local motel that served as a homeless shelter when people were evicted and on welfare. He slept on the couch. His dad was unemployed at the time and had the appearance of a 'biker', always wearing a ripped leather jacket with leather fringe and a bandana tied around his head. Dusty always smelled of cigarette smoke so I assumed dad smoked quite a bit. Dad had a raspy voice to go with the odor. Dusty worshipped his father and his father's friends. He thought they were the best people on the face of the earth. They let him ride on the back of their motorcycles, and sometimes they even let him sip their beer.

Besides not having a mother in the picture, Dusty had physical problems since birth. Life had not been easy for him. He was quite short and stocky and walked with a limp. He was excused from any real physical activity in gym class, although I did not know why for several months into the school year. The school nurse sent out a memo that allowed Dusty to excuse himself to go to the bathroom at any time, no questions asked. He carried an aura of mystery about him. You knew his life had to be a mess, but for some reason, nobody picked on Dusty. Everybody seemed to like Dusty. He had social status.

It is common knowledge that most middle school kids pick on each other for every reason under the sun. You might look different, you could be poor, you don't have good hygiene, your parents are jerks, you talk funny; anything will do. So I was curious. What was it about Dusty that gave him special dispensation from being picked on? What was the source of his social status?

Eventually, I learned what all the kids already knew about Dusty. First of all, Dusty was a great listener and conversationalist. He would carefully listen to what anyone said, and respond to it with a sincerity that was respectful, thoughtful and often funny. Dusty could have a meaningful conversation with a classmate, a teacher, or anyone else who was around. I figured he got this skill from hanging around his dad's friends all the time. The kids knew Dusty was a great friend: he was loyal to a fault and would never 'rat' someone out under any circumstances.

The kids also knew what was up with Dusty's physical condition before I ever did. It turned out that Dusty, among other ailments, had no control over his bowels and had to wear diapers everywhere and everyday. He took such good care of himself that I did not even know about this condition for several months into the school year. Here was a twelve-year-old kid dealing with more than some people have to deal with in a lifetime. He had earned the respect of his classmates, that was for sure.

Dusty's story was indeed unique, but it seemed like all my students had stories of their own.

Jan, the elective mute, was fortunate to have an intact family with mother, father and siblings all living together under one roof. Dad had a job and mom seemed devoted to her children. They had lived in their house for several years. Mom claimed that Jan talked constantly at home; school was the only place she did not speak. Jan was a very hard worker and completed most of her schoolwork, but sadly, I was never able to have a substantive conversation with her. If I could get a nod of the head and a smile, it was a good day. One day she brought in a picture of her baby niece to show me. That was a very good day. But, try as I might, I couldn't get Jan to speak in class. That was who Jan was – she didn't speak in school.

I already introduced you to Karlos the night of the open house. Karlos was a handful in class, what you would call a real *character*. He would often crawl under a table, cover his head and try to sleep. We were told never to visit Karlos's home by ourselves; we should always bring the principal with us if we needed to go there. One reason was that step-mom spoke no English. The second reason was because dad was apparently involved in moving large amounts of cocaine through the local area. Karlos used to joke about 'going into the family business' but I didn't find out what the family business was until a few months into the school year. Dad was arrested and sent to jail sometime around the holidays during my first year at the ALT school.

But Karlos was a talker, one of those natural-born salespeople you meet from time to time. One day in class he was acting out and having a tough time. I didn't know why he was misbehaving but I was patient and just trying to go about the business of conducting class. I saw him watching me, and finally he blurted out, "How old were you when you lost your virginity?"

Caught off guard (again) I gave him a look and said "I really don't think that's any of your business and besides, there is no way I'm going to discuss this with you here in class."

He smiled and seemed satisfied for the moment that he had shocked me. At least now I had some insight into what was on his mind.

Another one of my students in the class was called "Baby". For the life of me, I cannot recall her real name; we all called her Baby. Baby was attractive but wore a lot of make-up anyway. Baby was extremely sexualized even though she was only thirteen. There was talk of her going out with twenty-somethings. There was even talk of her going out with old men and talk of prostitution. There did not seem to be a mom or dad in the picture. Baby could care less about school and she certainly wasn't going to tell me anything about her personal life. There was talk she was pregnant. She was out for a few days and there was talk of an abortion. One of the other teachers commented that it seemed like she was going out with every male in the school. I was able to partially refute this on the grounds that she was at least not going out with me.

Rumor had it that another student in the class, Mitchell, was the father of her unborn baby. Mitchell was a strong, wiry young man, fourteen years old, but barely reading. He did not take school very seriously either. I remember walking into the class one day and seeing Mitchell rolling around on the floor making weird noises. "This," I thought to myself, "This, is about to become a father." Scary, but real.

Dominick, another one of my students, had already been in placement for a while. He had been beating up his mother and little sister on a regular basis and Mom had to call in the police. Dad was already in jail. I had to be careful of Dom's temper. He could explode at any time.

Adrian was an extremely hyperactive young man whose mom worked at a daycare and didn't want her son coded as ADHD. She did not want him medicated. When we requested a meeting with her to discuss Adrian's behavior, she brought in two younger boys with her who destroyed my classroom while we spoke with her about Adrian's unruly behavior. Mom pretended not to notice. Not once did she speak to them about their behavior. When the meeting was over and she left with her little monsters, we were glad we were not in her shoes. We could only imagine what living in her house must be like.

Loren had beautiful red hair and an awful case of acne. She did not shower regularly enough, and often had an unpleasant odor about her. Loren would be silly-giddy one minute, and crying and running out of the room the next, but there was no suggestion of a bi-polar diagnosis in her file.

Selina was a large girl, both in personality and physical stature. She always seemed to be in perfect control although very unhappy. She wrote dark, dark poems about loneliness and barren relationships. Her mother always cried when we had parent meetings. Things were tough at home.

One day I realized Selina was not in class; the kids said she was in the office. My teaching partner was not coming in to take over my class at the appointed time and I was beginning to wonder what was going on. I found out later that my partner, Brenda, had intercepted a suicide note and was with Selina and the nurse, waiting for her mom to arrive. Selina had a plan to kill herself with a rope in the basement at home after school.

I have not told you about all the kids in my first class, only a handful of them. Their stories are not pretty, but they give you some idea of how bad it was for some of my students. We all know that some kids have to deal with conditions like these. *Sixty Minutes* runs a program about them every now and again, so we know that they're out there. But it's a lot easier to pretend we *don't* know about them; they make us feel uncomfortable.

But teachers know about them. We know it every day. We just don't always know what to do about it.

I took some comfort knowing that at least my students had someplace to go each day where they could be safe and warm and receive a couple of free meals. And if I could provide a little learning, and a little love and encouragement along the way, that was OK with me. It was all I could do. It would have to be enough.

20

FATHERS AND SONS

I told you about Mitchell rolling around on the floor the day I heard he was going to become a father, right? Let me tell you a little more about Mitchell.

One morning I was in my classroom getting things ready for the day. One of my daily rituals included putting out fresh, sharpened pencils every day; they just seemed to disappear when my students showed up. It wasn't that the kids were writing so much that they wore them down. Pencils just disappeared. Sometimes I would notice them stuck up into the ceiling tiles and I had to stand on a chair and pull them down to recycle them. I often found them broken and discarded in a corner. I guess the kids thought I would stop assigning classwork when we ran out of pencils. They didn't know I had access to an endless supply.

Anyway, I had just finished sharpening pencils and was putting away the math folders when I looked up to see Mitchell entering the room. This was before school had begun for the day. It was very unusual for him to make an appearance so early, especially in *my* room.

"Hey, Mitchell, how you doing?" I asked, trying to be friendly.

"I got arrested last night, that's how I'm doing," he announced, pacing back and forth around the room.

I was in shock, not because he was arrested, but because he had never confided anything to me before that moment. Recognizing his attempt to reach out, I pulled out a chair, expressed my concern and interest, and invited him to sit down and talk to me about it. I could almost feel myself being snatched out of my 'teacher' mode and thrust into 'counselor' mode (or was it 'parent' mode?).

The details of the arrest seemed a little sketchy and not of any real importance; they involved some friends, a stolen dirt bike and resisting arrest. I gently asked questions and provided a little advice, letting him know that everyone makes mistakes from time to time.

As he described how angry his father was, I found myself increasingly in the father-role, trying to be the kind of father he needed: firm, somewhat disappointed, but still accepting and loving. Although he was too tough to admit it, Mitchell was obviously afraid of how his father was reacting to the situation. I flashed back to the image of his father at our last meeting: the solid ex-con, tattooed, earring in one ear, with biceps the size of my thigh. I shared Mitchell's fear.

Not quite sure what to do next, I pulled out a broken train engine that I had found on the rug the day before. Someone had taken the motor apart and it was in pieces. I showed it to Mitchell and asked if he wanted to try to fix it today, maybe it would help him keep his mind off his troubles. He immediately started working on it and I let him know how great it would be if he could get it running again for us.

Then the bell rang, summoning us to morning meeting. Another day at the ALT had begun.

21

HOLDING ONTO POWER

Experts have published all kinds of theories about working with at-risk youth. And every book or article I read had a different take, a unique perspective, something to add to my 'bag of tricks'. Ultimately, however, they all reached the same conclusion: there was no ONE SIZE FITS ALL approach that could be guaranteed to work in a given situation. Every kid had his or her own baggage and every plan had to be customized. That's what alternative education was all about.

I always enjoyed discovering new ideas to try out in the classroom. I read everything I could about different approaches to handling behavior issues. The problem was that I could never remember what the research said to do in the heat of the moment when the going got tough. Whenever I found myself in a difficult situation, I always felt like I was 'winging it'.

One day I was trying to get my students' attention in order to present the lesson I had planned, but the class was not cooperating. There must have been some big personal drama going on between some of them that I was unaware of, and I couldn't get them to stop chatting and arguing among themselves. I felt as if I was invisible.

I raised my voice to be sure I was being heard. No good.

I spoke very quietly, remembering from one of my readings that sometimes the whispering technique would quiet them down because they wanted to hear what you were saying. No success with that either.

I moved around the classroom so that I was standing next to the worst offenders. Still they totally ignored me as if I didn't even exist.

I was getting frustrated. I remembered one of the articles I had read suggested doing something unexpected to regain the power back in the classroom. I could try making a loud noise, dropping something - anything to cause a sudden distraction. It might work, I thought.

Without saying anything, I went into slow motion. I spread my arms out wide and slowly began to crouch down in the middle of the room.

Suddenly one of the kids shouted out, "QUIET, everybody! Rick is going to *DO SOMETHING!*"

I felt the eyes of the whole class upon me as I held my strange position. You could have heard a pin drop in the room at that moment. WOW! It was working, I thought. I continued my downward motion very slowly. I had regained the power of the classroom! I suddenly realized that I had absolutely no idea where this was going. Panic started to set in: they all expect me to *DO SOMETHING* now, and I had no idea what to do next.

I slowed down even more to gain time to think, but I kept moving ever so slowly toward the floor. I tried not to let my face show the pain that I was now beginning to experience in my legs from holding my weight in mid-air. Everyone remained silent, watching for the slightest motion as an indication of what was going to happen next. Eventually, I found myself sitting cross-legged on the floor.

They all looked at me. I looked back at them. Then, in a flash of insight, I knew what to do. I began speaking to them in a soft tone about what we were going to do that day, what my expectations were, and what the lesson was about. In short, I began teaching, albeit from the floor.

Some of the kids declared, "This is gay!" and tried to start their conversations back up, but it was no use. They knew I had gotten the power back, that I was the one in charge. Soon they all settled down and did their work.

From my lotus position I contemplated what had just happened. I knew I would probably never be able to use that trick again with this class, but at least it got me through the day. Just one more lesson to add to my increasing bag of tricks.

22

UP CLOSE AND PERSONAL

Have you ever had bad breath? I know I have because my students told me. Kids have this knack for being brutally honest. They don't hold back because you're a teacher. In fact, they let you have it point blank, right between the eyes, double barrel.

A few of my students made a point of telling me every day that I had bad breath. It was their form of morning greeting. They would even tell me this as I was sucking on a breath mint.

If I raised my voice at them, they would respond, "Your breath stinks!"

If I would sit next to them and calmly advise them of a better choice they could make in a particular situation, they would try to change the subject by waving their hands and holding their nose.

I often thanked them for telling me, saying that only a 'true friend' would care enough to tell me to my face. Then I would pop a mint into my mouth and offer them one as well, which they always grabbed. Of course, everyone in the room wanted one too. It's amazing how contagious my bad breath was!

At some point I realized that these interchanges were not really about bad breath at all. They were really about getting close to someone, especially if that someone was a teacher.

My students would scrutinize everything about me: the clothes I would wear, the common expressions I used on a regular basis, the type of shoes on my feet. They judged me by the old van that I drove. They wanted to see me without my glasses on. They wanted to know if I colored my hair. I loved to have them guess my age. I was somewhere between 28 and 72.

One day I was working closely with some students at a table and the girl next to me shouted out, "Oh my God! There's a hole in your cheek!" She turned to the other kids and shouted again "There's a hole in Rick's cheek! There's a hole in his cheek!"

Suddenly the whole class was huddling around me to get a closer look. Sure enough, they confirmed, there actually *was* a hole in my cheek.

"How did you get that?" "What's it from?" they were all shouting at me for answers.

Now, we all have imperfections in our skin and at some point in my life, unbeknownst to me, I must have had a clogged pore or a zit or something, and it had left a small pockmark in my cheek. There was, in fact, a small hole in my cheek. I never paid much attention to it, but here it was now, the center of attention for a bunch of middle school students.

I decided that the hole in my cheek should get its fifteen minutes of fame. It deserved it.

"When I was younger I had a piercing in my cheek," I lied to the kids. They looked at me in awe. "Yeah, I had it for a while, it was a big spike thing sticking out, but it got in the way so I took it out," I continued. They couldn't tell if they should believe me or not. "I can actually squirt spit out of it if I want to" I said and I puffed my cheek up with air as if I was about to spit out of the side of my face. The girls screamed and backed away and the boys weren't getting too close to me either at this point, just in case.

I smiled and said "Be careful if you ever get anything pierced. You never know when a piercing will go bad." I gathered up some papers and continued on as if nothing had happened. We had schoolwork to do. No big deal. So I had a hole in my cheek.

23

FROM THEORY INTO PRACTICE

My school principal had arranged my schedule so that every Friday afternoon I could leave school a little early to travel to Antioch and attend ProSem, which was short for "Professional Seminar". ProSem was more of a discussion group than an actual class. All the grad students in a teaching internship would meet and share how things were going for them in their classrooms. A discussion topic or interesting question was usually presented to stimulate our thinking. Mostly it served as a group therapy session, and I must admit, by Friday afternoon, I really needed it!

My input was always very popular during these discussions due to the nature of my internship. My professor and fellow graduate students enjoyed hearing all about my tales of survival. While they were all designing and delivering integrated lessons with clever craft projects and authentic learning experiences, I told them how I had to sit on the floor just to get my students' attention. I felt like my classroom was the ultimate testing ground where the rubbery concepts behind educational theory met the road.

One afternoon we happened to be discussing classroom behavior and the importance of applying 'logical consequences'. Logical consequences were part of a 'responsive classroom' approach to managing your class. In a true responsive classroom, the teacher would respond to a situation with a logical consequence to whatever had happened. For instance, if a student made a mess, you would not assign an extra homework assignment as a consequence; you would have them stay after class during recess to clean up their mess. It sounds simple, right?

OK, let's say in your classroom you have one computer and the whole class has to take turns using it for research, writing, whatever. I know it sounds pathetic, but sadly, that is the reality in a lot of classrooms, including mine. The teacher has to use this one computer also for grades, communications and as a teaching resource. One might consider it an important part of the classroom.

Now let's just say that the little rolling ball that operates the computer mouse is suddenly missing. You know it was taken by one of the students because it was in place and working that very morning, but you don't know who the culprit is. A logical consequence would suggest that no one gets to use the computer until the mouse ball is returned. Of course that means that many innocent people are adversely affected (including the teacher) and learning is impeded until the problem is resolved.

If the day's lesson plan happened to involve using the computer, you now have multiple classes of unruly students with little or nothing to do because you were not expecting this. It does not take years of teaching experience to know this is a recipe for disaster. The teacher had better come up with *PLAN B* in a hurry or it is going to become a very ugly day.

Now, if we assume that the little theif who stole the mouse ball *intended* to impede learning (which is highly likely) then restricting the computer use for the whole class feeds right into his or her wishes. Remember, at-risk kids have little value for learning in school, at home, or anywhere. They are most comfortable when they are not being challenged academically. What could be more entertaining for an afternoon than to see a helplessly frustrated teacher unable to teach the lesson for the day and observe the resulting chaos? Admit it, it sounds like fun, right?

And of course, there are always considerations of social status. Think of the power contained in that little rubber ball when it was held in the hand of a twelve-year-old. It might symbolize the ultimate in authority for a kid who feels he has no control over the circumstances of his life. It might make a puny, insecure little boy loom quite large, if only for an afternoon or a few days.

Yes, the situations I was dealing with in my classroom on a daily basis made for great discussions at ProSem. And as I mentioned earlier, the discussions were very therapeutic for me personally.

(For those of you who are curious about my dilemma regarding the missing mouse ball, the only logical consequence I could come up with was a work-around. I purchased an optical mouse that did not have a rubber ball that could be stolen. Problem solved, but immunity from prosecution granted.)

Another one of the topics we discussed at ProSem was well known as a 'Best Practice' in all the educational research. It was the inclusion of *CHOICE* in the work that students do. Obviously, if students *choose* to investigate a certain topic, it has much more meaning than if the teacher just assigned them to do it.

Back in my classroom, there was a particular student I was really struggling to reach. Nando was a tall, skinny boy who was heavily influenced by street culture and demonstrated very low academic levels in all areas. He lived with his Mom and sisters in the projects, and as the youngest in the family, they were all trying to keep close tabs on him to keep him out of trouble.

Out of the blue one day, he said to me, "We need to do more projects, you know, make stuff".

I thought about it for a minute and said "OK, Nando. What would you like to make?"

"Piñatas!" he blurted out. "We should make piñatas! We can blow up balloons, cover them in paper mache, paint them, and fill them with candy! I know just how to do it. Can we? Can we?" Picture this young wannabe gang member pleading with me to make piñatas in class.

In my mind this was a perfect opportunity to include some student *CHOICE* into the classroom. There was no reason not to do it; Nando was obviously excited about it; and if he bought in to the activity, other students would too. I even figured out a way to tie it into the content of one of the lessons we were covering.

"OK" I said. "I'll get the stuff and tomorrow we'll start making piñatas."

By now you must have some idea of how tough it was to teach at the ALT school. It was by far the hardest thing I had ever done in my life. Bringing a company public in my former life was a piece of cake compared to this. But the smile I saw on Nando's face that day and the excited look in his eyes made it all worth it. The bad stuff all melts away in those moments when you break through to a kid who hasn't had a breakthrough in a long, long time. It's hard to describe; it just happens.

The next day I brought in all the required materials. I had huge balloons, stacks of newspapers, buckets for water, paper mache, paint, brushes, everything. I set the room up so that there would be lots of space for the kids to work. I was so excited to be letting student choice drive this activity.

When the class came in I told them what we were going to do and how they could all thank Nando. It was his great idea, and I thought he was so smart to think of it. Everybody was excited and dove right into the project, especially the balloons. Very quickly I had to insist there would be NO water balloons today and anyone filling balloons with water would have to wait in the dreaded principal's office while the rest of the class had fun. Hurray! My logical consequence seemed to take care of that issue.

There was a loud pop. "Be careful" I warned. There was another pop; then two more.

"OK. That's enough!" I shouted. One of the teachers next door had come running into our room to make sure she was not hearing gunshots.

"From now on if you pop your balloon you will not be able to make a piñata" I declared to the class.

I assured my fellow teacher that everyone was fine, and as I looked over across the room, I saw Dusty lying on his back on the floor. He looked like he was having trouble breathing.

All of a sudden it hit me! Oh my God, Dusty is highly allergic to latex! The balloons are all made out of latex! Oh my God! What have I done? How could I have forgotten? How could I have been so stupid?

I went running over to Dusty. "Dusty, Dusty! Are you all right? Dusty! Are you OK?" I was on the verge of panic as I crouched on the floor next to him, ready to start CPR if necessary. I saw my short life as a teacher passing before me. Dusty lay lifeless before me for what seemed like an eternity, then slowly he started to break into a smile. Suddenly he burst out laughing.

"Gotcha!" he blurted out, laughing hysterically.

He had me, big time. "You're not having an allergic reaction?" I asked.

"I'm fine." He responded. "I'm not sure if I'm still allergic anymore or not," he said. "I might be, but I haven't had any reactions in quite a while."

Still recovering from the scare, I went around the room gathering up all the latex balloons from the kids. I was not going to take any chances. I certainly did not want to kill a student in my first year as a teacher. I bagged them all up and got them out of the school as quickly as I could. I told the kids to clean everything up and I would try to find some latex-free balloons we could use the next day.

I looked over again at Dusty. He was still laughing and some of the other students had joined him, including Nando. Did I tell you these kids had quite a sense of humor?

24

PARENT CONFERENCES

As the weeks and months passed, I found myself feeling more and more confident in my ability to teach these struggling learners. Each day was a challenge, for sure, and I had never worked so hard in my life, but all in all, I was pleased with the way things were going. Some of the kids seemed to be responding to my teaching methods, and those who weren't, well, I guess you could at least say we had a comfortable truce and they didn't think of me as the *enemy* any more.

Before I knew it, we were coming up on Thanksgiving. Our principal had warned us that the holidays were tough times for our kids and we should expect the worst. We also had to prepare for parent conferences which were scheduled for the two days before Thanksgiving break.

Up until this point, I had been primarily occupied with classroom management and the methods and content involved with teaching my students. Now I would have to switch gears and somehow communicate with their parents about their progress (or lack thereof).

I considered bluntly describing to the parents some of the spicy details of inappropriate conversations their delightful children were having in class. "So Mrs. Fernandez," I fantasized, "Does Juan discuss oral sex with his friends in front of you at home?" or "Has your daughter always been this bitchy, Mr. Smith?"

My teaching partner Brenda, with her many years of experience, was able to dissuade me from getting into any distasteful topics that might get me fired. "Put yourself into the parents shoes," she told me. "If your kid was one of these kids, what would you want to hear?" She also advised me to say something positive to each parent before saying anything bad, which was very good advice.

Truth be told, there were *lots* of positive things I had to report to this unfortunate group of parents. I had genuinely grown to *like* my students, despite - or was it *because of* - their awful behavior. In any case, I looked forward to my first parent conference with a mixture of excitement, fear and dread.

Selina's mom was first up. A large woman, she entered with a smile and handshake and a petrified look in her eyes. I could tell immediately that she had a history of bad experiences involving the school system. She sat down and braced herself for our awful words about her daughter.

We started off by saying how incredibly bright Selina was, and how we were so glad she was getting counseling through the suicide prevention program. Selina seemed much less explosive now and was getting most of her work done. Mom burst out crying. She couldn't express her thanks to us for recognizing that Selina needed help. She didn't know what would have happened if we hadn't intervened. She was sobbing and we were trying to comfort her by telling her things would be all right, that Selina was strong, a survivor. We told her what a leader Selina was and that at some point in the future this would all become a distant memory.

Mom rambled on telling us how her husband had just recently been laid off and her older children had moved back in with them. She continued crying as she said she didn't know how they were going to make ends meet. The holidays were coming up and there was no money for Christmas this year. Brenda and I had all we could do not to break down and cry with her myself. Her story just seemed to keep getting worse and worse.

We told her we would get her information about social agencies that could possibly help her, and that we would put her family into one of the Christmas outreach programs we were familiar with. We told her to focus on her family, and that things would work out; Selina would be just fine.

When the conference was over and she had left the room, Brenda and I looked at each other. Oh my God, this was just the first conference and we were both totally drained. How were we ever going to get through this night? Were all the conferences going to go this way?

Somehow we composed ourselves and proceeded through our schedule of parent meetings. Fortunately or unfortunately, depending on how you look at it, very few parents actually showed up for conferences. A sad comment, for sure, but totally predictable considering the student population we served.

I do remember one other conference that night. Kirk's dad came in and sat down quietly in the chair. He had little expression on his face and did not make eye contact with us. Dad worked hard as a custodian at a downtown factory to support his five children of whom Kirk was the oldest. We knew that at least two of the youngest kids had spent some time in placement when his ex-wife (and mother of the children) was sent to a rehabilitation hospital to de-tox. Mom was back now, living at home with them, along with her young boyfriend. (Honest, I'm not making this up.)

Brenda and I loved his son Kirk. He was bright, respectful, hard-working, and had a great sense of humor. We carried on and on about how well Kirk was doing, how much we enjoyed having him in class, how proud he must be of his son doing so well under tough circumstances.

Dad just looked at us with this blank stare on his face, his mouth slightly open. After an awkward silence, Brenda asked him if he was all right, if he was feeling OK since he wasn't responding or saying anything.

"Yeah," he said. "I'm fine." He paused. "It's just that I've never had a parent conference like this before," he confessed. "Usually all I hear is how bad my kids are doing. I've never heard stuff like this before. I'm not sure what I should say."

Once again, Brenda and I had to fight the tears coming into our eyes.

My brain was totally fried when the evening of conferences was finally over. I had gained a new appreciation for my students and the messy lives they led. I also felt a renewed sense of appreciation for my own family and the normalcy that surrounded my life. How close am I, how close are we all, to an alternate reality that we can't even imagine?

Someday, I began to think, I really should start writing some of this down. Nobody would believe it. But I know you believe me. Life's messiness traps us all from time to time.

25

GET INTO HEAVEN PASS

One of the really special things about working at the ALT was the incredible support and comradery building up between all the staff members. We knew we had to stick together if we were going to survive in this environment. We were all dealing with the same issues in our classrooms so it was important for us to share our ideas and strategies. We also shared a lot of laughter and tears.

After parent conference night, it was critical that the entire staff get together to share information and insights into what might be going on with some of the kids. Collectively, we might be able to put together more pieces of the puzzle and develop a coordinated approach for each student. Understanding the family dynamics and support systems for our kids could help us devise strategies for them to be more successful in school.

To be honest, the family information we had uncovered was very discouraging, even painful. The outlook for so many of our students was so bleak. Children of poverty have to deal with issues that many people might not have to face in a lifetime. And yet, they attempt to overcome them on a regular basis. Chaos and insecurity are normal for them. Relationships are often dysfunctional at best.

The anger and the fear at-risk kids carry around with them is often the driving force behind their obnoxious behavior. They push people away because they have been badly hurt by so many broken relationships. One needs to see beyond the vulgar language and oppositional behavior if one is to have any hope of moving them forward.

This is not easy to do. It seems like the nicer you are to them, the more they feel a need to crap on you. The more you help them, the more they resent you. At-risk youth rebel against all the rules and authority, yet what they are often craving is someone who will set the boundaries and limits for them so they can be safe, so they can be kids for a moment.

It is not surprising that their parents were not always able to set these limits for them. In the first place, many were still big kids themselves, literally. Some of the parents of my students were in their mid-twenties and decked out like they were going clubin', not to a teacher conference. Secondly, many of the parents had issues with limits themselves. It would be quite a stretch to think they could teach the skills of personal restraint to their offspring when their own lives were often spinning out of control. Then there was the issue of generational poverty, with familiar cycles of helplessness repeating themselves over and over. At times, it was hard to tell exactly who was enabling who.

But there we were, the dedicated staff of the ALT, in the midst of all this mayhem. We showed up every school day, wearing our smiles and our optimism, encouraging our students to do their best, sharing our homemade muffins along with whatever advice we could provide. The kids would trudge into our classrooms and tell us to "leave them the fuck alone" and the day would begin. We would teach no matter how hard they resisted. We would be the 'constant' in their messed up little lives.

At one of our teacher support meetings someone suggested the reason our staff was so close was because we faced a 'common enemy'. It was hard not to foster an *Us Against Them* mentality when the going got tough. And on some days it certainly felt like we deployed to a battleground. But we knew the 'enemy' was not really the kids - it was the culture of poverty and insecurity that produced them and followed them everywhere.

The kids were the real *heroes* in our stories. How many of *us* could survive the lives they were living? We'd be obnoxious and repulsive and angry too if we were in their shoes. Let's face it: teenagers are hard to deal with under the best of circumstances, let alone this.

So, yeah, the kids were bad. Someone joked at one of our staff meetings that, if there is indeed an afterlife, we would all be automatically granted entrance to heaven because of the work we were doing with the kids nobody wanted to work with. We could probably even get away with committing murder or other mortal sins and still be let in. Such was the reward for our efforts.

I personally found it extremely comforting knowing I had earned a '*Get Into Heaven*' pass already in my first year of teaching. What more could anyone ask for?

26

PEEK-A-BOO

One of the things I began to realize in my new role as a teacher of at-risk youth was that my students often exhibited symptoms of developmental delay. We all know there are certain stages of development everyone must go through to ensure 'normal' physical and emotional growth. A baby has to crawl before he can walk; she has to babble and make all sorts of weird noises before anything sounds like "mama" or "dada".

One day, my students were giving presentations as the culmination to a project they had been working on. I had invited some teachers and guidance counselors to come and watch their presentations to help create the aura of a 'real' audience. (I had invited parents to come in too, but none showed up.) I was glad I had invited other staff members so there would be some appreciative adults in the audience.

The classroom was set up with a 'stage area' where the kids were presenting, and an area with all the chairs set up in rows for the audience. The students who were not presenting made up a large part of the audience, and I had to keep 'shushing them' to quiet them down. I frequently reminded them how to be appropriate audience members. There was a lot to coordinate, and I had my hands full facilitating the event.

During the presentations I realized that one of my students had slipped out of my room unbeknownst to me and was in the next classroom. There was an adjoining doorway, which the two rooms shared, and the door was open so I could see into the other room from where I was standing. Every now and then, I would see Noah poke his head out around the doorway enough to see me and then he would quickly duck back behind the wall. I was busy with the proceedings in my room so I just ignored him.

After a few minutes, I noticed him peeking out at me again from a different location this time. He gave me a big smile, and ducked back again. This went on for some time, his peeking out and hiding. Noah was obviously getting a big kick out of his immature behavior. At one point he even went to the back of the other room and pretended to be tip-toeing across the opening to get to the other side of the doorway, where he peeked out from new locations on the other side of the doorway.

I waved at him to come into our room, not wanting to distract from the presentations going on. He smiled and waved back. I gave him the 'teacher look' with my eyes; he tried to give it right back to me. It was then that I realized I was actually engaged in a real game of peek-a-boo with Noah.

What you have to understand is that Noah was not a little child, in size or personality. He was a good-sized fourteen-year-old who shaved regularly and got up at 4am each morning to deliver newspapers. He had fought enough kids at the school that nobody wanted to mess with Noah. He was one of the *cool* kids with considerable social status. And there I was playing peek-a-boo with him. Amazingly, none of the other people in the room had any idea what was going on the whole time students were presenting.

Could it be that I was satisfying some instinctual primal need for Noah that had never been met when he was a baby? Had his mother (another drug addict) never played peek-a-boo with him because she was always too stoned? Had he never experienced this basic parent-child bonding experience? I was flabbergasted at the thought. What other basic developmental stages might he (and my other students) be lacking?

I decided to just let it play out and not get into a whole disciplinary power struggle with him. For the next hour I kept one eye on my students as they presented their projects, and I kept one eye on Noah and his antics. I still really don't know what it was all about; it was just one of those things that happened at the ALT during an otherwise normal day, a story I could share at home or during my professional seminar at Antioch.

In a way, the whole incident reminded me of chasing down the 'hiders'. I had a small group of boys whom I called 'the hiders.' They hid everywhere they could, every chance they got. It was a big game to them and a challenge they obviously enjoyed.

If I should happen to stick my head out into the hallway for a second to speak with another teacher, one of them would scoot down behind my desk and hide underneath. Or one would climb into the metal storage cabinet that was in the class. My favorite was when one would stand behind the curtain next to the window; his legs and feet sticking out from underneath the curtain - it didn't matter as long as I could not see the face: he was still considered hiding.

The hiders especially prided themselves on their speed at hiding as if it were an Olympic sport. Most of them could slip out the door and vanish literally in a second. By the time I got to the door, they were gone. It always amazed me how fast they could disappear around a corner or into another doorway.

If I were to slip into my role as an amateur psychologist, my interpretation of the hiders would go like this: The hiders were trying to assert their independence from me, the archetypal parent figure. Most children get to play hide and seek from a young age. The game is essentially a developmental response expressing the need to distance yourself from your mother. The child hides and 'pretends' he is 'out on his own.' As the child grows older, the radius of the playing circle gets larger. The game moves outside, then out of the yard into the neighbors' yards. By the time the child is a typical teenager, the parent often has no idea where he is. This would be considered normal development by the experts.

For some reason, my hiders were apparently never able to fill this basic human need to play hide-and-seek at the appropriate age. Perhaps it was the urban landscape with danger lurking on every street corner. Or maybe there were dysfunctional relationships in the family that somehow prevented the game from taking place. My hiders did have an unusually high percentage of dads in jail or parents that were somehow missing or unaccounted for.

"That could be it!" I thought, excited about my clever intellectual insight. The parents were actually the ones who were hiding, not the kids! And the kids could never find their hiding parents! That would certainly do an insecurity number on any kid.

When I eventually found my hiders or they returned on their own (which they always did) I would often ask them "What exactly is it you are running away from?" But they never knew why they did it. It was just something they would do when an opportunity presented itself.

"You know, you can't run away from yourself," I would sometimes say to them.

"I'm not running away from myself!" they would argue.

"Sure." I would say. "Sure. C'mon, let's get back to work. Game over."

Then they would usually come back to the room and settle back into their work. The game was over for the moment - but there would always be more opportunities for a re-match. If they needed to hide once in a while, I was OK with that. I knew they would always come back to me and they knew I would always be there for them when they got back. It was just another one of those strange little games that made for another typical day at the ALT.

27

TEACHING, ACTUALLY

Teaching. Wasn't *that* what I was supposed to be doing? I had to remind myself that I had left the corporate scene and the fat paycheck to become a *teacher.* Where was all the *teaching* among these silly games of peek-a-boo and hide-and-seek?

And yet I learned an incredible amount about teaching my first year at the ALT school. When your students have a very short attention span, a condition at-risk youth are notorious for, you had better be prepared to teach quickly and effectively if you harbor any hope of success, either for your students or for yourself. Regardless of the subject I was teaching, I learned to sneak in quickly, go after whatever it was that I wanted, and then make an artful escape. If that sounds a little like a *break and entry*, so be it. I don't mind the street metaphor. All I know is: it worked.

I always tried to start each science lesson with some quick attention-grabbing gimmick or activity. Research indicated if you didn't capture your audience in the first three minutes, your whole lesson could be doomed. So I worked hard those first three minutes. Sometimes it was a simple demonstration that raised questions. Other times it might be a game or an activity involving the participation of my students.

For example, one lesson began by taking a dish with some milk in it, placing a couple of drops of different food colorings in a few places in the milk, and then adding a drop of dish detergent. My students were absolutely mesmerized by the swirling colors that erupted when the soap broke down the surface tension of the milk. You would have thought we had just discovered the atom.

Once I had their attention, questions would invariably arise and we could discuss the content, the science of what they were experiencing. I would lead them into the process of doing science by writing down hypotheses, observations and conclusions. I would often let them work together which involved cooperation, planning and teamwork. I encouraged my students to conduct research into their topics and to try to push themselves to learn about things they did not understand. For some reason, they often preferred to tell me what they already *knew* rather than explore the unknown.

I always encouraged them to make mistakes in science. *That* was where the *real* learning took place. If you made a mistake, I knew you were learning something. At the very least, you were learning what *not* to do in the future; and then you could go try something else. If you never made any mistakes, you weren't learning anything.

Sometimes I would use the textbook to teach the content, but I often used it as a reference, not as a Bible. I might have students read individually, or in small groups, or we might read as a whole class. I might Xerox the passage we were reading so the kids could highlight the important parts in yellow marker. I might have them trace diagrams or illustrations out of the textbook, or even answer the dreaded questions at the end of the chapter.

But just as often, I would not use the textbook at all. I would use a video or find an online resource or bring in a stack of books from my local library on the topic. I would bring in real examples of stuff we were studying. The kids often had to make something that would teach the concepts I was trying to convey to them.

It was very creative. It took a bit of planning and a lot of assorted materials. It involved hours of work, not even counting the class-time.

My students loved it and hated it at the same time. They loved that they could work with their friends and that they didn't have to sit in their seats for the whole class. They appreciated the fact I allowed them to talk, ask questions and express opinions. They enjoyed it when there was some sort of fun contest or culminating activity. They really liked the fact that I assessed them in ways other than a standard test format. And they really, really liked the fact that I always seemed to have anything they might need for a project or to solve a problem.

"Rick, I need some string"' someone would ask and I would quickly produce a piece of string from inside my desk drawer.

"Who's yo daddy?" I would say as I gave it to the kid.

"You ain't my daddy!" the kid would reply.

"Rick, Rick, do you have a safety pin?" a student would ask. Again I just happened to have one to solve the problem.

"Who's yo daddy, Melissa?" I would say as I dropped it on her table.

"Not you, that's for sure! You ain't my daddy!" Melissa would claim.

"Rick, I need one of those things that help you draw good letters." In no time I produced my collection of stencils for the kid to choose one that was just right for his poster. "I'll use this one" he would say and look at me, smiling, waiting for me to say "Who's yo daddy?" which I always did.

"You're not MY daddy!" he'd shout, grinning from ear to ear.

Eventually, I earned the reputation as the 'go-to-guy' for anything that anybody ever needed in the school. Sometimes, in the middle of teaching a class, a student would come into my room from another class and ask if I had some obscure item. I was almost always able to produce some facsimile of whatever they needed from my collection of 'stuff'. And of course, as the student left my class with the goods, he would always hear me ask "Who's yo daddy?"

Now, I told you that my students loved my teaching style and hated it at the same time. In the interest of fairness, I must tell you what they hated about my classes. First of all, I asked a lot of questions and only rarely gave out answers. That drove some of my students crazy.

"Could you just tell us the answer?" they would frequently ask.

I would usually give a hint and tell them where they might be able to find the answer.

"Is this it? Is this it?" they would yell, pointing to a page in the book.

I might say something like "Does that say anything at all about the question you're trying to answer?"

"JUST TELL US THE GODDAMN ANSWER!" an exasperated student might scream at me.

I would smile, perhaps model a re-phrasing of their profanity, and ignore their plea until I found someone who had persevered and found the answer to the question or a solution to the problem. Then I would be all over that student with lavish praise and compliments, telling them how proud they must feel right now, really giving them the royal treatment. They might even get a tootsie pop or some token reward. In seconds, it seemed that everyone in the room had mysteriously come up with the very same correct answer, the one that had eluded them up to that point. I calmly declared it a 'miracle' and moved on.

My students also hated the fact that I worked them hard. I expected them to not just *do* the assignment; I expected them to do a 'good job'. Our educational system has taught many of our at-risk youth they can get away with the bare minimum of effort. Sadly for many, there is little incentive to succeed in school. In my classroom I remained relentless in my expectations for them to show me how smart they were, that there was nothing they couldn't do if they put their heart and mind into it. I often worked alongside them to model the skills I wanted them to learn. I encouraged them and suggested ideas that might help them reach their goal.

This is not to say I had the same expectations for every student. Fairness did not necessarily mean that all students were treated perfectly equal. I might expect one level of writing from one student and demand extremely different expectations from another student. Both were held to high standards for their own achievement, but that might look very different in appearance.

I expected my students to show me, and hopefully others, what they knew about any of the topics we were studying. I did my part in 'cutting to the chase' to teach them what they needed to know. But they always had to do their part and show me what they knew. Otherwise, nobody would ever know how smart they were.

But I knew they were smart. Wicked smart when they wanted (or had) to be. Their intelligence was just hidden below the surface waiting to be uncovered.

I haven't told you anything at all about how I learned to make an *artful escape* when I was teaching a lesson. I found out that there are times when you have to actively engage kids in the stuff they are learning about, and there are times when you just have to let them wrestle with it themselves. You have to trust your students, and you have to trust yourself, and you have to trust the learning process itself.

During my first year, I discovered that I could not *make* my students learn anything. I could only make them *want* to learn. The rest was really up to them. All they needed from me was a little guidance or encouragement and maybe a little "stuff". But once I had them engaged in their own learning, it was best if I could just slip quietly away and hope that nobody noticed.

28

MINIATURE GOLF MATH

I had finished all my graduate coursework at Antioch by December of my first year teaching. All the requirements for my Master of Education degree in the area of Integrated Learning had been met and I had submitted my credentials to the state for certification. There were no more college classes, no more papers to write. Now, all I had to do was teach. I thought I had finally made it to 'Easy Street'. Well, at least it *seemed* easier to me to just be a teacher and not a student at the same time. But of course, it was still a lot of work.

I loved the concept of Integrated Learning. It made so much sense to me. Instead of teaching isolated bits of knowledge, why not tie it all together and integrate art and music and science and math and literacy? Don't we want our students to be well rounded, to become whole people? Everything in life was connected anyway, whether we wanted to admit it or not.

With at-risk kids, the art and music could be motivating pathways into literacy and math. They loved to draw and they were always listening to and talking about music. Why not use them as the motivational tools they were? Perhaps we could teach them the grade level expectations they need to know and they wouldn't even realize they were learning until it was too late to do anything about it! *Gotcha!*

It all seemed so clear, so *real* to me. I was standing in front of the classroom speaking to the class. "WOW, kids, this is amazing! We're all done with our unit on fractions! You just showed me that you understand all there is to know about fractions."

"We did?" they were astonished.

"Of course! There's no way you could have replicated and analyzed the paintings of Piet Mondrian without understanding fractions! Congratulations! Your math test scores are going to go through the roof!" Somewhere, a buzzer was going off signaling the next class period.

Oh, wait. That's not the buzzer for class; it was my alarm going off: 6 a.m. Still half asleep, I rolled over to shut off the alarm. I had been dreaming again. I often had weird dreams lately about my teaching. I was often searching for students who were hiding. I had nightmares about food fights in the cafeteria with endless supplies of potato puffs and carrot sticks.

Another day was beginning. I had to remember to bring in the cardboard boxes and the felt. And the marbles, don't forget the marbles, I reminded myself. I often forgot my cup of coffee in the mornings, and I could live with that. But I couldn't live with the fact that I might forget some vital item or piece of equipment for a lesson I was planning that day. That would be an unforgivable act of stupidity on my part. I might as well go back to bed if I forgot something like the marbles.

I was going to integrate learning that day, come hell or high water. My plan was to teach math concepts using a miniature golf course. My students were going to create a tabletop version of a miniature golf course while learning about probability, ranges, and averages. Each student would be tasked with creating a hole for the golf course using the cardboard boxes and felt and an assortment of other odd stuff I had collected. We would use pencils for golf clubs and the marbles for golf balls. The students would have to determine what 'par' was for their particular hole by gathering data on how many shots it took for other students to get the marble into the hole. Then they would have to add it up and determine the average, which would become their par.

My students became very excited about this assignment. As their projects came to life, it was not uncommon for holes on our miniature golf course to have a par of '15' or even '20'. Such was the difficulty of some of the greens. What I had not taken into account when planning this lesson was how much some of the kids would get into the *building* phase of the project. For some, it was not enough to have a well-designed green with a slope and an obstacle or two. Students were building tunnels and bridges and the all-too famous waterfall often seen at the most popular summer destinations. I had students putting together two boxes to make their green longer, and then three boxes with another one on top of those. There were holes to drop through and jumps to navigate. Needless to say, the students' level of engagement was extremely high.

Not everyone got into the math portion as intensely; eventually though, pretty much everybody was able to arrive at an appropriate par for his or her green. I had to help some kids by leading them through the math process step-by step. That was OK, though; it reminded me that I was still teaching amongst all the chaos and laughter and yelling going on in my classroom.

The project took a couple of days for everybody to complete their green and to play the whole course. Some of the kids were extremely proud of what they had done. There were a few who were frustrated that their green was falling apart or that somebody had damaged, or even worse, COPIED something they had built. By the end of the project, most of the students had a pretty strong understanding what an average was and how to arrive at one.

Of course, my over-achieving ego couldn't just leave it at that though. Idealistically, I had this vision of taking them to a real miniature golf course to play a game or two as a culminating activity. There was even an ice cream stand there to celebrate the event. The place had just opened for the season, so we got a good rate arriving on a school day when most kids were still in school and the place was empty.

Everything was going according to plan as I grouped all my students into teams and equipped them with golf clubs. There were some inappropriate jokes about the color of somebody's balls, but there weren't any other golfers there yet, so their behavior was not a problem. The groundskeeper asked kids to stay where they were supposed to be a few times, not to climb on the cave, no big deal. Then some students began calling him a grouch and other unpleasantries. I tried to keep them focused on the game.

At this point several 'real' customers had arrived on the scene and I found myself continually reminding my students to watch their language. A couple of four-year-olds were playing with their grandfather nearby. They watched the antics of my students intently as I prayed for my students to show appropriate manners and self-control.

As students were finishing the course, I directed them to go over to the ice cream stand. I had arranged for them each to get a small cone, nothing else. I was arguing with Luis why they could not have chilidogs also, when I saw Dominic swinging his club near Adrian's head. Thankfully, he missed.

Knowing about Dominic's explosive temper and how he had beaten up his mother, I quickly ushered him onto the bus and had him wait there with the bus driver until everyone had finished their ice cream. When we were all finished we joined him on the bus for the ride back to school. It was another example of a logical consequence.

I asked Dom why he would do something so dangerous when we were all having such a good time. Adrian could have been seriously hurt, I reminded him. All Dominic could do was hang his head like a puppy that had just had an unfortunate accident on the rug. Then he gazed up at me with a little glint in his eyes and he said, "I missed him on purpose," as the smile broke through his mouth. "He can be so annoying," Dom confessed.

"Good choice, then," I sighed, knowing how annoying Adrian can be sometimes. "I'm glad you made the right choice." Progress with at-risk kids comes in small increments, I reminded myself.

29

ANOTHER PERFECT DAY

The school year was winding down and summer vacation loomed on everyone's horizon – especially mine. I was hopelessly infected with spring fever. I had not had an entire summer off since I was fourteen years old myself. This was one of the parts of my plan that I was most looking forward to. Ten weeks with nothing to do but relax, unwind and recharge my batteries. Oh boy! And this was only the first of many summer vacations Carol and I planned on sharing together.

I had already been offered a contract to come back and teach at the ALT school for the following year. My teaching position was secure. I knew in my heart that I had established myself as a teacher, but there were still some formalities surrounding my professional status that had yet to take place.

The first quietly occurred one afternoon when I arrived home after school. In the mailbox was a very official piece of mail from the State Department of Education. Inside I found a formal certificate with a fancy border announcing I was now officially certified as a teacher. I proudly held that piece of paper in my hands and considered the events of the past few years. I did it – I had become a teacher! It was now a 'done' deal. All my hard work was paying off, if not financially, at least emotionally. Carol and I celebrated that night with a cheap meal out.

The other formality consisted of my graduation from Antioch with my Masters of Education degree. The silly ceremony itself was exciting for me – the caps and gowns, the pomp and circumstance, all the hopeful speeches. I fought back tears when my name was called and I walked across the stage to get my diploma. From up on the stage I could see Carol and my kids in the audience. I held my diploma over my heart and then pointed to them. The diploma, the plan – it was for *all* of us, not just for me.

There was another ceremony at Antioch that I need to tell you about also. It was much less formal but no less important than the graduation itself. To celebrate the culmination of our studies, the education department at ANE had a tradition of hosting one last pot luck gathering where students and faculty got together before the graduates headed off on their missions to change the world. There was ample beer and wine and unusual vegetarian dishes, the ingredients of which one could only imagine. It was probably the last time we would all be together, so the evening held a very special and festive atmosphere.

The ceremonious part of this gathering had to do with our Antioch professors. Our advisors had each carefully selected a book for every one of the graduates that somehow spoke to the uniqueness of each one of us as individual teachers. As they presented us each with our specially chosen book, they spoke about why they had chosen that particular book and what it was about us that made us so special. Passages from the selected book were sometimes read for emphasis. It was a magical moment and there were lots of laughs and quite a few tears.

I was one of the last to be presented with my book. As soon as my advisor Don started speaking about some of the difficult challenges I had overcome and the unbelievable situations that I faced everyday in my classroom, I knew this would be another one of those moments I would never forget. In the end, he presented me with a perfectly appropriate book entitled *Another Perfect Day*, by Ross MacDonald. It was about a typical guy who overcomes some super-human challenges when things don't go as planned. I loved it.

Back in my classroom, near the end of the school year, a lot of the students were talking about what they were going to be doing over the summer. It didn't sound very exciting. They weren't heading out on exotic vacations or being sent off to exclusive camps. They might get to spend a weekend with their dad or go fishing down by the river. I tried to convince them that even though they didn't have any big plans for the summer, that didn't mean it had to be boring. Each day had the potential to be fun and interesting. I decided to have a little read-aloud with them and I pulled out my precious gift from Antioch, *Another Perfect Day!* I sat in front of the class and read the story in an exaggerated singsong voice, holding the book up high so they could all see the pictures as I was reading.

Oh, I had the usual chorus coming from the kids "THIS IS GAY, THIS IS SO GAY!" as I continued to turn the pages and tell them the story. But they got the idea. They knew what I was telling them. They understood it was going to be up to them to turn the summer into something fun and interesting.

It was undeniably true that I was looking forward to summer vacation with great anticipation. But I also had to admit that I was already starting to look forward to September and seeing some of those familiar faces in my class again next year.

30

HOW I SPENT MY SUMMER VACATION

Summer vacation was turning out to be everything I had imagined it would be. Carol and I packed up our stuff and set up camp near the beach on Cape Cod as soon as school let out. We immersed ourselves in the outdoors - bike rides, whale and seal watches, swatting bugs by the campfire while we roasted kosher hot dogs and sipped home-made margaritas made with diet soda.

Carol and I both loved to read, and now we found ourselves with unlimited hours to relax with our books. We read on the beach and huddled in the evenings under the limited light from our comfortable little camper.

I always tried to read something 'just for fun' while I was on vacation, but my serious side also insisted that I read a few things that had some intellectual meat. In this, my first summer as a card-carrying schoolteacher, that meant I had to read a few books on discipline in the classroom, or the prevalence of poverty in our culture and how it was infecting our schools. And of course, being a science teacher I read about general science topics that interested me. Besides, I would freely admit I was an unabashed nature-lover, so I enjoyed reading about science anyway.

One of the books that I read for 'fun' that summer happened to be a novel from the *Oprah Book Club* entitled *I Know This Much Is True* by Wally

Lamb. It was a strange tale about a young man who encountered a great deal of misfortune in his life and how he tried to deal with it. Having been through a good bit of personal despair myself, and having witnessed the unbelievable adversity facing so many of my students during the course of the previous school year, it was a story that resonated deeply within me. The main character in the novel suggests that God, if indeed a supreme being exists, can only be found in the hardest of circumstances. You don't stumble upon God when things are easy - you can only really discover the presence of a higher power when the going gets tough, sometimes really tough. He called these moments when humans can be completely overcome by despair the 'round places'. The round places in life were the difficult times that try to wear you down and test your character.

As Carol and I walked along the beach, I reflected on the events of the past few years and how I felt stronger and more alive now than I had felt in a long, long time. Could it be that all the challenges and hardships and incredibly heart-wrenching circumstances I had experienced had some larger purpose? Was I a part of a much larger plan that I was only beginning to glimpse?

We strolled along the edge of the beach where the waves meet the sand, keeping an eye out for sea glass as we often did. When we found some, we would pick it up and tuck it away in a safe place to add to our growing collection at home. Someday, Carol hoped to do something with it, but we had no idea what. We just liked having something to look for as we walked along with the waves pounding around our ankles.

We came upon a stretch of beach that was not too crowed and my eye was caught this time, not by a glistening piece of sea glass, but by a small stone. Its polished white surface was almost perfectly round; it looked like an egg of some sort. I picked it up to check it out and felt the roundness in my hand. I was thinking how nice it felt – how smooth, just the right weight, just the right size. It felt like it had always belonged in my hand.

My mind raced back to the book I had been reading and how it spoke about stumbling upon God in the 'round places'. Surely, this simple white stone had been worn down by the harsh circumstances of its life. Who knows how long the salt and the sand and the wind and the water had pushed it around? This small, egg-like object was an innocent victim to the overwhelming forces of gravity and erosion. And yet, here it was: perfect and beautiful and impressive in its strength to exist despite all odds. I stared at the stone, awestruck by the revelation I had just experienced.

Carol asked, "Are you all right?" noticing I had stopped walking.

"Yeah. I'm good." I finally responded. I wasn't sure if I would be able to put into words what I was thinking in that moment and the symbolism I discovered in that small white stone. I slipped the stone into my pocket and we continued along the beach.

We had not gone far when I found myself picking up another stone, this one also polished but black as the night, and not quite as spherical as the first. It, too, was nonetheless an amazing specimen of another 'round place.' Then I discovered the green one, and the speckled one, and the beige one. I found one that was an almost perfect equilateral triangle with the softest rounded corners. I found some incredibly tiny gems and ones that had intricate patterns of lines in them. I held each specimen in my hand to see if it had that 'perfect' feel to it, and then slipped it into my pocket.

I wasn't sure what I was going to do with these amazing discoveries, but I was sure they held a larger purpose than getting pushed around by the tide and the waves on the beach.

By the time we got back to our car, I was clutching the waistband of my shorts as I walked to keep them from falling down. My pockets were bulging almost as much as my spirit.

PART TWO

31

BACK TO SCHOOL

When school started back up in September, I hit the ground running. I knew what I had to do. There was no naiveté clouding my thinking this year – my innocence had been gradually whittled away during my rookie year by the razor edge of raw experience.

My list of students for the upcoming year included many names that were already familiar to me. This helped to increase my confidence. They were returning to the ALT school for round two and I was ready for them. I had already established good working relationships with most of them. I knew what they were good at, I knew what they struggled with and, most importantly, I knew which kids would most likely give me the most trouble.

There were new faces, however, and these were unknown entities, wild cards thrown into the mix. I was aware it would take time to uncover their true personalities, but I also felt there was little they could do to intimidate me. I had spent the summer reflecting on what worked in my classroom and what didn't. I had refined my methods and my lesson plans to accommodate their energy and idiosyncrasies. My bag of tricks was full and I was ready for them – all of them.

Take challenging behavior for example. I had arranged a meeting with the school psychologist where we devised a consistent behavior plan that the whole school could use to raise the level of socially acceptable behavior. Our plan identified four major areas of behavior: respecting yourself, respecting others, respecting learning, and respecting our environment. Students and teachers were all instructed on what the expectations were for each category, and students earned points every class period in all four categories. Our behavior rubric placed ownership for the students' behavior squarely on themselves, and it allowed us to recognize the kids who were responding appropriately with praise and motivational rewards. We knew that behavior would always be an issue at the ALT, but at least now we had a pro-active system for responding to it effectively and consistently.

Literacy would also continue to be a major challenge for many of our students. I had witnessed first-hand the lack of books or any reading material in their homes. A large percentage of our students only spoke Spanish at home. Reading and comprehension loomed as crucial skills for them to acquire if they were going to have any hope of staying in school and graduating. Together with my principal and another teacher, we wrote and received a large grant that would supply a state-of-the-art computerized reading skills program along with twenty computer stations to implement the program. We were ecstatic about the potential to improve our students' literacy skills, not to mention the increased access to technology. All the cards were falling into place.

I had devised some practical solutions to tackle specific problems in my own classroom as well. I had a new (and larger) room this year and I would only be teaching science. I strategically placed my desk and some old bookshelves to create an area that the students could not get in to, at least not easily. My personal stuff would be reasonably safe from theft, misuse or potential destruction. I purchased notebooks for each student to be used as Science Journals to increase writing across the curriculum. I hung a special small whiteboard for the sole purpose of itemizing the daily schedule and important announcements so everyone would always know what was going on. I even hung an obnoxious bamboo wind chime in front of the door to the adjoining classroom. If someone opened the forbidden door, I would be notified immediately of the offense and the escapee would be caught before slipping out of the room. (Oh, how the kids grew to hate that wind chime!)

To further my professional growth, I had signed up for a course at the local college specifically on how to teach science. The school district was required to provide the state department of education with some sort of proof that all its science teachers were "highly qualified" to teach science. If I took this course, they told me, I would be considered highly qualified. "Not bad, for my second year of teaching," I thought, even as I wondered privately how many unqualified teachers were "highly qualified".

I had also spent a good part of the summer researching 'best practices' and successful approaches for alternative education for at-risk youth. I was both surprised and encouraged to realize how many of the best practices being touted by the research were in fact being employed in some fashion in our own fledgling program at the ALT. So, with the encouragement of my principal, I prepared a proposal to present some of my findings at the National Conference for Alternative Schools. Surprisingly, I was indeed selected to be a presenter at the conference in Orlando that following winter. Me, a national presenter, in my second year of teaching?

I was so psyched – my plan was working out better than I had ever dreamed. I was on top of my game. I was ready for anything.

And then of course, the kids showed up. They apparently had plans of their own.

32

THE USUAL ASSORTMENT

In September the usual assortment of at-risk kids showed up in my classroom, but there were more of them this year. The ALT program had been expanded slightly, and since I was only teaching science this year, I would have twice the number of students to teach, forty-five to be exact.

Surveying my class lists, one would find that only eight of them came from what could be called an 'intact' family. In other words, thirty-seven of them did not live with both biological parents. And the eight kids who were living with both bio-parents were often not much better off. These were not folks who even remotely resembled the land of *Leave It To Beaver.*

Another statistic, even more frightening, was that eight of my new students had been 'crack' babies. Of course I could not be absolutely sure of this statistic – but it seemed reasonably likely based on the behaviors they were exhibiting, and the information I had at hand.

I suspected the mothers of several of my students were prostitutes, there were a number of them who spoke little or no English, and many moms were either unemployed or on some sort of disability. One mother claimed to be an actual witch, which I strongly believed to be true.

The fathers, stepfathers, mother's boyfriends and assorted male authority figures were not in much better shape. Dad seemed to be for the most part either in jail, or just out of jail and whereabouts unknown. Some kids had not seen their dad for many years, and a few did not even know who dad was. I could sense a great deal of anger at the various father figures that had passed in and out of their young formative lives.

On the bright side, one of my new students was an amazing natural musician. He could tap sticks and rulers and anything else he could grab, creating rhythms that amazed everybody. "I have to get this kid into a drum and bugle corps," I thought. Another one displayed amazing artistic talent, which I recognized as being beyond what one would expect from a middle school student. Several of the kids were extremely intelligent, despite their records of failure in previous schools. Something had to be going on to prevent them from being successful.

One of the boys, Aaron, prided himself on being a really good thief. He quickly showed me, and the class, how good he was by lifting everything of mine that was not nailed down. All my efforts at protecting my personal property did not make a dent in Aaron's ability to pilfer through my stuff and 'borrow' things. The weird part was that he always gave me the items back – he never kept anything. He just wanted to show me he could do it. I think it was a psychological attempt on his part to get close to me.

One day near the beginning of the year, Aaron had taken something and disrupted the class to the point I had to call him out privately to talk to him and see what was going on. He confided to me that he didn't know why he was doing it, he was just all messed up since his sister had just recently died. He told me she was just two years older than him. He admitted that he and his mom were a complete mess. He shared details about a car crash in the next town, something about a drunk driver. I adeptly switched gears into the consoling and supportive male authority figure and suggested he speak with one of the guidance counselors. I gave him a guidance pass and he was gone for the rest of the class period.

The next day the stealing continued and, in fact, escalated. Aaron had stolen another teacher's car keys, and his Mom had already been called and was on her way in for a meeting. As we sat down to talk, I gently told her how sorry I was to hear about her loss, that Aaron had told me about her daughter, and it must be an awful time. "How are you holding up?" I asked.

Her eyes grew wide and she said to me, "What are you talking about?"

"Your daughter." I said, struggling at how I should proceed. "Aaron told me his sister had just died in an awful car accident."

Aaron's mom burst out laughing. "That little liar!" she said. "When I get my hands on him he's going to wish *HE* was in a car accident. Aaron might hate his sister, but she's very much alive and driving us all crazy!"

Aaron was only one of the forty-five assorted kids I worked with my second year. He recently came back to visit me, showing up unexpectedly at my classroom doorway one afternoon with a couple of friends. He just wanted to stop in and say 'hi'. He was eighteen now, had gotten his GED, and was working in an electronics store until it went out of business. He looked good, he sounded good and I gave him a hug when he left. Out of habit, I also glanced around the room, taking a quick look to be sure that nothing was missing.

Apparently, even Aaron had grown up.

33

LOST IN SPACE

Learning was certainly taking place in my classroom, and I was pretty sure that some of it even had to do with science. On a few occasions I overheard students arguing about some obscure scientific point or intensely debating the different conclusions they came up with after observing the same phenomena. This was the process of doing real science at its best - and I absolutely loved it.

My students appeared to love it most of the time too - especially when I was not teaching out of the textbook. I became pretty adept at designing challenges that would lead them into a deeper understanding of their world around them. My challenges were hands-on, they involved creativity, and the students usually had the option of working with partners or teams. There was always some form of final product or presentations involved so that I could assess their learning, and ultimately, determine a grade for the almighty report card.

One of my favorite projects was the space station challenge. I wanted the kids to consider the factors that create severe environments in different parts of space. Gravity, for instance is determined by the size of a planet. Temperature ranges would be dependent on a planet's distance from its sun. A planet with oxygen would provide a vastly different environment from one that had none. I'm sure you get the idea.

Now if a space station were built in one of these remote areas of outer space, and you had to provide a place for humans to work and live, what would it look like? How would people communicate? How would they produce their food? What form of travel would they use? What problems might they encounter? These were the questions my students pondered.

I would bring in all sorts of junk for them to use to create their space stations and ask probing questions to get them to think and push themselves as they worked. The results were often phenomenal.

One group had constructed a huge cardboard dome over their space station to simulate darkness; then they punched small holes in it and poked Christmas lights through so it looked like stars. They had used some sort of spray-painted cottony material for the surface of their planet. They created a small slit in the cardboard to look through and admire their creation. It looked so realistic in the darkness they thought they could sell it to a real museum. We compromised by inviting a nearby kindergarten class to come in one afternoon to look at it. I sensed that my students were not used to feeling so proud of something they created in school.

Another group was comprised of four girls and Tim. The girls were very precise about what they wanted in their space station, but somehow Tim, as the token male, had become responsible for doing most of the building. The girls had designed a completely coordinated color scheme throughout the space station from the curtains on the windows right down to matching utensils on the desks and tables - it was gorgeous. Even the color of the miniature computer terminals had to match. I had never seen Tim exhibit so much patience as he did working on that space station with the girls. He received extra credit for all of his efforts and I am certain his learning extended far beyond the field of science.

Kirk had chosen to work on his space station alone. He had assembled a complicated system of buildings connected by tubes. He was trying to figure out how he could have smoke coming from the power plant. I asked him if he had ever tried using dry ice. His eyes grew wide and he begged me to bring some in so he could use it. “It would be so cool!” he pleaded.

The next day was more about dry ice than anything else. Everybody wanted to see it, to play with it. I had some students look it up online to answer their questions about how it worked. I snapped a great photograph of Kirk looking out over the smoke billowing from his power plant and used it in my presentation at the national conference on alternative education. His eyes glistened in the camera’s flash and his smile spread all the way across his face. That one picture said it all.

34

WHAT'S ON THEIR MINDS

During this, my second year of teaching, I began taking a science methods course at the local college to achieve 'highly qualified' status. The course actually turned out to be very helpful to me in several ways. Besides learning some great ways to incorporate hands-on approaches to teach basic concepts of science, the course also helped me to be able to assess what it was my students were learning, if anything. I learned how to ask probing questions to get inside their heads and find out what they were thinking – and with my at-risk student population, this was scary business.

I had already been dabbling in this area myself – I was always trying to figure out what they were thinking, usually with little success. In an attempt to demonstrate how a scientist gathers data and communicates results using graphs, I had created a quick lesson that I thought might be fun. We had been studying the human brain and about how different areas of the brain were responsible for different functions. So I prepared a simple drawing of a brain on a sheet of copy paper with a very scientific label: "The Teenage Brain". There were some basic squiggly shapes that marked some general areas within the brain, but that was it – nice and simple.

It was the students' assignment to color in different parts of the brain depending on what they thought about. If they thought a lot about sports, for example, there should be a large area of their brain devoted to sports. I told them if they thought about sex, or drugs or gangs – any of the taboo subjects – the assignment was confidential and they could list it, as long as they did so appropriately. Nothing too graphic, I admonished them. I told them I was going to gather the results and tabulate it for everyone to see. I even told them not to put their names on their papers because I didn't want to know who thought about what.

For some odd reason, no one refused to do this assignment. In fact, the more they got into it, the more things they wanted to add – there was so much that they thought about. They would see a classmate add something and I'd hear "Oh Yeah! I think about that too!" and I'd see them adding it to their 'Mind Map,' as I was calling it.

I gathered all the papers and spent several hours that evening calculating the results and entering them into a spreadsheet I could graph.

The next day I displayed a beautiful color bar graph that clearly showed what all the teenagers in my class were thinking about. By far the tallest column belonged to the category 'family'. There were a bunch of topics on the second tier: friends, personal appearance, money and the future all ranked pretty high. Surprisingly enough, the category of 'romance' fell fairly low on the list, despite all the bravado that I overheard from time to time in the classroom. At the bottom of the pile they listed health and food – very few of them ever thought about those topics. Privately, I questioned that last result since the kids were always asking me if I had anything to eat. I presented the results as objectively and scientifically as I could so that my students would have the feeling of being part of scientific research.

Now, I am not proposing for a second that the data we gathered represented any sort of a scientific finding. There was nothing in our results that would shock the scientific community, and of course, that was not my intent. But the exercise did get everybody thinking, and sharing ideas, and the results really could not be disputed. Most importantly for me, it gave me a quick peek into their brains to get a glimpse of what was going on.

I had another opportunity to get a much clearer picture of how they reason and figure things out thanks to an exercise I carried out for the science methods course I was taking. Our class at the local college was investigating the use of videotaping students as they were working. The intent was to assess the learning that was taking place as the students wrestled with some sort of problem. The idea fascinated me. I talked my professor into coming into my classroom to help me videotape the kids as they worked.

We had moved beyond the brain into the skeletal system. I wanted the kids to understand the functions of skeletons and how they support the body of any vertebrate. They were working in pairs and small groups to create models of skeletons such as you might see in a museum. I had gathered pictures of all kinds of skeletons for them to choose from and create a model out of all sorts of junk. There was wood, plastic and a lot of weird stuff I had brought in for them to use. There were hot glue guns in action all over the room.

I was circulating around the classroom helping students, asking questions, providing glue sticks, and keeping them on task. I was being a 'facilitator' of learning rather than standing in front of them delivering information about the functions of a skeleton. My professor moved among the students with the camera, videotaping them as they explained what they were doing and why they had chosen a particular approach to a problem. At the end of class, she told me how impressed she was by the kids, by their level of engagement, and she thoroughly had a great time. She left the camera with me so I could view the tape after class when I could give it my full attention.

I viewed the videotape at home that evening, not once, but several times. I studied how the kids communicated with each other; I studied their eye movements. I was particularly interested in how they observed each other ALL THE TIME. I observed that the kids appear to do most of their learning from watching each other and imitating each other. This was a bit of an eye-opener for me. I thought *I* was the instructor in the class and that they listened to *ME* to learn things. Not true. They practically ignored me – they scrutinized each other for signals, ideas and solutions to their problems. It was as if they had to keep up with each other. Maybe I should plan lessons where I *expected* them to copy from one another. Hmmm.

It was another fascinating glimpse into the mind of an at-risk teenager. I wondered if the day would ever dawn that I could say I knew what I was doing as a teacher, highly qualified or not. I began to think not. But I did wish I could hire a camera crew to work in my room alongside me on a regular basis. There was so much to capture in my microcosm of a classroom. We might not be at the cutting edge of human learning, but I could always guarantee there'd be interesting film at eleven for the nightly news broadcast, that's for sure!

35

THE FARM

Remember how I told you I often entertained my graduate classmates at Antioch by telling them my crazy stories of life at the Alt school? The other grad students always enjoyed hearing about my little 'gangstas' – it provided such a unique perspective for them.

One day at Antioch one of my classmates, Pete, came up to me and told me about a farm he was working on in Vermont. The farm had an educational program designed to teach urban kids about where their food came from, life cycles of animals, all the different types of activities that take place on your typical farm. "It would be a wonderful experience for your kids," he told me.

You might say I was a bit skeptical. "*MY* kids?" I arched my eyebrows. I was leery about taking my kids anywhere; they seemed to find or create trouble wherever they went. I could only imagine the havoc they would cause on Pete's idyllic, pastoral dairy farm.

"No, really." he pressed on. "We take in tough kids from all over, from Harlem in the Bronx, Roxbury in Boston; some even come from Chicago. The kids love it and you get to see a whole other side to them. Besides," he was really pressuring me now, "You don't have to pay for anything except how to get here."

With this latest piece of information I now began to seriously entertain the idea. A foundation had been set up by wealthy benefactors to provide a week in the country for city kids. All we had to do was help out with the farm chores. Meals, lodging, and all equipment were provided. Pete and I spoke for a bit, and I agreed to come up on a weekend and have a look. The thought of spending a week on a farm with my 'gangstas' was still hard to grasp.

A few weekends later, my wife and I and two other teachers travelled up to the farm to check it out. The more we saw, the more we liked. The cows were surprisingly beautiful – like enormous golden retrievers. The kids would be able to experience all sorts of hands-on activities and learn things we could never teach in a classroom. Another plus, the farm was in the middle of nowhere, so there was literally nowhere the kids could run off to. The entire staff was superb – they really knew what they were doing and had a ton of experience working with the issues of urban kids.

I was concerned about the overnight living conditions since it was *my* liability that would be at stake if I brought my students up here. There were five rooms with bunk beds for students, a couple of rooms for chaperones, nice clean, private bathrooms – this was do-able, I thought. There was a magnificent great room with huge cathedral ceiling and some old couches for relaxing. We could have meetings or organize games and activities right there if the weather wasn't cooperating. The huge kitchen came with a fabulous cook who would prepare all our meals. It all seemed too good to be true.

Now, in the day to day reality of human existence, we all recognize that awful things can happen to people – accidents, sickness, calamities of every nature, and even death. There are few among us who can claim they are totally untouched by some tragedy at some point in their life. These awful events fill the newspapers and TV coverage every day, and their horrors linger in our memory, in some cases forever. My students, of course, were no strangers to these harsh realities of life.

But we have to remember that *good things* happen, too – unbelievably good things. Discovering the farm for my students was one of those good things. We brought our first group of students up to the farm that spring, and we have been bringing kids back every chance we get. The farm turned out to be, as one student put it, "By far, the best field trip I have ever been on." But it was much more than a great field trip; it turned out to be a special place where we, as teachers, actually began to witness some of the transformations that were in fact taking place in our students. Whether with a group of boys or a group of girls, it was nothing short of magical.

First of all, the kids got to be kids again. Gone were the drugs and gang culture of the city streets. They had a comfortable place to sleep, lots of great food, fun stuff to do, and no parents around – just a few overworked chaperones to keep order. Each season at the farm brought different activities and with it new opportunities for learning. No trip was exactly like any other.

I will never forget that first trip with a group of boys in early March. Besides caring for the cows and other animals, we were also tapping maple trees to gather sap to be boiled into maple syrup. It had snowed while we were there and I had brought a couple of old toboggans along for fun. We had a little time to kill in between chores, so I told the boys they could try out the toboggans. They excitedly dragged them up the driveway. I watched dumbstruck as they put the sled down in the snow facing the wrong way, and all of them proceeded to sit on it backwards – they didn't even know which way a toboggan points down the hill! I demonstrated the correct way to ride one, and they all agreed that it worked much better that way. And then, they were off! The runs got longer, the jumps got bigger, the sled grew more crowded as they figured out how many people it could hold. They were having a blast, and so was I, just watching them be kids.

That night, after all the evening activities and chores were done, a small group still wanted to go out once more to sled in the dark. They wanted to try one of the bigger hills over near the barn. We found a place that looked promising – I had to make sure there were no electric fences they would run into in the dark. I always had to keep safety in mind since I had promised all their mothers I would return them safe and sound.

The boys dragged the sled up the hill and I stayed down at the bottom near the road. If a car should happen to come by on this dark, deserted road, I would be there to *save* them from catastrophe. At first, the sled did not go very far or very fast – the snow was too deep. But you know how things pick up once the snow gets packed down. Things quickly picked up. I was standing in the snow guarding the roadway and the kids came barreling down the hill faster than ever. They were flying. I realized there was no way they were going to stop before the road so I got in position to 'catch' them as they came down. They bulldozed right over me and shot out across the road and finally came to a stop in a ditch on the other side. They were all laughing hysterically. I recited a short prayer thanking God there were no vehicles out on that particular stretch of country road that moonlit evening. I knew I had dodged a bullet: no one had been hurt or killed.

"That's it," I told them, "We're done sledding for the evening," I said as I got up and brushed the snow off me. Together we dragged the toboggan back to the bunkhouse, amazed at how bright the Vermont night was with the moon shining on the snow-covered fields. This was definitely not your typical class trip, we all agreed.

36

FROM BOYS TO MEN

I have to admit I did things at the farm that a grown man has no business doing. I rolled my ankle one night playing manhunt; yes, *manhunt*. I heard a loud pop, and thought my ankle was broken. Laying sprawled on the ground in the dark, I wondered how I was going to explain myself. I spent most of that week using a crutch. On another trip, we came upon a huge grassy hill and we all started to roll down it – over and over and over – you know, the way kids do. I lost my eyeglasses when they slipped out of my coat pocket. I was blind without them, and had to resort to wearing my prescription sunglasses. Have you ever worn sunglasses at night? It was quite a challenge chaperoning my charges under the circumstances. I did find my glasses the next day, but it was certainly a night I would not wish to relive.

I rode a pig. I experienced the shock of an electric fence. I squirted milk directly and intentionally out of a cow's teat and into the face of my students. I witnessed the birth of a calf along with my students in the middle of the night and we got to name it. But at 6am the next morning I was still blasting my obnoxious wake-up music on the stereo, just like every other day at the farm, to get the little buggers up for morning chores.

Then there was the Halloween trip. It had been difficult to get the boys to come up to the farm because they would miss Halloween. Nobody wanted to miss out on all that candy. But in the end, we talked most of the boys into coming, loaded them onto the bus with their gear and headed off for the farm.

During the bus ride, I was informing the kids about basic stuff they needed to know about the farm, and I casually mentioned the old lady next door, just in passing. She was nothing they had to worry about; she was just a little crazy, that was all. She hadn't hurt anybody in a long time. If they should happen to see her wandering around the farm, just try to ignore her; she was just odd ever since her son died in the tractor accident, that's all. She probably wouldn't hurt them. I just wanted them to be aware, in case they saw her.

Of course, I just happened to have a scary, little-old-lady mask packed in my gym bag – what a coincidence! That night I snuck out of the great room while they were all watching a horror flick – it was Halloween after all – I slipped the mask on, covered myself with an old blanket for a shawl, and crouched outside one of the windows, waiting for some unsuspecting prey. After a short while, Dennis came along trying to sneak downstairs while everyone else was upstairs watching the movie. I made a small scratching noise on the window – just enough to get him to look up in my direction. His face immediately lit up in terror and he fell down – literally clawing his way along the floor, back through the doorway and into the great room. Even from outside the building, I could hear him screaming, "The old lady! The old lady! I just saw her at the window! She's right outside! She's outside the window! She is soooo ugly!"

I quickly ditched the mask and the blanket and circled back around to the other door and ran into the great room. "What's going on?" I asked innocently. "What are you all so excited about?" The boys were all crowding around Dennis, shouting all at once about him seeing the old lady. Dennis looked like he had just messed his pants.

"I told you she might be around," I said calmly and headed into the kitchen to get some snacks.

The old lady made another appearance later that night and scared another bunch of young street thugs. When the kids finally figured out it was me, they borrowed the mask and took turns trying to scare each other. It was all in good fun. It was part of the bonding process that made each trip special.

There was a lot of work that got done on the farm too, and I'm not just talking about stacking the firewood for the sugar shack or cleaning out the cow barn. But Pete did tell me that my kids worked harder than any of the other schools that visited. That was sweet. When my kids accomplished something nobody expected, I understood what real pride felt like.

The work that was the hardest, though, was the 'people' work. I remember on one trip, one of my students, Luis, had been having a hard time adjusting to farm life. He didn't like getting up so early; he didn't like being told what to do. Luis had a bad habit of 'tagging' things – writing his name in permanent marker wherever he could. It was his way of expressing his identity: Luis had been here. And there. And over there. All over the place.

While at the farm, Luis had been caught tagging his name, among other places, on the wooden shelter that stands looking out over a magnificent view of the whole valley. You truly felt like you could see forever from this spot on the hilltop. The farm called this place "The Top of the World." It was a special place and Luis had desecrated it with his selfish tagging.

So Luis was busted and he had to go back up to the shelter with soap and turpentine and brushes to clean up his handiwork. When he got back, he was in a foul mood. He got into a fight with one of the other chaperones, was refusing to cooperate, and finally stormed outside and sat down on the porch steps, slamming the door behind him.

I gave Luis a few minutes to cool down and then went out and quietly sat down on the steps next to him. I just sat there. He started saying how mad he was at us and how the farm sucked. He was ranting and raving and carrying on, and I just sat and listened. Suddenly he was in tears. He began ranting and raving again, but this time it was about his father in Columbia that he had not seen in several years. He never sends his mom any money and it's hard at home with his little brothers and he's under a lot of pressure to get a job so he can help out. "I hate my dad," he tells me. "He's such a jerk! I hate him."

"Luis," I said gently. "Is that what this is all about?"

He was sobbing uncontrollably at this point.

"Luis, I don't know your dad," I started, "but I can tell you this: if he hasn't seen you in a few years, he *must* be a jerk."

Somehow, I negotiated the minefields of that situation, and probably another hundred just like it during our stays at the farm. There was something about that farm that could strip away all the excess baggage and get right to the core of things. Lots of things. Big things. I always told my students at the end of the trip that I had brought a bunch of boys up to the farm, but I was coming home with a bunch of men. And, in many ways, it was true.

I want to tell you two more things that happened on our most recent trip to the farm. The first one involved Stevie, a small freckle-faced dynamo who had been having the time of his life. The night before we were leaving, Stevie had to gather the eggs from the henhouse with a few of the kids as part of the evening chores. Somehow, one of the eggs happened to end up in Stevie's room that night, hidden under his pillow. He was ratted out by one of his roommates and I went to fetch the egg, figuring it was going to end up getting thrown at somebody during the night and causing a problem. When confronted with the evidence, Stevie admitted taking the egg, but insisted he was not going to throw it at anyone. He told me he planned on taking it home and hatching it. I must confess it was not easy for me to reclaim the egg and put it in the refrigerator with the others for breakfast.

The second incident occurred as we were packing our things to leave. Chad had been one of the superstars that week, working hard, loving every minute. Although usually very quiet, he turned to me as we were rolling up sleeping bags and summed it all up. "There's something about this place," he said, deep in thought. "All the work, all the fun, it builds character, that's what it does. It builds character." My sentiments exactly, I told him.

37

THE LEAF RAKERS

A good deal of scientific research has been conducted about working with at-risk youth. Much of the data points to the importance of establishing stable relationships with students as an essential ingredient to a program's success. The research indicates the average at-risk student takes about eighteen months before he or she can trust a teacher enough to take the associated risks involved with learning. But once that trust is established, the results can be remarkable.

So I need to tell you about Nando and Luis, two of my students you have already met. In case you don't remember, Nando was the idea-man behind the piñata fiasco, and I just told you about Luis, who had a meltdown at the farm, largely due to his lack of a relationship with his father. Both of them were on the fringes of the gang culture and both of their futures were definitely at-risk.

Nando had been in my class for several years and, although we had our battles, we also had grown to respect each other. Nando was great in the kitchen or whenever there was a hands-on project to do. He was a hard worker and an extremely creative problem-solver. Of course, it takes time to build the level of respect we felt for each other – it is not something that happens overnight.

Luis was new to the ALT school that year, very outgoing, outwardly confident, good looking and full of himself. At first, Luis and I did not have the same level of mutual respect that I shared with Nando. But he and Nando were close friends, and Luis knew if Nando trusted me, then I must not be too bad of a guy, even if I was a teacher, and white on top of it. I kidded with Luis every chance I got, greatly enjoying his outgoing nature and sense of humor.

It was a Friday afternoon in the fall and I was casually talking with the class about everybody's plans for the weekend. I happened to mention that I would be spending the weekend raking leaves – there were a ton of them in my yard. Luis told me he used to live in my town and asked me what street I lived on. I told him, not thinking much about it.

The next day, Saturday, my wife and I took the dog and we enjoyed a vigorous climb to the top of a small mountain nearby. It was a gorgeous hike with the foliage in peak season. When we got home we were tired and decided to soak in our hot tub for a little while to stretch out our sore muscles before we had to start raking and bagging leaves. We were not anxious to take on the enormous project.

Our hot tub was located outside behind our garage. We were extremely proud of the fact that our children had all chipped in and purchased it for our twenty-fifth wedding anniversary. They had even constructed the deck surrounding it. It was a special place, cozy and private, full of warm water and warm feelings.

Carol and I were relaxing in the hot bubbling jets, when I noticed a couple of young men poking around the side of the garage. Nando was saying, "Yeah, this must be the place. That's his car out front."

Immediately recognizing Nando and Luis, I called to them and told them to come over. "What are you guys doing here?" I asked, puzzled and taken off guard by their surprise appearance in my home territory. They both looked sheepishly at the ground with strange smiles on their faces. It was as if I had caught them doing something they shouldn't be doing. Then I realized what it was: they thought we were naked in the tub! I told them to come over; it was OK, that we had bathing suits on.

Somehow, they had come up with the idea of showing up at my house to help rake leaves. They had taken the bus as far as it went, then walked and hitchhiked, and wandered around until they eventually found my house, I think by pure luck. It had taken several hours, but they were here now to help rake leaves if I wanted some help.

Knowing an opportunity when I saw it, I gave them each rakes and a box of leaf bags and showed them where they should start. They got right to work in the back yard, while Carol and I continued to lounge in the hot tub. I thought I had died and gone to heaven.

After quite a while, the boys had filled up two bags. They came up and said, "You really have a lot of leaves here."

"I know," I said. "I can't tell you guys how much I really appreciate your help."

"We think you should pay us something if we rake all these leaves," they told me. Nando was the spokesperson but I knew it was Luis who was putting him up to it.

"You're right," I said. "How much do you think it's worth?" I asked.

"How about a dollar a bag?" suggested Nando.

"You got a deal." I replied, thinking they would fill about twenty bags.

Hours later, it was getting dark and I knew they must be hungry. I went out to them and suggested they call it a day. I would buy them burgers and bring them both home. They jumped at the chance. There was a huge pile of lawn bags, all stuffed to the brim with leaves. They offered to count them up for me – all one hundred and two of them.

Luis told me "You don't have to pay for the two extra bags – one hundred will be enough."

"Uh…Thanks," was about all I could muster as I surveyed the mountain of black trash bags piled up at the end of my driveway.

I made an unexpected stop at the ATM machine that evening, bought them both supper as promised, and delivered them both safely home to their mothers. The boys had worked hard and they knew it. They were feeling pretty good about themselves that night, and I'm sure the fifty dollars in each of their pockets had something to do with it. Luis's girlfriend had a birthday coming up and now she was going to get a nice present. Nando didn't know what he was going to do with his windfall yet.

I had to admit, I was feeling pretty good too. It had been an expensive day, for sure, but I knew it had been worth it. After all, you get what you pay for.

38

MYSTERIOUS BLOODLINES

The leaf-raking episode was not the only time students had been to my house, but home visits by students were definitely a rarity. I tried to convey an aura of mystery about my personal life when I was around my students. I didn't want to give them too much personal information. Oh, I told them lots of stories about my past and present life – they were always full of questions. But I also tried to keep a safe distance, partly for my own sanity. These kids were emotional vampires and they could suck you dry in the blink of an eye.

For example, my students frequently called me a racist, which I found extremely hurtful. Of course, their use of the term had little to do with the generally accepted meaning of the word. I prided myself on being open to everyone, regardless of skin color or any other discriminating factor. They called me racist purely on the grounds that I was white – and in their eyes, all white people are racists. They usually called me a racist following an incident where the student didn't get his or her way. Then I was *really* a racist. Sometimes, even the white kids would call me racist.

I always responded with a short sermonette about racial equality, about my dedication to accepting everyone, and how nobody gets to choose their parents. Ultimately, we are what we are. One day the kids were giving me a hard time and calling me racist for some ridiculous thing and I realized I needed to try a new approach to get through to them. I got very quiet, sat down on my stool, looked at the floor and gave the loudest sigh I could muster. I looked up at them and then, very seriously, I said to them, "OK, guys. You need to know something about me."

They all quieted down and studied me, realizing I was very upset. But this was different – I wasn't angry or lecturing them this time. I was going to tell them something about myself, something important. I spoke very softly and told them I had been adopted when I was very young. My adoptive parents happened to be black. (I hated to lie to them, but I had to give this a try to see where it might go.) They were stunned and a few did not believe me.

"No you weren't!" they shouted. "Black people don't adopt white kids!"

"Well, they do sometimes," I answered. "At least mine did. Anybody can adopt anybody they want, regardless of color."

"How old were you when you were adopted?" one of them asked. This was a good sign – they were starting to believe me.

"I was very young," I replied, still acting very sullen and withdrawn.

"Do you know why your parents gave you up?" somebody else asked.

"Not really," I said. "I guess they just weren't ready for a baby. My adoptive parents were great and things usually work out for the best." I was surprised at myself for how skillfully I was pulling this off. I looked around the room at the faces staring back at me. I had their full attention. "You can see now why it hurts me so much when you call me a racist," I said, getting back to the point of the whole conversation.

"Have you ever met your real parents?" asked one of the girls. Oh no, I thought, they were just not going to give this up. I was getting in deep and didn't know how to get out, or even if I should, the ploy was working so well.

"Oh sure," I said. "We get together once in a while for celebrations and things. We're all OK now." I was trying to wrap this up. At last the questions dwindled and we were all able to get back to our classwork. I was relieved to have survived the inquisition with my mysterious background intact.

My students did not call me a racist as much after that talk, and word quickly spread throughout the school that my parents were black and I had been given up for adoption as a baby. My real parents didn't want me. At least, that was the storyline in the lunchroom. I know this because I overheard students telling other students about my heritage. Knowledge was power for them and they couldn't wait to tell the story of my background to one of their friends.

A few weeks later, the kids were in a silly mood; they were all telling 'Your Mama' jokes – you know, "Your Mama is so ugly . . ." That kind of thing. It was nothing too outrageous, just normal middle school obnoxious behavior. Eventually I came down on them, trying to get them to stop, and most of the class was finally able to get to work.

But Ronnie just wouldn't let it die. Ronnie was a popular and lively black boy – one of the class clowns. His antics often got him in trouble but he and I got along pretty well. He saw that I often laughed at his jokes and appreciated his great sense of humor. I reminded Ronnie to settle down and get his work done, and that I really didn't want to be making a phone call home just because he wouldn't focus and get to work.

"Phone call home?" Ronnie repeated. "I'm the one who should be makin' the phone call home," he declared. "I should be callin' *your* mama to find out why you're so ugly!" The class broke out in stitches at his bold pronouncement and Ronnie was enjoying every minute, basking in the limelight.

I don't know what came over me. I nodded and said, "All right." I took out my cell phone and began dialing the number for my parents. Suddenly, you could hear a pin drop in the class. Ronnie looked incredulously at me, then at the cell phone, and back at me again.

"You're calling your mama?" he asked.

"Yup. You said you wanted to speak with her, so I'm calling my mama."

Ronnie could not believe what was happening.

With the whole class watching and listening I spoke into the phone, "Hi, mom. Everything's OK, I'm in class right now and one of my students would like to speak with you. His name is Ronnie. I'm putting him on. Talk to him." I handed the phone to Ronnie, who was still in shock.

"Is this Rick's mom?" Ronnie began. I guess he thought it was a trick.

"Yes, it is," my mom answered, probably wondering what in the world was I doing?

Ronnie changed voices and spoke into the phone like a professional telemarketer. "This is part of a national survey and we're gathering information on teachers. We were all wondering if you could tell us why your son Rick is so ugly?" There was a loud collective gasp from the class. I could not hear my mother's response; I could only watch the priceless flow of expressions that were being displayed on Ronnie's face. Finally Ronnie said "Thank you" and handed the phone back to me. I thanked my mom and told her I would talk with her later and disconnected the call.

Ronnie reported my mother's response back to the class. Apparently, she told him what every kid would want to hear. "Well, he's always been very beautiful to me," she had told him.

There was a loud chorus of "AHHHHHH!" echoing around the classroom.

When I spoke to my mother later that evening, she told me she was taken off guard by the question and hoped that her answer was good enough. I told her it was great. If she had more time to think, she told me, she might have said something like "Because his mama is so ugly, that's why!" She had no idea how well that would have played into the day's events.

Looking back on the incident with my mom, I was surprised that one of the kids didn't question whether it was my *black* mama, or my *bio*-mama. I guess they figured it must have been my adoptive mom by the answer she gave. In any case, the fabricated story of my origins was still taken to be the truth.

Months later, on our summer vacation, Carol and I were bicycling on Cape Cod, and we happened to ride our bikes to the place where the ferry to Martha's Vineyard docked. I noticed an old black man, probably in his seventies, struggling to carry a huge carton with a TV in it. I offered to help him and he gladly let me carry it over where the other passengers were waiting to board the ferry. We were joined by his wife and had a lovely chat about being retired and living on the island for the summer. They were a delightful couple. They had been shopping at Wal-Mart and found this TV on sale, and they needed one for the summer. It was really too heavy for them to manage by themselves. They were so grateful for my offer of assistance.

I looked over to see Carol laughing hysterically as she struggled with our digital camera. In an instant, I knew what she was doing. I casually asked the old folks if they would mind posing for a picture with me. I explained I was a schoolteacher, and it was a long story, but it would really help me out if my wife could just snap a quick photo of us together. The three of us huddled together like long-lost relatives and smiled into the camera as my wife captured that special Kodak moment.

In my classroom, on my desk, to this day, you will find a small plastic photo frame with the picture of me with my 'adoptive' parents. I bring it out to show kids from time to time when one of them calls me a racist. Students who know the story use the picture as an opportunity to explain my family history to the new kids who can't believe it's true. That snapshot continues to serve as undeniable proof: Rick may be weird and mysterious, but he is definitely not a racist.

39

FAMILY SUPPORT

When I would get home from school each day, I usually needed to 'unload'. Call it therapy, processing the day, or letting off steam, whatever you want to call it. I needed to talk. I told my family pretty much everything that was going on at the ALT school, whether I had a good day or a bad one. I often had no idea what kind of a day it had been.

Carol and the kids served as both a sounding board and a release valve for the pressure, but I especially unloaded on Carol. We would go for long walks with the dog in the evening and I shared the day's events and my interpretation or my ideas on how best to handle situations. She became very good at learning when I was truly looking for advice or when I just needed her to listen as I vented. I suspected then, but now know for sure, that I will never be able to express how deeply I appreciated Carol and my kids' unwavering support for me throughout this crazy journey I was on.

Listening to my stories, however, was one thing. Making an actual visit to the war zone that was my classroom was quite another. I think my own children were somewhat frightened of my students. I spoke casually of fights, assaults and parents in jail on a regular basis. In our own family life I had been able to spare my children the ugly realities that most of my students accepted as part of their normal routine.

The first time my son, Scott, and my daughter, Jenna, visited my classroom was a typical school day – loud, active, and unpredictable. We had plans to go somewhere after school, so they had come into school near the end of the day so we could all go together. Scott and Jenna huddled safely in a corner of my classroom observing the mayhem. I was anxious to hear their opinions of the kids after school let out.

"So, what do you think?" I asked them after the last student had darted out the door for the bus.

They looked at each other as if they didn't know how to respond. Finally, Scott said, "I think they all need a swift kick in the ass, that's what I think." Jenna just rolled her eyes and nodded in agreement.

I told them ass kicking was not part of the school district's discipline policy, but I could understand how they might feel that way.

"You get used to them after a while," I told them.

Another time, Carol was meeting me at the end of the day so we could run errands after school. She had visited my classroom on several occasions and so she was able to connect a lot of the faces in my room with the stories I had been telling her. I had to go outside for bus duty because some staff were absent, and we needed all hands on deck. We had received word that there might be a fight after school with some kids from the other middle school. It was just a typical afternoon dismissal at the ALT.

There were still students in my room awaiting dismissal, so I asked Carol to stand in the doorway and not let the kids out until they were formally dismissed. Uneasily, I left her and went outside to keep the peace.

The kids outside from the other school were finally dispersed. (It's funny how the arrival of a police cruiser will do that.) Our students were eventually dismissed and everybody headed home. I returned to my classroom to make sure Carol had not been assaulted or trampled by stampeding students. She was standing in my room laughing.

She told me about the conversation she had just had with Justin, a tall, lanky mess of a young man. Justin lived with his grandmother, and struggled in all his classes. I would diagnose him with a severe case of ADHD, but he was not medicated, at least not with any prescription drugs. Justin was also well known to have diarrhea of the mouth. He had no control over whatever flew out of his mouth.

Justin had been looking at Carol as they awaited dismissal, calmly studying her. Finally he asked her, "You live with Rick?"

Carol answered "Yes, of course. We're married."

Justin shook his head and looked at the floor. Then he declared, "God, if I was married to Rick, I think I'd kill myself!"

Just then, the bell rang and the kids all herded out the door, leaving Carol to ponder the incident, which is when I returned and found her laughing.

The next day in class, I thanked the whole class for being so respectful to my wife during her brief visit. I turned and looked directly at Justin.

"And Justin," I said, "I want you to know that you have nothing to worry about." He looked at me not knowing where this was going. "There is no way you and I will *ever* be married, because if we were, I can assure you that I would have *already* killed myself, so you won't have to."

Justin smiled, looked down at his book, and pretended to read. We had a pretty good day that day.

40

ALL WORN DOWN

It was never easy knowing when you could kid around with a student and when you had to take them dead seriously. I would often have to change gears abruptly when I realized that a situation was much more serious than I had previously thought. A casual conversation with a student could take a sudden turn into unexpected territory – and I learned to be on constant vigil for any danger signals.

I had been drawing and painting with a small group of students as part of the after-school program for several weeks. There were about six or seven girls and boys who were extremely talented in the visual arts and I had agreed to offer an art class one day a week after school. It was a way to build more connections with some of the kids and besides, I was getting paid a little extra for it. Considering the pay cut I had taken, I desperately needed every dollar I could earn those first few years.

The kids painted with acrylics and watercolors mostly; one girl was consumed with drawing cartoon figures. I surprised them by painting right along side them on my own work, which I had been anxious to get back to anyway. I demonstrated how to stretch a canvass and various techniques of working with the paint. We all felt like *real artists*. And, of course, while we would paint, we would talk.

One day, it was nearing the end of the session, and I was cleaning up and washing out the brushes. Most of the kids had left for home, but Lenny was still finishing up a drawing he was working on. I had agreed to give him a ride home since he lived too far to walk.

Out of the clear blue, Lenny said to me, "Rick, I have something I want to show you, but you have to promise not to tell anyone that I showed it to you."

"I'm not sure I can do that, Lenny." I answered. I explained to him how I was bound by law to report any information I came upon if I thought a student's safety was in jeopardy.

"What is it, Len? Is it something I need to see?" I could tell from Lenny's expression and body language that we were in 'serious' territory and that he was thinking carefully about what he should do.

"He's going to hate me when he finds out I showed this to you,"

Lenny said as he handed me a small, folded up piece of paper.

"Nobody will hate you for doing what you thought was the right thing," I responded. I unfolded the paper and began to read the handwritten note.

It was written by his close friend, Zachary, and it expressed the depth of Zack's despair. His life and family were a mess and he could see no point in continuing his life if it was always going to be filled with sadness and misery. I knew immediately that action would need to be taken quickly if disaster was going to be averted.

I asked Lenny a few quick questions. When had he received the note? When did he last see Zack? Did he know where Zack was now? Lenny thought Zack was going home after school. Home for Zachary right now happened to be the motel where homeless people sometimes stayed. Len even knew a phone number for Zack's grandmother because Zack's immediate family didn't have a phone.

I called Zack's grandmother. The answering machine picked up. "SHIT!" I thought, probably out loud. I couldn't think how to phrase an appropriate message, so I hung up.

"Do you think you could point out the apartment where Zack lives if I drove us there?" I asked. Len said he thought he could. "I want to stop at Zack's to make sure he's alright before I dropped you at home." Len looked uneasily at the floor. I told him that he did not have to get out of the car or talk to Zack if he felt uncomfortable - it would be his call. "But I need to speak to Zack right away," I said, and Lenny nodded in agreement.

When we arrived at Zack's family's motel room, Lenny agreed to accompany me to the door. Zack, his sister and his mother were surprised at our unexpected visit, but everything seemed as normal as it could be. Zachary's mom was an extremely large woman who was wearing nothing but an extra, extra large tee shirt. I was somewhat embarrassed by her appearance although she did not seem to be. I asked if we could speak with Zack privately outside about a matter at school, and he stepped outside with us.

"This is about the note, isn't it?" started Zack.

I nodded. " I've read the note and I need to know that you're alright." I emphasized that Lenny and I were there because we CARED about him, and that this was serious and he needed to get some help to get through this. I explained to him that I was required to report this to the principal but first I wanted to make sure he was safe. Zack assured us that he would not hurt himself that night, and that he would seek help. He actually seemed relieved that somebody else now knew about his pain, and he told Lenny that he was not mad at him.

I wrote my home phone number on the back of the note – it was the only piece of paper I had available. I handed it back to Zack and told him he could call me at any hour of the night if he felt he was going to hurt himself or just needed to talk. We hugged and shook hands with Zack promising he would not do anything that night. He would seek professional help in the morning.

I dropped Lenny off at his house and assured him that he had done the right thing. "Someday Zack will understand how good a friend you've been to him."

As soon as I got home, I called Pam, my principal, and related the events of the past 2 hours. She was glad that I had called and began to inform me of the school district's protocols for circumstances such as these. We had a responsibility to see that Zack's parents knew exactly what was going on and that Zack be brought to a crisis intervention center at the hospital immediately. I suddenly realized the personal risk I had just taken, writing my phone number on the back of his suicide note. If anything should happen . . .

A few minutes later, she was picking me up and I was again on my way to the motel where Zack's family was staying. Pam had called ahead to the police so they could meet us there. They would insure that Zack would indeed be brought to the crisis center right away without incident.

When we knocked on the door, Zack answered and knew immediately why we were there. Mom appeared in the doorway shortly after and we briefly explained what was going on. She started to cry and hollered inside for Zack's dad to come out. A minute later he was standing with us in his boxer shorts. He had been sleeping, he explained, because he was working the night shift for the local cab company.

None of them were particularly happy about having to go down to the hospital, right then and there, to get Zack evaluated. But they did – maybe the police presence was, once again, the deciding factor. They followed us to the emergency room in their old beat up car. Pam and I sat with them in the waiting area. Zack's mom was thanking us profusely for our concern and our help through the whole process. When the person from the suicide prevention unit came out, I hugged Zack for the second time that evening and we left them, knowing our role that evening was at last completed.

Several days later, Zack was back in school. He came into my class and handed me another handwritten note. My skin prickled as hairs stood on end all over my body. This time, though, it was a thank-you for being there note. I was deeply touched. The moment called for something special.

I went over to my desk and reached up on top of a cabinet where I kept some of my personal belongings. Sitting up there was a hollow, fluorescent green alien head. Yes, that's right, a plastic alien head I had picked up somewhere along the line. I had a lot of weird stuff in my classroom, but this green alien head, which kept a constant vigil over my room, was certainly among the weirdest.

Inside the alien head I had stored my collection of stones from the beach. I placed the head on the table next to Zack and began examining the stones, looking for just the right one. He quietly stood by watching. At last I found it. I took a black sharpie out and wrote my phone number on the stone and handed it to Zack. He immediately began rolling it around the palm of his hand. I told him where the stones came from and how they got to be so smooth and polished. I explained about the pressure of the sand and salt and water constantly pushing it around until it was all worn down. His stone would not be special if it hadn't gone through some really tough times. And yet here it was, all beautiful and unique and strong: just perfect!

"Just like you," I said softly. "I want you to have one. You can keep it in your pocket or wherever you want. If you're ever having a tough time, maybe you can pull some strength from it."

Zack rolled it over in his hand and studied the number written on it. He glanced up at me for second before returning his gaze to the stone. "And I can call you?" he asked.

"Anytime," I said. "Anytime you ever need someone to talk to."

Zack smiled as he held it tight in his fist and our eyes met again. He said nothing and said everything: he understood the significance of the stone. While I was speaking to Zach, another student, Carla, had come over to us and was standing next to Zack. She had apparently overheard me telling Zack about the stone.

"That's sooo beautiful!" Carla sighed. Her crooked teeth gleamed through a huge smile, but I could see the tears in her dark eyes.

41

VISITORS

The alternative school, being new and somewhat controversial, had a lot of visitors. Sometimes, I would know ahead of time when guests would be visiting my classroom, and other times the principal would just show up in my room with an unidentified person or a small group of people interested in what we were doing. We had parents and prospective students visiting, guidance counselors from other schools, local politicians, and people from various service organizations. There were teachers who thought they might like to work with at-risk youth. A few times, it was someone from the newspaper trying to stir up some local controversy. I had the superintendent, members of the school board, and even people from the state board of education, including the commissioner himself, visit my classroom at one time or another. I got used to having unexpected visitors.

Our more outgoing students were often recruited to act as tour guides for our visitors. They could convey more about our program in five minutes than we teachers could in a formal two-hour presentation. The student ambassadors ate up the attention that was bestowed on them by our guests and it greatly boosted their feelings of self-importance. Of course, we had to be careful whom we picked for these assignments – we didn't want a student to offend a visiting dignitary with his language or remarks. Our guests usually found their guides to be warm, funny and refreshingly honest. It was good P.R.

My principal, Pam, loved to bring guests into my classroom because she never quite knew what they were going to see, but it was always 'alternative'. They might see my students building marble-coasters as they explored laws of physics. Or the students might be gathering data about pendulums by swinging marshmallows on strings as they tried to get a blindfolded teammate to catch it in his mouth. One group of visitors showed up the day we were having our catapult competition - the kids had built catapults and various shooting contraptions and were competing for distance and accuracy. Marshmallows were once again incorporated into the challenge – this time as the ammunition. But I was mindful of the inherent dangers. Students would forfeit all their points for the assignment if they shot anything other than a marshmallow from their catapult. Like I said, you never knew what you were walking into when you came into my room.

I had learned how to create PowerPoint presentations in my former life as a corporate manager, and now as a teacher, this skill had become an invaluable resource for me. I began creating my own PowerPoint lessons for any topic I needed to cover – and of course, even my PowerPoints had to be 'alternative'. I injected humor into them by using funny or unusual photos I would find online. I inserted pictures of my students with cartoon bubbles to put words in their mouths or thoughts into their heads. Needless to say, my students loved to see themselves and their friends in my slide shows. It was a lot of work, but seeing the kids engaged and actually following along with the lessons made all the effort worth it. It was especially rewarding when a distinguished guest would pop in and see the kids actually enjoying their learning.

I created games to be played with the LCD projector and PowerPoint. One was a takeoff on a TV game show called *One Versus The Mob.* I prepared slides with multiple-choice questions on whatever topic we were investigating and the kids would compete to answer the questions correctly. I did not have a million dollars to give away, but I probably did give away close to a million candies. My students didn't know it, but I was actually using the game as a method for reviewing a chapter before a test. The game also taught them strategies to improve their test scores on the standardized tests they were expected to take.

One group of classroom visitors seemed particularly impressed with that last idea. A few members of the local board of education had stopped by to see how the school district's money was being spent at the ALT school. They happened to catch my class in the middle of a heated game of *One Versus the Mob.* The kids dazzled them with their knowledge of earth science, specifically tectonic plates. Anything that increased students' test scores for the district was OK in their book.

Being on a limited budget, our school had very little money for technology. The LCD projector had been purchased with money I had been awarded through an education grant. I became very dependent on that projector – using it for my PowerPoints, for my games, for science videos, for on-line demonstrations. I even had the kids creating their own reports and presentations they could show to the rest of the class. Occasionally the projector was lent out to other teachers for them to use in their own classrooms, but I was definitely hogging the equipment. I told myself I was making sure it was secure. It could disappear in a split second if someone wasn't watching it and keeping it in a safe place.

After Christmas vacation, I returned to my classroom, refreshed and ready to get back into the school routines. Unpacking my things and getting ready for the day, I was in great spirits. I walked behind my desk to the shelf where I kept the projector. I wanted to set it up for the lesson I planned to teach that day. I was surprised to find that the projector was not there.

One of the other teachers had borrowed it, I thought, and they neglected to return it. I reminded myself that it really did belong to everybody, not just me. As I went from classroom to classroom searching for my prized possession, panic began rising in my chest. No one had seen it recently or used it. I returned to my room thinking maybe I had inadvertently misplaced it.

As I looked around the room, I realized that the room was somewhat chilly and glanced over at the window behind my desk – open a little. Strange, I thought, in the middle of winter. I remembered checking all the windows the day before vacation to make sure they were locked. I was on the ground floor so I was always careful about my classroom being locked. And the things in front of the window had been moved a little, too. This did not look good, I thought. I peered outside the window. Sure enough, there were still some footprints in the deep snow right outside my window.

I was upset at this point, coming to terms with the reality that my LCD projector had indeed been stolen. But I was more upset at the fact that it was undeniably an 'inside' job. Whoever had taken it had skillfully left the window unlocked so he could get in over the vacation when no one would be here. He knew exactly where to look for the equipment. Nothing else was missing, only the projector. The knowledge that the thief was one of my students haunted me for weeks. I did so much for them, how could they do this to me – to all of us?

The principal and I tried to get the kids to talk, to tell us who the culprit was. I laid on all the guilt I could, trying to get any information out of my kids, but to no avail. They were not going to rat out one of their own, even if it meant everyone would suffer. I told them I would not prosecute; I just wanted the projector back, no questions asked.

I had my suspicions and watched and listened for clues that might solve the mystery. I even checked e-Bay each evening to see if someone was trying to unload it and make a quick sale online. It was no use – it was gone – I would just have to go on teaching without it. But the disappearance of that one projector left a hole in my heart and served as a clear reminder that there were some things that I could never change.

Eventually, I applied for and was awarded another grant. I used the money to buy three more projectors for the school. I kept one for myself and still had two to lend out to other teachers if they wanted to use one. And this time, I learned another important lesson – I also bought a large locking cabinet we could keep all the equipment in. From that day forward, I always tried to be a little more careful about who was visiting my classroom, expected or not.

42

ARE WE HAVING FUN YET?

Attending the national convention for alternative education was an eye-opener. I had been traveling for many years in my former corporate position, so it was not like I had never been away for business before. I was quite familiar with hotels and airports and restaurants. But this trip was different.

Yes, the hotel was stunning. Yes, there was a huge pool with a swim-up bar, great restaurants and lots of things to do. And of course, yes, it was held in Orlando, Florida, smack dab in the dead of winter. This convention had a lot going for it; that was true.

I think I only made it into the pool once. I never quite made it to the swim-up bar or any of the exciting attractions Orlando is famous for. I hardly even got any sun the whole time I was there, despite my determination to come back with a tan in the middle of winter, or at least a few freckles. The alternatives conference was about something much larger than a warm winter vacation.

To start with, the array of workshops offered was impressive. There were courses for administrators, teachers, counselors and students. Some of the presenters were experts in the field of alternative education and many of them had been published. It was difficult to choose which workshops to attend; they all sounded – and were - so interesting and informative. I was attending the convention with our school psychologist, and we decided to go to different workshops just to broaden our coverage of the event.

My first surprise revelation was about how "on track" our young program seemed to be in comparison to other alternative programs across the country. The ALT was only in its third year at that point, and yet it seemed to be light years ahead of what many school districts were trying to establish. I'm not saying we had it all figured out, by any means. It's just that we seemed to be hitting all the right buttons according to the research and model programs. I felt pretty good about what we were accomplishing back home and I couldn't wait to inform our staff what a great job they were doing.

Even more than this, however, I was struck by the size and scope of the problem we were dealing with. At-risk kids were not only a growing problem in my school district – their numbers were increasing dramatically all over the country. And not just in cities and urban areas either. The numbers in rural communities also seemed to be growing exponentially. Poverty, drugs and alcohol, the breakup of families, teenage pregnancy, histories of academic failures – all these issues were undermining millions of young Americans from achieving success. The numbers were staggering.

Fortunately, many of the professionals working with at-risk youth had somehow managed to retain their compassion, their stubborn dedication, and their sense of humor along the way. While burnout and emotional exhaustion were common to people working with our disenfranchised youth, it was also apparent that the rewards that come from working with these young people were truly immeasurable. As we shared our stories both in and out of the workshops, we realized that our struggles, our successes and our failures were all essentially the same. We were all in this together.

This is not to say that we all agreed on our methods to attack the problem. Some schools took a very prescriptive military approach, others focused on job training, and still others created independent programs for each individual student. Some districts had a lot of money at their disposal; others had little or no money to work with. There were rural schools with one classroom for a few alternative students, and city programs with multiple school buildings servicing thousands of at-risk kids.

When the time came to present our workshop about 'best practices' in alternative education, the school psychologist and I were both nervous. Not only were we presenting for the first time, we were presenting to the cream of the crop – people who really knew what they were talking about. We were feeling at once both intimidated and confident in our material.

As our presentation began, we spoke about our program at the ALT with pride and with passion. I demonstrated some of my teaching methods and even incorporated the audience into a short demonstration that was entertaining while being informative. I displayed some slides from my PowerPoints to show how I mix science content with literacy, middle school humor and teenage interests.

After the workshop, one of the attendees came up to speak with me as I was packing away my equipment. She told me she was a school principal and that she really enjoyed the workshop. Before coming to the convention, she had been going around her building, observing her teachers and the students, and felt that something was missing, but she just couldn't put her finger on what it was until just a few moments earlier during my workshop.

"Really?" I said, somewhat flattered. "What is it?" I asked, genuinely curious what it was about our humble presentation that could provide her with such an insight.

"You were having fun," she told me. "It was obvious. My teachers and students aren't having any fun. I'm going to go back and try to get my teachers to have some fun while they are teaching. The kids need it. We all need it. Thank you so much for pointing it out to me."

I shook her hand and gave her copies of my handouts. I told her she was welcome to contact me and wished her luck.

As she walked away I thought to myself, "WOW! She's right! I *do* have fun. I don't think I could possibly teach these kids if it wasn't fun. It would just be way too hard." I shook my head and continued packing up. That was the night I finally made it into the pool. It was time to have a little fun.

43

LIFE IN THE BASEMENT

Back at school, I dove into my teaching and my students with renewed fervor. I shared my insights and packets of materials from the convention with the rest of the staff. I prepared a report for the superintendent's office regarding best practices for alternative education with specific descriptions of how we at the ALT school were addressing each of those needs. I told my class stories about the other programs – I wanted my students to know they were not alone, that there were struggling students all over the country and many were worse off than we were. They would be amazed at how well we were doing with so little.

Of course, the kids didn't really listen to me – after all, our school was located in a basement. What school worth its salt was located in a basement? The ALT students perpetually complained about going to school in a basement. And to a great extent, they were right. Our facilities and classroom resources were less than ideal. The space we were leasing was located underneath the local Boys & Girls Club. There was only one bathroom for one hundred students. Half the classrooms had no windows, and those that did only had one. There were no closets, there was no intercom system, and there was no auditorium for assemblies or special events. There were no lockers for the students and no playground outside for recess. The kids all looked forward to the day they would finally be able to go back to a *real* school.

What the ALT school lacked in windows, though, it made up for in doors. There was the door at the main entrance and doors at the end of three hallways. There were doors to get into the gym, the cafeteria, and all the kids' favorite places in the Boys & Girls Club: the games room, the teen room, the computer room, the kitchen and the indoor pool area. There were doors all over the place, even between classrooms. I already told you my strategy for limiting the use of the door in my room with the obnoxious wooden chimes.

For the 'runners' and 'hiders' this was an ideal situation. They could run and disappear out a door and be out of the building before we could even report they were gone. From a security point of view, all these doors were a nightmare.

Speaking of security, I told you that there was no intercom in any of the rooms. Instead, most of the teachers carried walkie-talkies. We frequently used them to call for assistance or report missing students who had just slipped out a door. But of course, we had to be very careful about what was said over the walkie-talkies – there was a certain etiquette that had to be followed.

For example, it was forbidden to suggest that a student had not taken their 'meds' that day over the walkie-talkie – very poor etiquette. We were never to use the word "fight" over the airwaves, as that word could ignite all the students in the school to come running out of class to see what was going on. Instead we could ask for "immediate assistance" and someone would come running to help. "Code Red" meant no students were allowed out of a room for any reason. It was usually called when a student was getting arrested or when someone had gotten hurt and needed an ambulance. Once it was called when the mother of one of our students had collapsed in the bathroom from an overdose.

At one point, we were having a problem with kids sneaking out of the building to have a cigarette out behind the building, where they could be out of view. Again, it would be poor etiquette to announce this over the walkie-talkie, so we came up with a phrase we could use in such an instance to alert the office to do a sweep of the outer perimeter of the building. Someone suggested we say "The elves are up on the roof," and, as absurd as it sounded, it stuck.

So one day the principal was in her office meeting with the head of Special Education Services for the district. In the middle of the meeting the principal's walkie-talkie announced, "There were some elves up on the roof." Pam had somehow forgotten our new code word for kids smoking outside. She and her guest thought some of our students had actually escaped and were climbing up on the roof. Then she realized what was going on and had to reassure the director that the students were safe and it was nothing to be concerned about, just an inside joke. Understandably, she made up some pretense and chose not to bring her guest outside to help search for the offending smokers.

As you can imagine, the walkie-talkies were a constant target for our students. Our young thieves could snatch one off our belt without our feeling a thing. If you accidentally put your walkie down for a moment unguarded, it was gone. We would lecture them about returning it immediately, no questions asked; it just needed to be returned for everyone's safety. Sometimes the teacher would have to walk out of the room and announce that the walkie was expected to be back on the desk when he or she came back into the room. Otherwise, there would be serious consequences. Usually that worked. It would always show up eventually. It was another one of those games the kids loved to play with us. It was called *Annoy the Teacher.*

There were a few students who loved to grab a walkie and make their own announcements. At the end of the day, we would all be awaiting the announcement for dismissal and instead hear a student trying to disguise his voice as he called the principal some vulgarity. Or we might be treated to loud farting noises coming from the walkies, followed by the standard request for all teachers to please check their walkie-talkies. Our days were full of these games.

I like to think that these things would have occurred even if we were not teaching in a basement. Surely, the 'real' schools have issues like these. But I was perplexed at how often the kids vocalized their annoyance about the 'basement' appearance of our building. They reminded us all the time. They might not care about their learning, but they sure cared about where it was supposed to take place.

For me, it didn't really matter where the school was located – we were doing some pretty amazing work. If we could just trade some of the doors for more windows, I would have been happy. But the building's appearance mattered to the kids, even the ones who were constantly trashing it. They might spit their gum out and leave it on the floor of the classroom, or discard their trash on the floor of the cafeteria, but that didn't stop them from complaining. They still felt they deserved something better.

I felt these yearnings were a good sign – wanting something better for themselves even though their circumstances were so bleak. And so, I tried valiantly to keep up with their messes, scurrying around between classes to straighten things up before the next group arrived. At the end of each day, I could usually be found picking up the gum and washing graffiti off the desks. I was determined my room was going to look like a place of learning. I would keep it looking as nice and inviting as it could possibly look– for a basement that is.

44

COOKING FOR MEN

I have always loved food – and not just because it can be delicious. I also love the healthy, nutritional aspects, and the social aspects, and the psychological aspects of a good meal. I like making food that is colorful and interesting to look at. Mysterious spices or unusual combinations intrigue me. I enjoy seasonal varieties that show up in the produce aisle. And I take great pride in saving money when I shop for groceries.

Obviously, I did not act like the typical macho male that many of my students were familiar with. The first time I baked homemade muffins and brought them in to school, none of my students believed that I had made them myself. They did admit they were good, though, and they seemed impressed that I could recite the recipe from memory. But as far as they were concerned, real men don't cook.

The after-school program was looking to expand their schedule by adding some different activities for the kids to participate in after school, and I offered to teach a cooking class geared specifically for the guys. I thought it would be fun and may even teach them some life skills they might need some day. At the very least, I could be sure they were getting a decent meal that day. They always seemed to be hungry in my classroom.

Only a couple of boys showed up for the first class. There were a few girls asking – no begging - to join us, but we turned them away – this was 'Cooking for Men'. We planned on cooking 'man' food, you know, lots of meat, huge servings, that sort of thing. And we wanted to do it ourselves, without female intervention. Men could cook; that was the whole premise.

I taught the guys how to wash up before cooking, and how to keep a clean work area. Since we did not have a kitchen to use, I brought in electric frying pans, griddles and crock-pots to cook in. Sometimes we even made dishes that did not have to be cooked – like miniature cheesecakes – those were a big hit.

I taught the boys the proper way to cut onions and other vegetables. In fact, I told them that the first thing a guy does when cooking, no matter what he's making, is to chop up an onion. That's always the first step for every recipe, I said.

"No way," one of them countered when I told them this.

"Absolutely," I said as I demonstrated how to peel the outer skin cleanly away from the juicy meat of the onion. For the first few weeks, all the dishes we cooked called for onions, so after a while, they began to believe me. Their onion chopping skills improved, too because we chopped a lot of onions.

That first day when only a few boys showed up, we made a chicken and broccoli dish with Alfredo sauce. The guys could not believe how good it tasted. I let them bring home the leftovers. The next day at school, some of the leftovers showed up at lunch and were shared among the students. Apparently, that was all the advertising I needed.

The next week and for every week after that, I had a crowd of about twenty boys for my 'Cooking for Men' class. Thankfully, one of the guidance counselors began to stay after school to help me, and I was grateful to have another adult to help out. On one particular week, we had decided to make my famous chili. I divvied up all the work between the boys, some chopping, some frying meat, and some opening cans of beans and tomatoes. Some boys were assigned to be the cleanup crew as we cooked so my classroom would not get overly trashed.

Once all the ingredients were placed in the crock-pot, I told them it would have to cook all night before we could eat it. They were very disappointed – they were hungry and ready to eat raw chili right then and there. Fortunately, I had anticipated this, and had brought some nacho chips and salsa they could eat in the meantime. It all worked out great.

I brought the crock-pot home that night, driving very carefully so as not to tip the chili on the way home. The chili cooked all that night and smelled delicious when I went into our kitchen the following morning. I placed the crock-pot back in my car, on the floor on the passenger side, to bring it back to school. I had told the boys they could have it for lunch that day.

Once again driving slowly and carefully, I made it most of the way to school with the chili intact. Yes, that's right - most of the way. On the last curve as I was getting off the highway I watched in horror as the pot tipped over and chili began oozing out all over the carpet of my car. My new, clean SUV, my 'MAN CAR'. I had just bought it a few weeks earlier – the kids had actually called it a *chick magnet.* Chili was pouring out everywhere onto the floor of my chick magnet. I tried to remain calm as I drove the short distance that remained to school.

I parked the car in the school parking lot and tipped the pot up trying to salvage as much of the chili as I could – there was not much to save. I ran for paper towels and started sopping up as much as I could. I sprayed the carpet with cleaner. The more I blotted the carpet, the more I got up. I wondered if my car would ever smell nice again. I could not believe what had happened. "How do I get myself into these situations?" I asked myself.

Only two kids got to try the chili that day at lunch. They told me it was very good. They wanted to know where all the rest of the chili went – did my family eat it? I told them my car ate it, and I had to promise we would make more.

We cooked all sorts of good food in that class and had a lot of laughs. We made Italian dishes and cheese steak bombs, Mexican fajitas and omelets. We mixed fruit smoothies, pudding desserts, and my grandparent's homemade fudge. I even taught the guys how to prepare my famous hot dog-potato-cheese casserole that sustained me during my starving college years. The guys couldn't believe how good it was thought we should make more. They were sure we could sell it and get rich.

Those young budding chefs felt good about learning to cook. They were proud of their creations. They loved sharing some of what they made with their friends and families. Some even began to talk about running their own restaurants when they got older. I liked hearing that, thinking that cooking might provide a stable income for some of them in the future.

But for me, the best part was helping the boys to understand that cooking and 'manhood' were not mutually exclusive – that real guys *can* cook. It's just that real men try not to spill it in their chick magnets.

45

ON BEING A TEACHER

I don't know exactly when it happened, but at some point I stopped consciously thinking about being a teacher. Teaching just sort of became part of my being, an undeniable aspect of my character. I was a teacher. I spoke like one, I acted like one, and I thought like one. I spent evenings and weekends planning lessons and gathering materials for my classroom. I shopped in teacher stores and read teacher magazines. I was even dressing like a teacher - casual but preppy, lots of turtlenecks and sweaters.

On the last day of the school year, we had planned a school-wide awards assembly to celebrate the students' accomplishments. Many of the students would be getting awards and the teachers had been asked to present them and deliver poignant remarks along with the certificates. I decided to dress up a bit for the special event, so that morning I put on a nice sport coat with a dress shirt and tie.

The tie did bring back some memories. Now, I do confess there was a small part of me that was feeling bad for my huge collection of forgotten neckties hanging lifelessly in my closet. Once upon a time, those ties were a highlight of my sad day – did I feel like being bold and wear something splashy and bright? Or perhaps the day called for something more subdued, a classic blue stripe or a conservative pattern with a lot of grey. Then there were the power ties that could only be worn with certain shirts and for certain meetings with certain coworkers. Managers who have spent time in corporate power circles recognize the look of power when they see it.

I did not miss the daily chore of choosing which tie to wear. In fact, I could barely remember my previous life as a corporate manager. Of course, I still pined for my old fat paycheck, but that was about the only thing I missed. I did not miss the commute, the office politics or the endless meetings and reports. And I certainly did not miss wearing a tie. Teachers did not need fashion statements around their necks to define their identity.

This, however, was a *tie* day. It was special, the day for the year-end awards. We had invited our students' families and friends as well as former teachers and district officials. We even invited a few local politicians because the ALT school was once again being mentioned as a possible target in the annual budget-cutting negotiations for the district. We needed all the positive public relations we could get. And of course, there was free pizza for lunch for anyone who attended, so we expected a great turnout.

When the students got off the busses that morning, they could tell right away that this day was not a typical day at the ALT school. They could tell from the way we were setting up chairs and audio-visual equipment for the assembly. They could tell from the way the teachers were dressed up. And they could tell from our mood – they knew there was nothing they could do that day to push our buttons. We were smiling and calm, steady through any waves that would come our way. Hours away from summer vacation, there was no way we were going to let the kids upset us on the last day of school.

I had been chosen to present the Science awards, and the awards for the Farm, and also the Citizenship award. Between the sports awards, the academic awards, and the various participation awards, all the students were certain to receive at least one award. This was not an accident – many of them had never received an award of any type before. Above all else, we were determined to find some way to recognize the achievement of each and every student. Everyone would experience success and feel a sense of accomplishment - whether they wanted to or not.

We had to reach a bit for some of the awards. That's where the 'Citizenship' or 'Most Improved' awards came in. But we always came up with something for everyone. And, like any other graduation or award ceremony, some students managed to win more awards than others – so in the end, the highest levels of achievement were indeed recognized. It just took a while to get through all the speeches and awards.

I sat in the audience among my students for most of the ceremony. I reminded the kids to be quiet, gave them teacherly looks from time to time, modeled how to clap and cheer appropriately for award recipients, and occasionally had to coax students to go up front to receive their awards. It was all part of being a teacher – I was just doing what teachers do.

From my seat, I was able to look back and see the parents and grandparents, the aunts, uncles, brothers, sisters and close family friends of my students in the back of the audience. There were dozens of little kids. Everybody was straining their neck and flashing their cameras to capture the image of their little cherubs as they won their awards. Families were shouting out and chanting nicknames. Mothers and grandmothers were crying, while dads and stepdads and other unidentified adult males were positively beaming with pride. I couldn't help but be deeply touched.

I thought for a moment about my own kids and their various accomplishments. High school and college graduations, soccer tournaments, awards for creative competitions, starring roles in plays, National Honor Society – the recognition and awards were too numerous to count. I felt so proud of my own kids at that moment, and happy that Carol and I had been able to share each of those moments with our children. It was what families were supposed to do.

I was happy that my students and their families could share that moment together too, however fleeting it might be. I knew exactly how those parents in the audience felt. Pride in your children's accomplishments knows no socio-economic boundary. It doesn't really matter if your kid receives an honor certificate or an attendance award. What matters is that you share the moment and show your pride, and that your child knows it. Being a parent is not always something you plan for or consciously think about – you just do it, sort of like being a teacher.

46

CASA DE CINCO

One of the unexpected benefits of my becoming a teacher was that my life had become very cyclical. There is a certain rhythm in the world of educators that is, at once, both comforting and bursting with a promise of anticipation.

I was no longer following a linear path from promotion to promotion, job to job, rising up some invisible corporate ladder. There was no end game of eventually becoming the boss or finally landing the 'perfect job'. And I was certainly not one of the mindless zombies riding into work on the subway or sitting in commuter traffic, ticking away the hours until it was time to punch out and return home. The underlying rhythm of my life had dramatically changed.

I say that this realization was unexpected because I didn't see it coming. It was never covered in any of my teacher preparation classes and it required a totally different mindset from most corporate environments. People who have been teaching for a number of years seem to take the impact of these cycles for granted. Of course you get new students every year. Of course you get to recharge your batteries every summer. Of course there are seasons and holidays and patterns of learning that occur every year. That's just the way it is.

But it was new to me. I eagerly looked forward to my new crop of students each fall. Who would they be? What could we accomplish together? I was excited to build community in my classroom, to celebrate holidays together. I couldn't wait to share my excitement for science with my students and help them arrive at a greater understanding of the world around them. I looked forward to the first snow day, the first buds of spring, the first day of summer vacation. The school year was all about looking forward.

There are teachers who do pretty much the exact same thing every year. They have their routines and systems and assignments that have been successful in the past and they just duplicate it year after year, rotating a new bunch of students through their program. It certainly makes sense not to re-invent the wheel every year. And, in all fairness, I must admit that I, too, repeated some of my lessons to a certain extent. It was part of the predictable cycle of teaching.

But a teacher can also mix it up a bit, try new things, explore new approaches. Even the most conventional methods of teaching can be 'tweaked' a little to become more effective for a given group of students. I found this to be especially true when working with at-risk students.

For example, I told you how I had helped devise the school-wide behavior system that scored students for every class, every day on the four categories of respect: yourself, others, learning and the environment. This system had become a major part of our school culture. Kids knew what it meant when they got a 'four' – it was a good class for them; they had earned all of their points. It was very rewarding when I would bump into a student at the end of the day and he would proudly exclaim, "Hey, Rick, I got all fours today!"

"That's great, Luis!" I would respond with a pat on the back. This was exactly how the system was supposed to work. Luis was taking ownership for his behavior and was feeling good about behaving appropriately. Luis was on his way to becoming a successful and productive member of society.

Not all days were like this, of course. Some afternoons I would be entering my behavior grades into the computer wondering if my students would ever get themselves straightened out. Keying in zeroes and ones into the spreadsheet instead of fours was very discouraging.

Sometimes I could see patterns in the behavior scores – the numbers seemed to be low near the end of the day, or one student seemed to pull the whole class down with him. Or I could look back at the scores and say, "Wow! Look at that, everybody was on task and respectful in that class. What did I do right?" The behavior scores were a great tool for me to self-reflect on the impact my own personal behavior had on the students.

If I was calm and patient and in a generally good mood, it often rubbed off on the students. If I was irritated by a student or upset about something, that would have an effect too. My principal used to remind us at our staff meetings, "*You* are the weather in your classroom." And it was surprisingly true, as painful as it was to admit, that it wasn't only about the kids – the teacher played an important role as well.

Somewhere along the way, I had gotten the idea of 'tweaking' our system of behavior scores. Getting a 'four' was great – it was what we expected from our students if they were going to be successful. But what if I pushed them a little harder? How could I acknowledge when they were being REALLY great? How could I recognize *outstanding*? If I could get some of my students to personally experience behavior that was above and beyond the normal expectations, what would happen? Could I effectively change their habits? It was surely possible – I had already seen it on a few occasions. Not often enough, to be sure, but enough to know it was possible. How can I raise the bar, I wondered?

The idea of a *five* sprang forth from somewhere in my head. What would a *five* look like? It would have to be 'WOW!' behavior. It would indicate going above and beyond what was expected, and doing it on your own, without the teacher prompting you to do it. I could give a *five* for outstanding work on a classroom assignment. I could give a *five* for helping another student without being asked to do so. I could give a *five* for an ingenious idea, or a question, anything that I was 'WOWED!' by. I decided on three basic requirements for getting a *five* – the student had to already have a 'four', the student had to do something extraordinary during class to WOW me, and the student was not allowed to ask for one, they had to earn it entirely on their own.

I was already aware of a simple but universal educational tool that teachers had been using for decades, possibly centuries, in the classroom to recognize and motivate their students. It was called a sticker. Over the years, this method of behavior management had proven so successful that parents frequently adopted it in their homes to teach everything from potty training to earning allowances. I still remember my own grade school experiences when the teacher would come around with her special stamp and ceremoniously imprint it atop a paper deemed worthy of praise and admiration. Everyone worked harder if there was a sticker involved.

So I set up a huge chart in my classroom on a wall where everyone could see it. I called it my *Casa de Cinco* - my "House of Five". I listed every one of my students' names on it because everyone was always welcome to enter my *Casa de Cinco.* I explained the rules to each of my classes. If a student 'Wowed' me during class with some behavior or example of work that was above and beyond, he or she would earn a *five* for the class instead of a 'four'. When they earned it, I congratulated them, and ceremoniously present them with a sticker and a handshake. I always offered to let them place the sticker up on the chart next to their name. This allowed everyone to compare their own progress with those who had the most stickers.

My students were obviously smart, even brilliant at times, although many of them had been failing in school for years. I knew they would quickly figure out that the sticker was just not enough of a reward for this herculean effort on their part. I would have to devise an incentive for them that would be more than a sticker on a chart. I anticipated that it would probably take quite a while for a student to earn five *fives,* so I highlighted the fifth column on the chart. I told them that when a student had achieved five *fives*, I would buy them breakfast. Whatever they wanted. That got their attention – they were always hungry and interested in free food.

For some of my students, *Casa de Cinco* worked like a charm. They busted hump trying to impress me with their artwork, their effort, even their handwriting. They went out of their way to help each other, to clean up messes that were not theirs, to offer to help me with any projects I needed done. And even though I loved to give out fives, I did not give them out easily. I had to be really impressed by something the student had done. But if I felt they earned one, I let them and everybody else know it. I believed *fives* were the essence of the most important idea that my students could learn – that they were always in control of their actions and, ultimately, their own futures.

Most of my students found ways to impress me over the course of the year and experienced the thrill of placing their hard-earned sticker on the chart. A handful even managed to earn a free breakfast, which they would proudly enjoy in front of their peers at morning meeting. Who would have thought a breakfast sandwich and a coolatta could have such an impact on a troubled youth?

The truth is, *Casa de Cinco* did not work for everybody. There were students who never managed to get a single *five* from me, despite the fact that there were days I would search and search for something, anything, they did that could impress me. They just could not seem to break their own cycle of hopelessness and despair.

"I don't give a fuck about your stupid sticker!" I heard on more than one occasion.

"Don't worry." I patiently told them. "I won't give up on you. You can do it." I knew there would be more opportunities for them to 'Wow' me. Maybe it would happen tomorrow or maybe next week. There was always next year. Even the most hardened students would eventually come around. They would Wow me when they were ready, and I would give them a sticker they could put up next to their name and I would shake their hand and congratulate them. In my heart I knew some day I would get to buy them breakfast. It was possible. Anything was possible.

And besides, it gave me another thing to look forward to. There was always something to look forward to in the cycle of teaching.

47

TEN FIVES

Chino had a potty mouth. He was constantly uttering some crude remark, trying to get a rise out of me or anyone else that happened to be around. Sometimes he did it for show in front of other students, and other times he dropped his vulgarities in the middle of an otherwise normal conversation. Girls were often 'fucking whores' even when chino did not know them. I was a 'fucking prick' even if I was giving him a snack. I was a 'goddamn dickhead' when I was pushing him to do his work. That was just Chino being Chino.

Chino's mom was Dominican and kept close tabs on him. She would have died if she ever heard his language in school. His dad was Guatemalan, lived in Florida, and he only saw him in the summer for a few weeks. Chino was very good at manipulating both his parents. Despite very little money in the family, he was always stylishly dressed and had matching shoes for every outfit.

Chino also had his good points. He was very smart and would work his butt off when he wanted to. He could turn on the charm better than Eddie Haskell (if you are old enough to have watched *Leave It To Beaver.)* He would often help other students complete their work after he had completed his own – and, of course, this was a sure-fire way to get me to give him a *five.* He was also a lot of fun – he just seemed to enjoy life. But above all else, Chino was an outstanding soccer player.

The ALT school had a good number of skilled soccer players and they would sometimes arrange pick-up soccer games after school with a bunch of kids from the other middle school. The ALT school did not have an official soccer team but the other middle schools did. I stayed after school a few times to watch them – they really were quite good. They were even able to beat the teams from the other schools on a few occasions.

One day, Chino and a few of the kids approached me as I was grading some papers at my desk.

"Why we don't we have a soccer team? All the other schools do." Chino was the spokesman but the burning question came from all of them. "It's like we're not good enough, like we don't really matter."

I told them I didn't know why, it probably had to do with money or the fact that we had fewer students than the other schools. But inside, I could feel their pain. They pleaded with me to find out if the ALT school could have a soccer team and if I would coach it. I was flattered to be asked and, caught up in the spirit of the moment, said if we could get it approved as an official school team, I would be happy to coach them, but I had a confession to make. I had never actually coached a soccer team before.

"That's OK," said Chino. "We'll tell you what to do."

I did know a little about the game of soccer because my own four kids all played quite a bit, even on elite teams where parents were expected to knowledgeable about he game too. My daughter had gone on to play in college. Carol and I spent many weekends traveling from one soccer field to another to try to catch all of our kids' games. We loved watching the games and rooting our kids on. I convinced myself the training and exercise would be good for me – I needed to lose some weight. So that's how I became the ALT soccer coach.

Our team was like a scene from *The Bad News Bears Play Soccer.* I tried to get as many boys and girls as I could to come to practices, with the hope of eventually scheduling a few games with the other middle school teams. There was a field in a park nearby we could all jog to. I usually jogged with Chino and a few others who were the serious players. Most of the kids walked and got there whenever they could. I bought a coaching book and ran them through some good training drills. I even set up some scrimmage games. It was fun, and it was great exercise, but we were terrible. I did lose a few pounds running around and keeping the kids moving.

Chino grew rather frustrated. He was used to playing on 'real' teams and his skill level was far beyond what any of the other kids dreamed of. After several weeks, the team began to fall apart, before we were even able to schedule a game with one of the other schools. Some of the kids would show up sporadically for practice, some not at all. We never were able to field enough kids for a whole team. Chino saw me hopelessly trying to keep the team going. I was encouraging even the most uncoordinated players and trying to come up with more fun drills for practice. But Chino recognized it was an impossible task. Thinking back on it now, I believe that was probably how I earned his respect. I just would not give up.

Back in the classroom, Chino was working harder than ever. His language had improved and he hardly ever called me a prick anymore. In fact, he went out of his way to speak respectfully to his classmates and me, and he was more helpful than ever. He started earning some fives.

The day after he had earned his fifth *five*, I brought him breakfast, per the usual *Casa de Cinco* deal. As he sipped his coolatta and stuffed the breakfast sandwich into his mouth he asked, "What do I get for ten *fives*?"

"Nobody has ever gotten ten *fives* before, Chino." I told him.

"I'm gonna do it," he said, his mouth full of eggs and cheese. "What do I get?"

"I don't know, Chino. What do you think would be fair?" I offered.

"Dinner." he answered. "Dinner with a friend, and I get to choose the restaurant."

"Ten *fives* are a lot of *fives*" I said, feeling like I had been set up.

"So it's a deal?" he asked holding up his hand for me to slap.

What could I say? "Deal." I told him as I gave him a 'high five'.

I really made Chino work hard for his *fives* after that, but he had figured out the system. He would always find a way to 'Wow' me, and the *fives* were piling up. Other kids were starting to earn more *fives* too – they were actually copying him and his methods to impress me. Sometimes their efforts and use of the English language were hysterical.

"May you please pass me a new pencil, please?" a student would ask me.

"Hey Rick, would you like some help cleaning up the room, please?" I would hear at the end of class.

Sure enough, near the end of that school year, Chino had earned his tenth *five*. He had been phenomenal during class. His work was superb and his manners were impeccable. He looked at me when class was over to see if he had done it. I pretended not to be paying attention. He waited patiently, watching my every move. He was smiling because he knew he had done it, but I was ignoring him.

Finally, I gave him a look and nodded my head. You would have thought he won the lottery. He was talking a-mile-a-minute, but there were no f-bombs escaping his mouth this time. He was not going to blow it!

The next day after school I brought Chino and Estuardo, one of the other soccer players, to a great Mexican restaurant in town. Chino was trying to impress me. When the waitress came over, he insisted on ordering our dinners in Spanish. The waitress chatted with him for quite a while and I assumed he was just flirting and trying to impress her too. Mr. Personality.

We enjoyed a great meal. Estuardo and Chino were adorable. They were silly, but not obnoxious. Chino had ordered appetizers (unbeknownst to me) in addition to our meals and we were stuffed to the gills. As we were finishing our dinners, there were suddenly a couple of singing guitarists at our table and the waitress was back with a huge dessert. She placed an enormous fancy sombrero on my head and began spooning desert into my open mouth while the waiters sang to me in Spanish. The boys were beside themselves laughing across the table at me.

Apparently, the conversation Chino had with the waitress concerned my birthday, which she and her compadres were now helping us celebrate. I went along with the joke – the dessert was too good to pass up. I told her to bring some for the boys, as well. We all ate fried ice cream with whipped cream – with me sporting that huge sombrero on my head the whole time.

We were finishing up and I had asked for the check. A worried look had come over Chino's face and finally he said to me, "You know, you have to give the sombrero back. You can't keep it."

"Sure I can." I said. "She gave it to me. It's for my birthday."

"It's just for you to wear in here. You can't keep it." I could tell Chino was beginning to be afraid that I might embarrass him in public.

"Oh yeah?" I joked. "Just watch me. I'm going to walk right out that door with this thing on my head and nobody is going to say anything about it."

"No, you can't do that." Chino was starting to panic. "It would be stealing."

"So what?" I said. "You guys steal all the time. Why can't I?"

Estuardo was petrified, literally – he couldn't move. I signed the receipt, got up, and headed for the door, the boys nervously at my heels. As we passed the hostess I paused and gave her a look. Then I graciously took the sombrero from my head and waved it across my chest as I bowed my head. "Gracias," I told her as I placed the hat on the counter. I could hear the boys begin to breathe again.

They laughed all the way home. They laughed the whole next day in school, telling everybody about our dinner adventures. For once, I wasn't such a fucking prick after all.

48

HURRICANE KATRINA

When Hurricane Katrina blew into New Orleans, I, like millions of others, had relatives living there. Fortunately, my nephew and his family were able to escape before the levies broke, and they had come north to stay with family until New Orleans was habitable again. Along with so many others, they had lost everything in the storm.

I asked my nephew and his girlfriend if they would come in and talk to my class about Katrina and what it was like. They were nervous at first, but then agreed.

Their story was moving. They spoke of details only a survivor of the hurricane could know. They created pictures in our minds of the devastation and the sense of uncertainty about the future of New Orleans. My students were mesmerized by their tale of survival. We had all read and heard about the disaster, but here, in front of the classroom, were some people who had actually been there.

After my nephew and his girlfriend left, I spoke with my class about how everyone in the nation seemed to be helping out in some way with the disaster relief. People were going down there to build houses and clear debris. Each day you heard about individuals and groups who were raising money and supplies to help out the victims who had lost everything.

One of my students suggested the ALT school should do something to help too.

"Maybe we could hold a fundraiser and send the money to the Red Cross, or something," he suggested. I told him that was a GREAT idea. I was not going to miss an opportunity for my students to experience the satisfaction of meaningful community service.

We brainstormed ideas with the class about what we could do. One student came up with a fabulous idea: we could make jewelry with beads and gimp and hemp (yes, hemp – the string kind) and sell it to raise money for the hurricane victims. All the kids loved the idea, especially working with hemp.

I bought beads and hemp and booklets on making necklaces and other similar items. I found small plastic cases for kids to keep their beads and supplies in so that they couldn't steal each other's beads. We scribed little red crosses on some of the white beads and put them into the jewelry to signify the Red Cross. We learned some macramé knots together and how to make gimp key chains. Kids who knew how to tie the knots became teachers, showing others how to do it. The kids mostly made necklaces. Some of them were quite fashionable.

When students were finished with their schoolwork, they could make necklaces. When students were done eating lunch, they could make necklaces. Necklaces were made when they didn't want to go outside for gym class. They were made during homeroom and advisory. There was always somebody in my classroom working on the Hurricane Katrina fundraiser with beads.

This was not a tidy enterprise – there were beads everywhere in my classroom. I was scooping up beads between every class, trying to salvage as many as I could. I was stooping down in the middle of my lessons dozens of times because I spotted a nice clay bead under a table or behind a shelf. I swept my floor at the end of each day before the custodian could get to my class just so I could go through the dustpan and save any good beads. It became a compulsion.

As the number of necklaces grew, I realized we needed a way to display them. I set up some black foam board displays, and students pinned their hand-made jewelry up to show them off and sell them. It looked like a kiosk you would see at the mall.

Teachers bought them, both male and female. Visitors touring the school would invariably be led to the display to admire the student's work – and, of course, how could they refuse to buy something to support the cause? We sold them during lunch and we sold them anytime someone showed the least bit of interest. The money jar was getting full – and I kept a close on watch it. A student was always assigned to be in charge and responsible for how much money there should be. I was very careful about keeping our proceeds locked up when no one was selling our handicrafts.

One day I heard about an outdoor fair being held in town – it would be a perfect venue for us to sell our beads. A couple of kids volunteered to help out – including Manny. Manny was a class clown and having trouble getting any work done in class. Ironically, he turned out to be the hardest worker at the event. As evening approached, the weather had turned cold, but there he was, selling necklaces to everyone who walked by, wearing nothing but shorts and a muscle tee-shirt. I finally insisted he put on my fleece sweatshirt because he was shivering so hard. Manny earned my respect that night, and I often referred to his hard work and determination for the rest of that school year. I had gotten a glimpse of the 'real' Manny – a character very different from the class clown everyone else knew.

We raised a total of $270 selling our beaded necklaces and other jewelry items. While that may not seem like a lot of money, I knew that those necklaces were worth far more than that. Their true value was more accurately appraised on the faces of my students in the photograph that appeared in the yearbook later that year. The camera captured us posing with the woman from the Red Cross as we presented her with a huge plastic bottle full of money. I made sure that Manny was front and center in that photograph.

Hurricane Katrina was a terrible disaster for a lot of people. But you'd be surprised how often good things spring out from the bad. It did for us at the ALT school; that was for sure.

49

HURRICANE ON THE HOMEFRONT

Shortly after Hurricane Katrina devastated New Orleans, a force that sent everything in our lives into a spin also struck my home life. Though not as dangerous, it likewise had the power to scatter much of our lives apart and leave us picking through the aftermath for evidence of whom we once were. The odd thing was that Carol and I willingly brought this storm upon us, and would do so again in a heartbeat.

Our oldest son, Matt, had been living in Brooklyn, NY with his wife Meghan and their two delightful children. I say 'delightful' not to imitate contestants on a TV game show introducing their family to the audience, but because my two grandkids were genuinely adorable, sweet little kids - *delightful* in all aspects. Perhaps all grandparents feel this way about their first grandchildren, I don't know. I just know they were more delightful than any other little kids I knew.

Carol and I always enjoyed our visits to the big city where we would take Anna and Jacob to parks or museums or the Bronx Zoo. They loved to have books read to them and of course, we were happy to oblige. It was hard having our grandkids living in the big city, four hours away from us, so we visited them as often as we could. What else could we do? Matt had a job in the city; Meghan was finishing up grad school at NYU. Kids grow up, they move out, they make their own lives, their own choices. It was as it should be, even if it was painful for the grandparents.

Of course, when we visited them we never missed opportunities to put in little digs about moving back closer to home. Always half-joking, always half-serious.

"Who wants to raise a family in the city?" we would say. Or "Kids should grow up knowing that their family is more than a bunch of pictures on a wall. They need to be able to play outside. If you were closer, we could help out more with the babysitting." We issued the typical litany of distant relatives.

During one of our weekend visits, Matt told us he was planning to go back to school to get his MBA. "Great!" we responded. With a growing family we had anticipated he was going to need a larger income than his current job was providing. It was just a matter of time.

"But there's a catch," he continued. "We're going to need a cheap place to live while I'm in school. Can we move in with you for a couple of years until I'm through school and can be working full-time again?"

Carol and I gave each other shocked looks but didn't need to discuss this before responding – we knew instinctively the answer would be 'Yes'. Our children would always be welcome in our home, under any circumstances. It is called unconditional love, something all children should have access to, but unfortunately, not all do. Besides, the upstairs of our house was empty now with all the kids grown and off on their own. We had the room. And we had enjoyed several years together as empty nesters – the prospect of a little more noise and activity around the house sounded interesting.

We understood that all of us living together under the same roof would present some challenges, and we would have to lay out some ground rules and logistics. There would be additional expenses to consider, food and utilities, that sort of thing. But all those things paled in comparison to unlimited access to our grandchildren.

And so they moved in with us. Matt was accepted into Grad school, Meghan got a teaching position near us, and we all tried to be very considerate of each other, respecting each other's privacy and learning how to get along together. We decided to hold family meetings where we could discuss any issues, plan menus, assign chores and responsibilities and coordinate schedules. We actually did have a meeting or two, but you know how life has a way of going on, with or without meetings.

It was a bit crazy and cluttered in the house, especially at first. Our home became much louder than when it was just Carol and me and the dog, but it was generally happy noise. There was stuff everywhere, of course. Kids' toys, discarded shoes, laundry, extra furniture was squeezed in wherever it would fit. Shopping, cooking, and washing dishes increased dramatically. Carol and I had new responsibilities like dropping the kids off at daycare or preschool. Our lives had changed quite a bit, but it actually went along quite smoothly considering how much we were all impacted.

We knocked out the back of the house and build a small addition so Carol and I could have a little space of our own and a private bathroom. That led to remodeling the kitchen, which was badly needed anyway. And, of course, we needed a new bathroom upstairs for Matt and his family.

When I left my corporate position several years earlier, Carol and I had prepared for the drastic reduction in my income. We were not living luxuriously, but we were squeaking by. But the dramatic increases in our family budget were now causing me to seriously reconsider my change of careers. Was I crazy to leave my well-paid position to become a teacher?

"We'll get through this," I confidently told Carol as I finagled our finances each month, although I had no idea HOW we were going to do it.

I have to admit, Carol found it easier to adjust to our new circumstances than I did. She had always loved being the nurturing mother and she missed the good old days when the kids always came running to her for help or advice. She was enjoying all the activity and commotion. And she especially loved every minute with her grandkids.

And to a large extent, I did too. But the constant clutter had also started affecting my mind. I would put something down only to find it had been moved to another place or covered by someone else's stuff. I couldn't find my cell phone and would need someone to call me so I could hunt for it while it was ringing. I lost my car keys and didn't have a backup so I had to drive my wife's car to work. (They were eventually found between the cushions of the couch.) I was forgetting my thoughts in mid-sentence. I thought I was losing my mind.

Strange as it seemed, my classroom became my safe haven. As noisy as it could be, as cluttered as it was, it was all mine. I was in control there – it was MY SPACE! Even when my students told me to 'Fuck Off!' or to 'suck their whatever', I was still centered in the feng shui of my classroom.

In time I became better able to handle the stress at home. I saw beyond the mess, enjoyed my son and the excitement of his young family. I took pleasure in shopping and cooking for a crowd, and managed to carve out some quiet time just for myself. I learned how to mind my own business and when to keep my mouth shut.

Our combined living situation was not just challenging for Carol and me. It had to be extremely frustrating for Matt and Meghan as well not to have their own place - four adults and two little kids living under one roof was no picnic. We all became better at sharing and communicating and helping each other out. We were a family in every sense of the word.

As I look back on it now, I realized what a blessing it was to have my son and his family move in with us. Fate has a strange way of weaving events together to affect the outcome. We didn't know it then, but we were all going to need each other close by, and we couldn't have been any closer.

50

THE ARRIVAL OF BUDDY

Cows did nothing for me until my first visit to the farm. But now I'm definitely a cow person. Likewise, I wasn't a snake person either, until Buddy arrived. Buddy magically turned me into a snake person – whether I wanted to become one or not.

Buddy was a Ball Python snake about a year old and about eighteen inches long. She had been named Buddy before it was discovered that she was a girl, and by that time the name had stuck. So she was a female snake living with a man's name. She had been living with Brian's sister. Brian was in my Physical Science class. He was a big, lanky ninth grader, who was very oppositional to any form of authority. He was especially cranky when he needed a cigarette. Brian was one of the kids who frequently initiated the walkie-talkie report of 'elves on the roof'.

Brian's mother had kicked his older sister out of the house, and the guy she was currently living with didn't want a snake as part of her baggage. So Buddy was technically abandoned. Brian's mother wanted her out of the house – NOW, and so Buddy was on the verge of becoming homeless.

Of course, that's where I came in. Brian offered her to me as a classroom pet. She could become our mascot. With her background story, I felt that she would fit right in. She could live in her aquarium tank in our classroom. Brian would help take care of her – he knew all about snakes. He assured me she would not be a problem. We would just have to feed her mice from time to time – dead ones were OK – we didn't have to catch live mice for her to stalk and devour in front of the children. With some reservations, I said OK; we could give it a try, but just temporary to see if it works out.

True to Brian's word, Buddy was a wonderful addition to our classroom. I held her the first day – the first time I had ever held a snake. I was nervous, of course, but I wanted to make sure she was not going to bite anyone, so I offered myself as a sacrifice. She gently wrapped herself around my arm and seemed to be enjoying the attention. God help me, I started talking to her like you would any pet. "Who's yo daddy now, Buddy?" I said to her, much to the amusement of my students.

My classes loved Buddy. I would let them hold her after they had completed their work or if a kid needed something small and vulnerable to hug for a while. I had to rotate her feeding schedule so that all my classes had the chance to witness Buddy snatching a dead mouse and swallowing it whole. I had to admit, it was quite fascinating. In time I had, indeed, become something I never thought I would ever become: a snake person.

At the end of that school year, I had a lot of travel plans for my summer vacation, and Buddy presented somewhat of a problem. I did not want to be bogged down taking care of a Ball Python all summer. Several of my students offered to keep Buddy for the summer and I chose one who was experienced with pets and really seemed to want to take care of her. Randy lived nearby, was very dependable and had a mother who was willing to let him keep Buddy in his room for the summer.

On the last day of school, I had arranged with Randy to bring Buddy over to his apartment as soon as school let out. Before that could happen, however, there was to be a school-wide breakfast, signing of yearbooks, and students helping teachers pack up their rooms. In the commotion of the day, someone neglected to put the top back on Buddy's aquarium tightly. When Randy came to my room to bring her home with him, we discovered she was missing.

We searched everywhere, with no luck. Other students came to join us but we could not find her anywhere. With a heavy heart, I finally sent the kids home and broke the news to my principal: Buddy was missing. This did not go over well with her or any of the other staff members when they heard the news. Who wants a snake loose in their school?

The next day I was back in my classroom to finish packing everything up for the summer. It also gave me a good chance to scour every inch of my classroom, still on the lookout for Buddy. There was only one more box left to move, buried way back behind my desk. As I pulled it away from the wall, there lay Buddy covered in dust.

Ecstatic to have found her, I picked her up and was relieved to see that she was still alive, although there were a few small scratches on her body with some fresh blood – nothing major, just some bumps and bruises from her escape.

I called Randy with the good news and, in about three seconds, he was standing in the doorway to my classroom, ready to take Buddy to his place for the summer.

His apartment was in a housing project nearby and there were about twenty kids running around the yard when we got there. Some of them were Randy's younger siblings but a lot of them were just neighborhood kids. Randy assured me Buddy would be safe, that he would take good care of her. I carried the aquarium upstairs to his room, which looked like it had been tidied up for Buddy's arrival. I gave Randy some frozen mice to put in his freezer and told him to call me if he needed anything. I wrote down my phone number and headed home excited to start my summer vacation.

Ten o'clock that night I got a call from Randy.

"Buddy doesn't look too good," Randy told me. "Her head is all swollen and it looks like her brain is going to explode."

I tried to assure Randy that it was probably nothing; maybe she had hurt herself while on the run. I told him to relax and we'd see how she was doing in the morning. Reluctantly, he said OK and hung up.

An hour later, Randy called again. "She looks like she's going to die," he told me. "I can't sleep with her here looking like this. Can you call a doctor? She needs to see a doctor."

I asked him a few questions about her condition and told him I would see what I could do.

Have you ever tried to locate a snake veterinarian at eleven PM on a Friday night? I tried the humane society who referred me to a reptile expert over an hour away. The answering message told me to call back in the morning. There was somebody listed on the Internet, but they were not answering either. The emergency pet hospital said that they were open and would see her, but the person on duty was not really familiar with snakes. It would cost $250 for the visit and that did not include any medication or treatment if necessary.

I called Randy back and told him that I had not had any luck finding a doctor who could see Buddy that night. "Let's just go to sleep and see how she is in the morning. It's all right if she dies and I know you did everything you could to help her. It's not your fault if she dies." I tried to sound consoling, but at this point, I really just wanted to get some sleep. It had been a long and tiring day.

"No," Randy said. "I can't sleep next to her knowing she's dying. Can you come and get her?"

The last thing I wanted to do at midnight the last day of school was to drive the 40 minutes to Randy's house, pack up Buddy and her belongings, and bring her back to our house. But that is exactly what I did. When I got there and saw Buddy, I could see why Randy was so upset. Buddy truly looked like her head was going to explode. My guess was she had gotten an infection from her wounds and there was a kind of lock-jaw/meningitis thing happening. I was no snake expert, but I could see she was miserable.

I brought her home and, after a few days, Buddy seemed to be improving. No doctors or medication, just quiet recuperation. In a week or so, she seemed to be back to normal. She ate a small mouse and was drinking water. I called Randy to see if he still wanted her for the summer. He was thrilled not only for Buddy's recovery, but that he would still get her for the summer. For the second time, I brought Buddy to Randy's house, carried her up to his room, made sure they were all set, and left the two of them to enjoy what was left of summer vacation.

Buddy and Randy had a great summer vacation together, at least according to Randy's account. She returned to our classroom in September healthy and appropriately snake-like. She had grown some over the summer so I knew she had been fed. Randy said Buddy had made an ordinary summer vacation special. I thanked him and complimented him on doing such a good job taking care of her. She was obviously very happy, I told him. "Look at how she is smiling."

"Snakes don't smile," he told me. "That's just how their mouths are."

"She looks like she's smiling to me," I answered.

We watched her for a while – it was probably only a few seconds but it seemed like a lot longer. We were smiling at her, and at each other, and I swear to God, Buddy was smiling right back at us.

51

SNAKEMAN

Let's face it, snakes have gotten a bad rap ever since the Garden of Eden. People think of them as slithery, deceptive, vicious creatures – sort of like my students. But when you get to know them, they're really not so bad, once again mirroring my students. Snakes, like any other living creature including at-risk students, just do what they need to do to survive in a hostile climate.

Buddy and I had developed a comfortable working relationship. I would give her mice, water and regular replacement of the heat lamps in her tank. In exchange, she provided hours of entertainment and some level of comfort for my students. They would hold her and spray her down with water. Her shedding skin was often the subject of study under the microscope. Buddy was also a popular stop for any visitors to our school, especially prospective students.

Somewhere along the way I became a snake man. I still was not crazy about snakes other than Buddy, but I had a snake in my classroom, so I must be a snake man. Personally, I thought this was extremely ironic – me, a snake man. But often we don't get to choose our own labels. We just become what fate or others want us to be.

One night I was relaxing at home and there was a knock on the door. I got up to answer it, holding back our large golden retriever, Bailey, so he would not jump all over the unexpected visitor. On our front porch stood my neighbor's brother, Bill, holding what looked like a pillowcase. Bailey was trying his best to retrieve both Bill and the pillowcase.

"I caught something in my basement I thought you might be interested in," Bill began. "I heard you were a snake man – that you liked snakes and had one in your classroom. I thought you might want this to show your kids." He was holding out the pillowcase for me to peek inside.

At the bottom of the case I could see a snake, pretty large, with amazing red, yellow and black markings. It was slithering around the bottom of the pillowcase looking vicious and deceptive, but I had to admit, it was striking in its colorful markings.

"I don't know what it is," Bill told me, "but it gave me a pretty good bite when I picked it up."

"It bit you? Are you all right?" I asked. The angry snake continued to squirm around inside the pillowcase.

"Yeah, I'm fine. It didn't really draw much blood. It is a nasty critter, though."

"It does look cool," I said, not really knowing what to think or say.

"So you want him?" Bill asked. "You're welcome to keep him so you can show him to your kids. You can do whatever you want with him – I sure don't want him in my basement."

Bill had handed me the pillowcase and was halfway down the steps before I could say, "Uh, I guess so." He was already across the street by the time I uttered a lame "Thanks."

My first thought was to find something secure I could put the snake in. I found a large box in the garage that would work, but I had to duct tape up some holes in the sides. I did not want this creature getting out in my house. I also cut a small piece of screen and taped it across an opening I had cut in the top so it would have plenty of air. The whole time I was working on the box that would hold the snake, I also had to awkwardly hold the pillowcase with my new friend in it. Once the box was secure, I opened the pillowcase and dropped the snake into it. It was definitely a beautiful specimen, whatever it was. I put the top on quickly and duct-taped it so it was nice and snug.

Carol was not going to let me keep the snake in the house overnight, and I didn't blame her. I thought about leaving it in the box outside on our deck, but it was getting very cold and I did not think it would be a good idea. I decided to put the box in my car for the night. I made sure all the duct tape was in place and the top was secure so it could not get out, and left it there for the night.

Inside, I dug out my *Stokes Guide to Reptiles and Amphibians* and began trying to identify the mystery snake safely stored in my car. It turned out to be an Eastern Milk snake, not poisonous, luckily for Bill.

I awoke the next morning thinking about how I would present this special learning activity to my students. I would bring my guidebook in with me and see if they could identify it. We could observe it and compare it to Buddy – perhaps a Venn diagram activity. I knew my students would definitely be engaged in the lesson today. This was going to be a great day!

I went out to my car with my backpack and my morning coffee, and put them on the passenger seat. I opened the back door to take a quick peek at my prize before heading off to school. I couldn't see it at first – it must be in a corner, or maybe along the top of the box. I shook the box, but no snake dropped to the bottom. I shook harder. No snake! This could not be happening. I carefully took the top of the box off – duct tape and all. The box was empty. I ripped the box apart thinking that somehow the snake would appear.

Don't panic, I said to myself, as I began looking under the car seats and anywhere else I thought a snake might hide. It had to be in the car, I thought. It will come out eventually. But I did not have the time to wait. I had to get moving if I was going to get to school on time. I took a deep breath and got in the car, started the engine, and began the usual drive to the ALT school, although the drive felt anything but usual that day. It was a challenge to stay calm as I drove. It's just a snake, I kept telling myself, just a snake. It's just a big, vicious, biting snake lurking somewhere in my car.

I got to school safely without being bitten or driving off the road into a ditch. I thought about leaving my car doors open all day so the snake could get out. Perhaps it was worth the risk of my students stealing all my CD's and anything else they could find. But if I did leave the doors open, how would I know for sure that the snake was out? I had to have proof it was gone – there could be no rest until I was certain it was out of my car.

Inside the school, my snake adventure was the story of the day. All the other teachers and staff thought it was hysterical that I had a vicious snake lost somewhere in my car, and that I actually had driven to school with the snake somewhere inside it. My students didn't laugh. They saw my predicament as some sort of a challenge, an obstacle they could remove for me. They were determined to find that snake and get it out of my car. They were sure I'd be 'wowed' and they could earn some *fives*.

I thought about it for a second; then I said, "OK. For today's lesson, we're going outside to my car to see if we can catch the snake. There will certainly be some sort of reward for anyone who can find the snake."

My students were down the steps and all over my car in a flash. They looked under the seats, under the rugs, everywhere – even under the hood. No snake. I repeated the assignment for the next class, also with no results. Disappointed, I drove home that night very much aware that the snake might attack me at any moment. I was not enjoying this.

Later that evening, my daughter suggested I look for the snake now that it was dark. Snakes are nocturnal so maybe it would come out in the dark. I went out to my car to see if I could see any sign of the snake. Low and behold! There it was on the floor behind the driver's seat. Just lying there! GREAT! I ran back inside to get a big plastic storage bin and a poker from the fireplace to scoop it out with. That snake was history!

When I got back to the car, the snake was gone. Shit! No sign of it anywhere. I let out a huge sigh. Well, at least I knew it was still in the car. I spent the next few days knowing it was still in my car, driving back and forth to school. I guess you could say I was getting used to it – almost. One morning, there was a fairly large snake turd right next to the driver's door. It had to be a snake turd – what else could it be? I could almost hear the sucker hissing "Nah nah na nah nah!" I considered this an act of war.

I decided to outsmart my opponent. He must be getting hungry, I thought. And I knew what snakes ate - mice. As a matter of fact, I had just caught a mouse in a mousetrap and it was in the freezer waiting to become Buddy's next meal. I would use the mouse to set a trap.

I put the mouse in a large, opened cooler on the back seat. It was perfect. Once the snake crawled in, I could shut the cooler door and he was mine! I began checking the trap in my car between every inning of the Red Sox game I was watching on TV. I checked it during every commercial. No luck. When it was time to go to bed, I shut the cooler for the night. I was no fool. I was not going to let that slimy creature eat my mouse when I was not around to catch him! Let him get good and hungry!

I repeated the process the next day. I had nothing better to do that weekend than catch that damn snake. I set the trap up again Sunday morning, checking it all day and all night. With a heavy heart, I finally closed the lid of the cooler to go to bed. Tomorrow was a school day and this snake hunting was exhausting. I went to bed depressed and frustrated.

Monday morning I went out to my car ready to be disappointed again. I considered trading the car in without telling the dealer about the snake. I was getting ready to admit defeat. I glanced in the car and to my surprise, coiled on top of the cooler was my fine red, yellow and black friend. The mouse-bait inside the cooler was pretty raunchy by this time – it smelled like spoiled marinated tips. The snake was trying to figure out how to get into the cooler. He could smell his meal and he was just waiting to pounce.

This time I was ready. The large storage bin was right there at the side of the car. So was the fireplace poker. I opened the door and grasped the snake with the poker. It wrapped itself around the iron prong and I dragged it into the storage bin in one fell swoop. I quickly secured the top, pressing down hard to seal it in – to hell with enough air to breathe!

Eastern Milk snakes are no dummies. He pushed his head up to the rim and searched for a way out, his tail supporting him from the bottom. He was still beautiful, even if he was vicious and slithery and deceptive. Most important, he was still very much alive, but now he was mine. He frantically searched for a way out, but he knew he was trapped.

I brought the snake inside to show Carol my irrefutable proof that she could now safely ride in the car with me. I brought him to school and showed him to everybody – teachers, staff and students. I was so proud I had outsmarted a snake. My students were impressed as I told them the story of his capture. After everyone had a good look at my adversary, I carried him out back to a nearby marshy area, wished him good luck, and let him go. He quickly slithered away into the wees.

A few days later, two girls from another class showed up in my room.

"Rick, Rick, do you have a box we can use?"

"Sure. What do you need it for?" I inquired.

"Look," one girl said as she started to pull something out of her coat pocket. "We found this at the bus stop. We thought you might want it for your classroom. We know how you love wild creatures!"

I shuddered. I was having a déjà vu, expecting her to pull out a snake. But it was not a snake. It was a small white bunny rabbit with pink ears and what appeared to be a rather large dog bite in its abdomen. It cowered pathetically in her arms.

"No, that's all right." I told them. "I definitely don't want a rabbit in my classroom. I can't have animals with fur because some people have allergies. And look at his belly, he really needs to go to the animal shelter to have that cut taken care of."

The girls nodded; they knew I was right.

"Besides," I said, "everybody knows I'm a snake man."

52

ALMOST PERFECT ATTENDANCE

Parent conferences at the Alt school were held each year on the two days preceding Thanksgiving. We would call all the parents of our students and try to get them to sign up for a designated time to discuss the academic and social progress of their son or daughter. We always made sure there were examples of student work displayed prominently in the classroom and that things were put away. It was important for the classrooms to look neat and interesting.

Getting ready for parent conferences involved a lot of extra work, but we wanted to create a good impression for the parents. Many of our students' parents had been at-risk students themselves when they were in school and still did not think kindly toward school, the teachers, or education in general. We wanted to change all that. If we could win the parents over, they could become invaluable allies in our efforts to work with their children. At least that's what all the research about best practices suggested.

Subconsciously, I deviously craved that the parents understand how incredibly difficult it was to teach their little bastards. I wanted them to feel some of our pain, or at least commiserate with us. They need to appreciate what we do at some level, I thought. Can they give us a little credit?

All the slots in our conference schedule had names penciled in. During my first year when Brenda and I teamed together, we had 26 students; that meant we had close to 26 appointments scheduled into fifteen-minute slots over the course of an evening and the following morning. We would be lucky if we could grab enough time for a bathroom break.

As it turned out, only four parents showed up for their conferences the first night and three showed up the next day - seven out of twenty-six. As poor as that sounds, it was the best turnout for any of the teams in the school that year. It was another sad comment on the plight of our students.

We were not pleased with the low turnout, to say the least, and we decided to do something about it. In fact, the next year we managed to have almost one hundred percent turnout – all the parents showed up. All we had to do was offer food, lots of food.

The month prior to parent conferences, the staff at the Alt School began to organize a food drive to provide every one of our families with a complete Thanksgiving dinner. We found a large grocery retailer willing to donate over one hundred turkeys. We found donors for stuffing, cranberries and pies. The staff brought in canned goods and coordinated with other organizations to do the same. Every family was promised a turkey with all the fixings - all they had to do was come to their child's teacher conference to pick it up.

Once again, it was a lot of work, but well worth all the effort. Some parents told us there would have been no Thanksgiving dinner if not for our food baskets. For others, it gave us the opportunity to demonstrate that we were not the awful teachers their children complained about. Those turkeys opened up a line of communication with parents we would not likely have reached in a traditional school setting.

There were still a few food baskets left over at the end of conferences. We had planned to have extras for some of the larger families, and we knew some of the kids would need two baskets because mom and dad could not be left in the same room together, let alone agree on how to split up one food basket. I was asked to deliver one of the extra turkey baskets on my way home to celebrate the holiday with my own family. It was for one of my students whose parents were divorced and he split his time between both parents.

I found the address and went up a dark, crooked set of stairs to the second floor apartment. I knocked and my student came to the door. Dad was not home; no parents were, just an older brother sleeping in the back room. I carried in the food basket and then went back to my car to get the turkey. I returned carrying the eighteen-pound turkey and told my student we would need to keep it cold – we should try to make some room for it in the refrigerator.

"No problem," he said. He opened the refrigerator door and I saw that there was indeed plenty of room in the fridge. In fact, there was nothing in there, nothing except half a bottle of ketchup. I thought about my own refrigerator at home and how frustrated I would often get as I struggled to find a place to fit anything in – another fringe benefit of my son's family living with us.

I could not forget the sight of that empty refrigerator – the image haunted me. The next day at home, as I tried to make room for our own Thanksgiving leftovers, my heart was full of thanks. There was so much I took for granted every day, and I felt especially blessed – not only for the material comforts that my family enjoyed, but for the unconditional emotional support as well.

The Thanksgiving baskets became a yearly school tradition after that year. It became just another part of what we did at the ALT school, another way of being alternative. We bragged about our almost perfect attendance for parent conferences – it was one of the highest in the entire school district. And best of all, we always knew we would eventually have at least one opportunity to meet our students' parents and get a brief glimpse at their home life.

I could never be certain if any of those parents ever truly felt our pain or understood how hard it was to teach their children, as I secretly hoped. But at least they knew their kids were in good hands. That counted for something in their books. And then again, so did the free turkeys.

53

MORE GIVEAWAYS

The turkeys were not the only giveaways that the ALT school offered to families of our students. Almost all of our students qualified for free lunch, which also meant the kids got a free breakfast every morning if they could get to school on time. Girls had access to free feminine supplies at the nurse's office. Staff members were known to take students to the shoe store on occasion. There were trips to department stores to buy jeans, jackets and winter coats, socks or underwear – whatever the situation or the season called for. Somehow, the ALT school managed to provide what no one else seemed capable of.

All too often, the teachers kicked in a substantial portion of their meager salaries for snacks and incentives for the students. We were always treating the kids to bagels or juice, sub sandwiches or frozen slushies. I became adept at checking out the day-old rack at the local supermarket for cookies or pastries I could get for half-price. I bought those huge packages of peanut butter crackers at the discount store to have on hand to hold off the hungry young stomachs growling in the middle of one of my science classes. I can't learn anything when I'm hungry, I thought, so how can we expect them to master the curriculum on an empty stomach?

Having food wasn't all about satisfying physical hunger, though. There was a social element to it as well. I used snacks to help build community, to establish trust with students, to reward good effort, and to show my students that I was human. Proper manners were modeled as I served all the ladies first, much to the dismay of my hungry gentlemen. I taught my students how to eat healthy things like carrots sticks or apples with peanut butter. I provided real juice instead of the soda or caffeinated, high-energy drinks they were used to drinking. Sweets were often saved for celebrations.

The ALT school also provided a lot of giveaways for our students in the form of incentives for good behavior. There were field trips to the movies, ice-skating, bookstores and a nearby amusement park – all in addition to any 'educational' field trips we might offer. There were gift cards to the mall and free coupons for the coffee shop or fast food restaurants for various incentives. There were candy bars for students who brought in a permission slip on time. There were snow cones or bags of popcorn for students with good behavior scores. It was not unusual to see a pizza being delivered to a class who had somehow earned it. One teacher presented each student with a book for his or her birthday, and for some it was the only birthday present they would get.

Believe it or not, we did find time to teach with all of these freebies floating around, and truth be told, the incentives usually helped motivate the students to accomplish more work than they would have if there had been no reward. The plain fact was that at-risk youth in particular responded well to behavioral incentives. We hoped and prayed for the day our students would do something just for the intrinsic reward involved, but sadly, that type of thinking was not a part of their daily reality. They were trapped by their desire to satisfy their basic needs. And we were trapped by our desire to fill them.

Besides being expensive, we knew that extrinsic rewards were not the solution and constantly tried to expose our students to less tangible motivators. Our staff became experts at finding opportunities to compliment our students. In fact, one of our guidance counselors taught us all about the 5:1 rule. You had to say five positive things to a student for every one critical or negative comment. You can imagine how hard this was to do when a student was determined to be a constant thorn in your side.

"Nice sneakers!" I would say. "How did you ever manage to do that fancy thing with the laces? I don't think I could do that! They look amazing!"

During an argument with a student, it was not unusual to hear me say, "I like your thinking, it's very creative. You really should go to law school."

Heaven forbid a student should come in with a new haircut, or a new hair color, or even a new belt buckle and we didn't notice and tell them how great it looked. It might take weeks to undo the damage of your oversight. The way that our students soaked up all our compliments, any compliment, was a concrete reminder about how starved they were to hear something positive coming from an adult in their life.

We tried our best to be that positive force that could put them on the path to changing their whole outcome on life. They just needed to see themselves differently.

Not often, but every once in a while, a situation would arise where I would present a student with one of my stones. It had to be just the right situation and just the right student. I did not want to diminish the significance of the stones in any way. Sometimes I wrote my phone number on it; sometimes it was just a stone to hold onto when things got tough. When Will moved away to live with his dad, I gave him a stone so he would not forget us. When Tony's parents both went to jail and he was put in placement, I gave him one with my number on it. When Jeff was leaving us to transition back into the bigger, traditional middle school, I made sure he had one in his pocket.

So our giveaways didn't always have material value.

When the Christmas holidays rolled around, the kids' unruly behavior invariably escalated. The stress of families in poverty was visible in our classrooms every day. I tried not to focus on any of the commercial aspects of the holiday, but it was impossible to avoid the hype of the latest video games and electronic gadgets bombarding us from the TV. Even my most impoverished students knew what 'style' was when it came to jeans or sneakers or hooded sweatshirts. But most of them were going to get none of that on Christmas morning. They would be lucky if there were any presents to open at all.

I don't know what we were thinking when we came up with the plan to become Santa Claus for our most needy families. Again, we enlisted the help of local charitable organizations and everyone we could think of to help. We adopted our neediest families and a local coffee shop generously encouraged its patrons to adopt more families. We made lists of our kids' clothing sizes, and sizes for their brothers and sisters and mothers and fathers. We shopped, and searched for bargains that would match up with the items on our lists. We bought wrapping paper and bows. We made sure that all the sales tags were removed from each and every gift so that a strung-out parent could not return their child's gifts for cash – sad but true. We wrapped and we wrapped and we wrapped some more. It was very festive.

One of my colleagues and I had the pleasure of delivering Christmas to two of the families. My car was loaded up with wrapped presents when we arrived at the motel where my student, Dusty, was living with his dad. Dusty was not home at the time, but his dad was. As we unloaded the gifts, Dusty's dad was beside himself, overwhelmed by both the number of presents we were delivering, and by the unexpectedness of our visit. We left him crying as he tried to hide all the gifts in the motel room so that he could surprise his son. He told us that, thanks to us, he was looking forward to the holiday for the first time in many, many years.

We went back to the ALT school and loaded up again, this time for another of my students and his family living in the projects nearby. We were holding stacks of wrapped presents when we knocked on the door, and my student happened to be the person who opened the door. He looked us up and down without much expression and motioned for us to come in. There was a tiny artificial tree on a table in the living room and we put the presents on the floor next to it. He followed us back out to my car and we all filled our arms again with another load of gifts. We brought them in and placed them on the floor next to the others. It was quite a stack of gifts for him and his sister, mother and father, and the pile of presents made the small tree seem even more dwarfed.

There was still little reaction from my student. Mom was apparently upstairs in bed and no one else was home. As we headed for the door, we wished him and his family a happy holiday.

"Thanks," he said.

That was it. Not much of a reaction, I thought. Oh well, it was still the right thing to do, and it still felt good. God bless us, every one!

54

DR. MARTINEZ

One of my former students was having trouble at the big high school. He was failing his classes, mostly because he was not managing to get himself to school in the morning. The ALT school only went up to tenth grade and Julio was in eleventh grade. He had been at the ALT school for sixth grade, went to the traditional schools for a few years where he struggled to get by, and then came back to us for tenth grade. Julio was a bright young man, but was prone to making some poor choices when it came to partying and staying up all night. In so many ways, Julio was your typical at-risk student.

Julio had also gotten himself involved with the courts. He was not much of a talker so I never knew exactly what his troubles were all about. All I knew was that he had a probation officer who wanted him in school. And Julio himself said his goal was to graduate high school. He just needed to find an alternative path that would work for him.

One of the high school credits Julio was missing in order to get his diploma was a science credit – he had failed physical science in ninth grade while at the big high school. I was asked if there was any way he could earn a science credit from me even though he was older and technically in eleventh grade. I was teaching ninth grade physical science and I immediately recognized this as an opportunity for both Julio and myself. Julio became my intern for the semester and I appointed him my teacher's assistant. In this way, being in class with the younger kids did not embarrass him, and I was able to bestow an aura of responsibility on him. At the same time, he began taking some classes at the adult night school to get his other high school credits. He was getting his act together.

I assigned Julio the job of helping me prepare materials for my ninth grade class. I directed him to make posters and instructional aides. He conducted research into topics we were going to cover and created PowerPoints presentations I could show to the class. I coached him on how to present the material without just cutting and pasting from online resources, assisting him with grammar, spelling and punctuation.

Julio was working hard and he knew it. He also understood that I truly appreciated his help. I began referring to him as 'Professor Martinez' when we were speaking with the younger students. Eventually, I promoted him to 'Dr. Martinez' because he was working so hard.

In my mind, this was exactly what alternative education was all about. Julio was learning more than he would have in a traditional classroom, and he was motivating himself to do it. Plus, he had the flexibility of a program that met his needs. In was a win, win, win situation – Julio won, my students won, and I won.

Julio had no trouble earning his science credit from me that semester. I'm not sure if his success stemmed from the individualized attention that I was giving him, or if it was because of the format – it was as if he was working on an independent study project. Maybe it was just because his head was in a better place. I'll never know.

What I do know is that it worked for Julio. I wondered how many others were out there struggling to maneuver their own way through the maze of traditional education. If we could make learning accessible for all students, and let them taste success at the same time, everybody gained.

I lost touch with Julio after that semester, but I heard rumors through the grapevine that he had gotten into trouble again with the law, something to do with an underage relationship. He supposedly did some time at the Youth Detention Center – the state facility for juvenile delinquents. Obviously, I could not change all the forces that were crushing Julio, pulling him along with the current. But I like to think that I gave him some hope, a glimpse at an alternative future for himself, maybe even a way out. He needed something to reach for, but it was just beyond his grasp.

One day, clear out of the blue, Julio stopped by the school to visit with another former student, Vince. Like Julio, Vince had done a little time at YDC. They both looked good now, clear-eyed and smiling. They were back at the high school and planning to graduate this coming spring. As I shook their hands, I noticed they were both holding a piece of paper in their other hands. From the looks of it, they were here on some official business.

"Check this out," said Julio, thrusting his sheet of paper in my face.

It was a report card from the high school. Julio's grades were all A's and B's. I could not hold back my enthusiasm and I hugged him, squeezing him as hard as I could.

"Look! Me too!" chimed in Vince. Sure enough, he had nothing lower than a C and I hugged him as well, telling them both how proud we all were of them. They were both beaming.

I had no doubt in that moment that Julio and Vince would indeed become high school graduates, and perhaps Julio would eventually attend community college as well. I wouldn't even be surprised if someday he was teaching science, maybe in an alternative setting. It was possible.

There was a large and colorful mural hanging prominently inside the main entrance to the ALT school. I had helped the students create it to brighten up the place and make the entrance to the school more inviting. We had brainstormed a bunch of ideas for the mural and this particularly uplifting phrase was the one chosen by the students. The slogan read *If You Believe You Can Achieve.* Julio was living proof that anything is indeed possible; when you believe you really can achieve.

IF YOU
BELIEVE
YOU CAN
ACHIEVE!

PART THREE

55

EVERY PARENT'S NIGHTMARE

I was now in my fifth year working at the ALT school and loving it. Teaching there was still the hardest thing I had ever done in my life, but *that* was probably what I loved about it the most – the challenge. The job and the kids could be overwhelming at times, for sure. They could easily suck the life out of a person by taking over your brain, your heart and every waking hour. But it was also exciting and fulfilling in ways that were difficult to describe.

At home I labored to keep a proper balance. On one hand there was the ever-present lesson planning and worrying about my needy students. On the other were my family responsibilities, not to mention my physical and emotional health. The two were not always easy to reconcile. Regular exercise helped.

Carol and I loved to walk and bike, and we often worked out together at the gym. On many evenings after dinner, we immersed ourselves in the crowded pool at the health club, taking water aerobics classes together. We enjoyed everything outdoors and we climbed mountains or kayaked whenever possible. It was all part of our 'plan' to grow old together while staying as healthy as we possibly could.

We woke to an unseasonably warm Saturday morning in April. Carol and I decided we would venture out on our bikes for the first ride of the season. There were still huge piles of frozen snow in the supermarket parking lots, yet the temperature was in the low seventies. The trees were beginning to turn red with their spring buds. Winter was definitely over. We had just purchased new bikes the year before and we were psyched to get out on the road.

As we were getting ready and filling our water bottles, the phone rang. Our tax accountant was on the line and he had some bad news to give me. He had completed our tax return and we owed money to Uncle Sam – a lot of money. I figured we would probably owe some, but I had not realized we would have to pay so much in taxes this year.

"Oh well, it's only money," I said philosophically. I think he was shocked at how well I was taking the news. We discussed payment options and came up with a payment plan we would have to live with. I was not going to let my tax return get in the way of this beautiful day and ruin our first bike ride of the season.

Carol and I buckled on our helmets and went outside. We jumped on our bikes, pedaled through town and started heading toward a nice, quiet area where we could ride without a lot of traffic on the road. It was one of our favorite local routes to ride. The fragrant spring wind in our faces and the increase in our heart rates were exhilarating as we contemplated all the warm weather to come. Another summer vacation was at last in sight, looming on the horizon.

At the top of a long hill, I paused to drink from my water bottle and waited for Carol to catch up to me. I was startled by the sound of my cell phone ringing in the pack on the back of my bike. I had forgotten that I had even brought it. Should I answer it, or should I just let it ring? Carol was still a ways back, working hard to get to the top of the hill. I decided to answer it, thinking it might be the accountant again needing some bit of important financial information.

I recognized the voice of my oldest son, Matt. He had just gotten a call from the Cheshire Medical Center in Keene. They would not tell him much - only that our daughter, Jenna, had been in an accident. We were supposed to call them back as soon as possible. That was all he knew.

It took a moment for that to sink in as I looked back down the hill. Carol was obliviously pedaling her way up but it seemed as if she were in slow motion now. I explained to Matt where we were and told him to start coming to get us. We would turn around and head back toward home so he should be looking for us along the way.

I broke the news to Carol. There were no more thoughts about a beautiful Saturday morning bike ride in April. There was only fear and worry. Carol had spoken to Jenna just that morning. Jenna had said she was just hanging out, doing laundry and schoolwork. She was thinking about going out for a jog. Surely it was just something minor, an inconvenience, we hoped, we prayed. But we were scared to death.

We met up with Matt and quickly threw the bikes into the trunk. We raced home not knowing exactly what we were travelling toward. Jenna was due to receive her own Masters of Education next month. For a graduation gift, I had given her my old Mazda as a trade-in. She had just recently bought a brand new car, her first. She was going to be so pissed if she cracked up her new car. My thoughts rambled, not wanting to think about the possibilities of what might have happened to her.

When my call got through to the medical center, the woman I spoke to was very reassuring. She told us that Jenna had been hit by a car while jogging. Jenna was conscious and talking, and there did not seem to be any paralysis: her head and spine seemed to be in working order. She was pretty banged up however, and they were going to airlift her to the main medical center at Dartmouth.

"Airlift her," I stammered, "you mean in a helicopter?" This could not be good, I thought.

"Yes, we med flight people up there all the time," she answered, trying to sound reassuring. "They have the best doctors and equipment for this type of situation."

"This type of situation . . ." The phrase kept echoing inside my head.

I was having trouble thinking clearly. Carol was already packing an overnight bag. The woman on the phone told me to head straight to Dartmouth – we would probably get there about the same time as the helicopter with Jenna. "Just go to the emergency room" she told me. She told me again that Jenna was a real trooper, that she was alert and talking to the doctors. She was in no immediate danger. I thanked her and said I could tell that she had children of her own. "Yes," she said, "and I can only imagine how frightened you both must be right now. But rest assured, your daughter is in good hands."

Carol and I said very little to each other during the two-hour drive to Dartmouth. We were catatonic. There was nothing really to say – our heads were flooded with questions that could not be answered and thoughts we could not imagine. All we could do was pray and worry and try to get to the hospital quickly and safely.

We sat and paced and fidgeted for about an hour in the emergency waiting room. People were coming and going with bandages and casts and crutches and wheelchairs. After a while, we were told the helicopter had just landed; they were bringing her in. We grew more frantic with each passing minute. They told us they would let us see her as soon as possible. More time went by. Carol and I did our best to keep it together but the receptionist could see the hysteria growing in our eyes. He made some phone calls. Finally, he told us we could go through the doors to the right and someone would meet us there.

We found ourselves in a large emergency room with a lot of activity – everyone seemed to have something urgent to be doing. A nurse in scrubs met us and warned us to be prepared – this was going to be difficult for us. We assured her we were prepared for whatever we had to do. "There was a lot of blood,' she told us. "They're still stitching her up."

"Yes, we understand. Can we please see her? We need to see her," I pleaded.

She led us into an area portioned off by screens and curtains and complicated medical equipment. Several doctors were working on Jenna, one stitching around her eye and forehead. Two others were stitching up her back. Jenna saw that we were there and Carol squeezed in to hold her hand. We tried to look and sound reassuring to her, but she certainly was an absolute mess.

The doctor in charge of the trauma unit gave us a brief rundown of her injuries. The car that hit Jenna had broken both bones in her right leg, cracked several ribs, and crushed her duodenum. Her head had hit the windshield and she had shattered her cheekbones and eye socket. There was a serious crack in her skull when her nose had been forced back into the cranial cavity. There was a danger that air had leaked into the cranium with the resulting risk of meningitis. If that all weren't enough, she had been thrown about a hundred feet, riding along the top of a chain link fence, which ripped open large gashes on her side, back, and legs. She had landed in a cemetery, of all places. There would most likely be more injuries that would present themselves during the next few days, he told us. The next few days would be critical.

We stayed by her side as various doctors and nurses performed their duties, and we tried to make small talk. We cracked jokes about what some kids will do for attention. We asked questions about medical procedures on her behalf, and about complications to recovery we had never heard of. We told the doctors what a great kid she was, a star soccer player, about to get her Masters degree in Education. Everyone had the same look on their face: how could something like this happen?

I called Matt with an update. He told me that Jenna's roommate had just called him, and that she and a friend were already on their way to the hospital. I looked over at Jenna, at her blackened eyes, the blood matted in her hair, the bandages, the medical devices she was hooked up to, the interns still stitching up her back. It had to be hundreds of stitches. There was no way she was ready for anyone visiting yet.

I got the phone number from Matt and called her roommate back. Becky answered and she told me they were already on the interstate, driving to the hospital. I told her to go back, that Jenna was not yet ready for company. I tried to sound optimistic as I gave her a brief update on Jenna's condition. I told her we would let her know if she could come the next day to see her.

I put my phone away and noticed I was standing in front of a large sink. I suddenly realized that I was not feeling very well at the moment and bent down to splash some cool water on my face. Carol asked if I was all right. "Yeah, I just think I need to lie down for a minute," I answered. The room started to spin out of control and I found myself lying down on the floor of the emergency room. A nurse appeared from out of the murkiness and she and Carol helped lift me into a bed she had wheeled up next to me. She waved some smelling salts under my nose which brought me back to the nightmare reality I was experiencing.

At that point I remember letting go and sobbing uncontrollably. "You spend your whole life taking care of your kids, trying to protect them and keep them safe," I sobbed. "Still you can't protect them. Still this happens. It's not fair! It makes no sense! I'm sorry, don't worry about me. Just take care of Jenna." I carried on for about fifteen minutes, the torrent of my emotions flooding out into the busy emergency room with all the bright lights and high tech instruments. Across the room, doctors continued to work on Jenna. I felt so helpless. The nurse brought me some orange juice to drink. Carol went back and forth between Jenna and me, checking on us both.

The nurse was very kind and assured me that this happens all the time, that it can be a terrible shock to the system when you see your loved one in such a state. I probably had a sudden blood pressure drop that brought me to the ground. When they finally let me get out of the bed, it was just in time. Another accident victim was being wheeled in and they really needed the space for him.

I went back over to where the doctors were still working on Jenna. Her sad, blackened eyes looked up at me and she mumbled, "I figured you were going to pass out," a little smile creeping onto her lips.

"I thought I was doing pretty well," I protested. I was ecstatic to hear a bit of humor returning to her frail little voice. For me, despite her terribly mangled body, Jenna's teasing signaled that the healing process had already begun. I clung desperately to the belief that she had already started on her long journey back.

56

BLOOD FROM A STONE

It was close to midnight when Jenna was released from the emergency room. She then underwent a series of CAT scans to determine the extent of her internal injuries. Eventually she was placed in the pediatric Intensive Care Unit, the ICU, for what little was left of her first night. The trauma doctor in charge felt she would get the best care there, even though she was 24 years old, because it happened to be less crowded that night than the regular ICU. Carol and I escorted her to her room and the three of us prepared to settle in for a long night.

The nurse on duty was not at all happy when I asked if a cot could be brought in, but she quickly realized there was no way we were going to leave Jenna. Carol stretched out on the small couch next to the window, and the nurse brought in a cot for me to use, which we tucked in along the wall. Carol and I took turns helping Jenna take small sips of water and holding a plastic tray under her chin when she felt the need to throw up, which was quite frequently. We were told she had ingested a great deal of blood and this was probably what was making her so nauseous.

Jenna was heavily sedated and Carol and I were exhausted but none of us were able to get much, if any, sleep. We spent a fitful night listening to odd noises coming from the patient in the next room and helping Jenna with the dry heaves. It was so surreal that I thought I really *was* sleeping and that the whole series of events were just a nightmare – I would surely wake up in the morning and everything would be back to normal.

Nurses came in from time to time to check her vitals and administer pain medication. Each visit was a grim reminder that this was all really happening, and that our lives may never get back to normal ever again.

Even today, I can't erase the images of that first night in the ICU from my mind. Dim light filtered through the window from the nurse's station outside the door. Monitors beeped while LED lights on various instrument panels flashed or held steady with their own hidden meanings.

From time to time I held the puke-colored plastic tray under Jenna's chin while she battled another round of the dry heaves. I wiped her chin, offered her a sip of water. I felt overwhelmed by the unfairness of it all. My mind screamed, wanting to know who had done this to my beautiful daughter – who, who, WHO? But on the outside I knew I had to be strong for her. Over and over again that night I reassured her that somehow, we would get through this. "We'll get through this, honey," I whispered to her in the semi-darkness. "We'll get through this. We'll get through this."

I remember lying on that small cot, studying the ceiling tiles, listening to a muffled commotion in the next room about a patient soiling his bed. I couldn't help thinking someone is going to pay for this. If Jenna pulls through, at least she'll be set for life. Somebody's going to pay, big time.

It was strange how some tasks quickly became routine. Carol and I checked the small plastic cup placed under Jenna's nose regularly to be sure that cranial fluid was not leaking from her skull. The doctors had told us it could be a serious sign leading to complications. When Jenna needed to go to the bathroom, I left the room to give her a bit of privacy as the nurses rolled her onto her side so they could slide a bedpan under her. We learned how to control the suction tube that Jenna could use to help keep her throat clear. We became skilled at operating the hospital bed, raising or lowering it a bit to provide Jenna with whatever small amount of comfort it could offer.

In the morning, Jenna began to receive visitors. First were the team of trauma doctors, followed by the orthopedic doctors, the plastic surgeons, the neurologists and various other specialists. Everyone said Jenna was doing as well as could be expected considering what she had been through. The orthopedics wanted to schedule surgery right away for her broken legs. A titanium rod would need to be inserted inside the larger bone to hold it together, we were told.

A detective from the Keene police department showed up around 9am. He was there to gather samples of Jenna's hair and clothing to be used as evidence. He told us he also needed to gather a sample of her DNA, just a cotton swab of the inside of her mouth. Opening a small notepad to jot down some notes, he gently asked Jenna if she remembered anything at all about the accident.

Jenna bravely told him how she was jogging on a quiet back road facing traffic, as she should. She saw the vehicle approaching her, tried to get out of the way, but there was a fence and she had nowhere to go. She remembered being hit and the next thing she remembered was being in the ambulance.

The detective nodded and scribbled a few things in the pad.

"What can you tell us about the driver?" I asked the detective.

"He is someone known to the local police department," the detective told me. "You should know he was crying at the scene, so he seems very remorseful. He's a nineteen-year-old kid with a drug problem, and he doesn't have any insurance. He was driving a junk box of a car that probably should not have been on the road. His parents are both drug addicts – they have nothing. I'm not sure if there's anything you can do. I'm sorry to be the one to have to tell you all this."

I was having trouble speaking or even breathing as I let the weight of his words sink in.

"What are you saying?" I finally asked. "That we're on our own here? That we're going to be responsible for all these medical bills? Jenna is the victim here – she did nothing wrong!"

"I know, I know," the detective said. "The problem is you can't get blood from a stone, you know? You can go after him if you want, but by the time you hire a lawyer, well, good luck is all I can say. He's got nothing to go after."

"You've got to be kidding!" I was incredulous. "Jenna's life has just been changed forever. We're lucky she's alive! We're not looking to go after anybody, we just want some justice!"

"I know, that's just how it goes sometimes. We're still awaiting results on the blood tests for drugs or alcohol. We'll do our best to bring charges against him, but the reality is there are no guarantees. It doesn't look like speed was a factor - in fact your daughter is lucky he *wasn't* speeding. If he had been speeding the outcome would have likely been much worse." The detective was trying to bring us some measure of comfort, but he was failing miserably. "Probably the most he would be charged with is reckless endangerment," he concluded.

I asked him to step outside where we could speak candidly without Jenna hearing our conversation. She had enough on her plate.

"Look," I began, "Up until yesterday, Jenna was a star athlete, a soccer player. She was expecting to graduate in a few weeks with her Master's degree and was already offered a teaching position for next September. She has been working as a long-term substitute in a local school and she has a job lined up for the summer. She has expenses – a car loan, student loans, rent. And you're telling me there's nothing we can do? Good luck? That's it?"

"I'm sorry," the detective said.

"And if Jenna, God forbid, should die?" I asked point blank. "What then? Will he be charged with manslaughter? Will he be found responsible then? What will it take for my daughter to receive justice?"

"Now, now, let's hope it doesn't come to that," he said without emotion. Jenna's case had abruptly become a routine matter of police business now. He left us with his business card if we needed to get in touch with him.

Carol and I thanked God that Jenna was still covered under our health insurance because she was still technically a full time student. But she was scheduled to graduate in a few weeks. Would she still be covered by our plan? We shuddered at the thought of the medical expenses she was incurring, with no end in sight.

Later that day, after countless phone calls to family to let them know about Jenna, I called my principal, Pam, on her cell phone. She was wonderfully supportive as I told her I was going to be out of work for a while and I didn't know when I could be back in to teach.

"Whatever you need," she told me. "Don't worry about school. You just take care of Jenna. If there's anything you need, just ask."

"There is one thing you might be able to help me with," I said.

"Anything," came her immediate response.

"Can you get me the name of a good lawyer?" I asked. "I think I'm going to need one."

57

ONE DAY AT A TIME

The next day Jenna was moved to another room, this one in the orthopedic wing. At first she was put into a double room to be shared with another patient. The floor nurse quickly surmised that Jenna was not going to be a typical patient when he realized her parents were not going to leave her side. Somehow he finagled us into a single room where Carol could sleep on a cot and I could sleep down the hall in the lounge.

Jenna lay in the bed badly bruised, swollen and unable to move anything except her arms. Groups of doctors and interns came and went regularly, asking the same questions.

"How would you rate your pain on a scale of one to ten with ten being the highest?" they all asked. Even with the morphine pump, she was ranging between fours and fives.

The plastic surgeon asked if we could bring in a recent picture of her – it would help with the reconstruction of her broken facial bones. That was a request I never expected to hear in my lifetime.

Jenna could not see well enough to watch the TV in the room. She did not want to listen to any music. She wasn't really capable of doing anything. Carol and I sat in the room looking at her, trying to figure out how we were going to piece our lives back together. We took turns walking down the hall to the lounge where we could make our phone calls out of earshot of Jenna – everyone wanted updates on her condition. We didn't want her to keep hearing us talk about it over and over and over. And besides, we never knew when we were going to suddenly break down in the middle of a conversation, which turned out to be quite often those first few days.

Carol's brother, who was a family practice physician in Maine, became our primary medical consultant for all the procedures and new terms that were being thrown at us. He answered our questions, reassured us, and educated us on what to expect. His presence, even if it was through a cell phone, was immeasurable.

Carol and I tried to focus on the positive. Jenna was alive, her vital signs stable, and her brain seemed to be working OK. Everything else could be fixed and would heal in time. Carol summed it up perfectly, "For an unlucky girl, Jenna was very lucky."

Minutes seemed like hours. Hours seemed like minutes.

I came back from the lounge with a magazine I found laying there. It might have been a *National Geographic*, but I am not sure, I was walking around in a daze. There was an article about scientists studying the possibility of advanced thought in various animals. Jenna had spent a lot of time working at several wildlife zoos and as an intern at SeaWorld in Orlando. She loved working with all kinds of animals. While working at the zoo, she had even carried around a baby kangaroo in a pouch tied to her waist for a few weeks, bottle-feeding it. Its mother had died and she was serving as a surrogate.

I sat down close to her bed and began reading the article out loud to her. I told her she could listen or not, but I was going to read it out loud anyway, just to pass the time. While I was reading and occasionally holding up the magazine for her to see the pictures, I could not help but flash back to happier times reading to my children when they were young. Carol and I would read to them every night. Each of our kids had their own favorite stories and we would read them over and over until they dozed off to sleep or at least were ready for bed. And now I found myself reading out loud to my twenty-four year old daughter a story about whether or not chimpanzees and other animals could really think and communicate.

Later in the day, Scott, our second oldest son, arrived with his girlfriend Amy. They had driven several hours from Connecticut. I met them at the main entrance of the hospital and tried to prepare them.

"Now remember, Jenna looks awful," I told them, "but the doctors are very pleased with the progress she's making." As we quickly walked the long corridors to Jenna's room, I kept warning them to prepare themselves, knowing full well how futile that warning was – nothing can prepare you to see an injured loved one looking the way Jenna looked and not feel the pain of their injuries. Amy started to cry as soon as she came into the room once she saw Jenna all swollen, bruised and bandaged.

But somehow, we got through it together. My oldest son Matt and his wife Meghan joined us after awhile also. Thankfully, they did not bring their young children with them – they shouldn't see this; no kids ever should. We spoke of Jenna's condition and progress, and her upcoming schedule of surgeries. We cracked stupid jokes. Mostly we just let Jenna know we were all there for her. Scott and Amy offered to take over her car payments for her until she was able to pay them herself. Carol and I cried a little when we heard that. All parents like to think that they brought their kids up right, but most never really know. Carol and I, however, now had proof.

I had asked Matt to bring us a recent picture of Jenna, which we had at home, per the surgeon's request. One of the benefits of being a classroom teacher was that you always had great photos of yourself taken along with the rest of your class. Jenna had just sent us her latest school picture. It had been taken where she was teaching as a long-term substitute. This recent school picture happened to capture not only Jenna's physical beauty, but some of her sparkling spirit as well. When the plastic surgeon who had requested it came by later in the day to check on Jenna, he taped the picture up on the wall where everyone – even Jenna - could see it. Carol and I thought it was a bittersweet gesture.

A little while later, one of the interns came into the room to draw blood. He looked up at the wall and asked, "Is that her?" as he continued with his duties.

"Yes," I replied, "That's Jenna." I didn't know what to say. I wanted to cry or scream or grab him by the shoulders and shake him shouting "Of course, you idiot, can't you see that that's my beautiful daughter whose blood you're drawing right now?" But this was new territory for me, and instead, I was quietly grateful for the kind plastic surgeon who knew that my daughter was still hanging in there somewhere underneath all the bruises and stitches.

"We can get through this," I kept reminding myself, but I knew we were staggering around in a vast unknown wilderness.

58

SEEING FOR MYSELF

Jenna was scheduled for her first surgery early the next morning, Monday, to repair her broken leg and insert a titanium rod. The doctors told us the surgery would take several hours and we would not likely see her until early afternoon. She would be pretty groggy most of the day.

Carol and I decided I should return home late that night before the surgery. If I hurried, I would be able to be back at the hospital by the time she was out of surgery. We both needed some new clothes and other personal items. It was becoming increasingly apparent that we would be staying with Jenna at the hospital for at least a week or more – we had no idea how long. I also had to arrange some lesson plans for my students and take care of a few things at school. And of course, there was the matter of finalizing our taxes, which needed to be filed the next day, cleaning up some remnants from a former life.

I zipped home, packed some more clothes, slept for a few hours, signed the tax return, and headed in to school to leave some plans for a substitute. I wanted to get in and out quickly before any of my students arrived. I knew it was going to be difficult to face my colleagues without breaking into tears. I didn't want to talk about how awful the weekend had been. I secured some things in my classroom, and ran off copies of worksheets and assignments I thought would keep the students busy for the week. When I bumped into my co-workers, all we could do was hug - I couldn't speak. Everyone understood and offered encouraging words and prayers.

I was back on the road before the students arrived, just as planned. I did not, however, head straight back to the hospital. I decided to take a detour to Keene, where Jenna had been living – where she had been hit. There were some things at her apartment that I needed to retrieve. I wanted to let her landlord know what had happened, and I planned to stop in at the police station to check on the status of the investigation.

I shook my head when I saw Jenna's apartment. Clothes were scattered all over the floor of her room. "Just like normal", I thought. But nothing was normal anymore. Normal had been stolen from us on Saturday. I managed to find her purse with her wallet and checkbook, and her laptop. I thought she might be up to using the computer at some point. I checked to be sure that her bearded-dragon lizard had water and lettuce in the aquarium where he lived. I dropped in a few crickets for him to catch and eat. I found her landlord's phone number and called him. I was grateful to be able to leave a message on his answering machine. "Why was talking about it so hard?" I wondered to myself.

At the police station, I was ushered into a small room to await the detectives working on Jenna's case. In time, two officers appeared and I updated them on Jenna's progress. They were happy to hear that her condition was no longer listed as critical. They told me that the lead detective on the case was away on vacation, so there was no information they could share with me at the time. He'd contact us when he returned.

"OK", I thought, taking a deep breath. They said the matter was still under investigation. "Uh-huh," I was beginning to get the picture. The lead detective should be back sometime next week, and they assured me again he would call me with any information he could share. I tried to be as polite as I could, given the frustrating circumstances I was facing.

"Can you at least tell me who placed the 911 call?" I asked. "I would like to thank them and let them know how Jenna is doing."

They told me they thought it was someone who was out walking, perhaps with a dog, and heard the crash. They did not know who it was. There was also a doctor on the scene quickly, they said, one who just happened to be driving by. "If you want to see the scene, we can tell you where it happened."

"Thanks," I said. "I know where it happened. I looked it up on *Google*. I'm planning to go there when I leave here to see for myself."

"The whole place is marked off with paint and tape," one of them told me. "You can't miss it. Let us know if you need anything." He reached for his coffee mug as I stood up.

"I need to know you're going to arrest the son-of-a-bitch that nearly murdered my daughter," I thought to myself. I shook their hands and left.

The road Jenna had been jogging on when she was hit was just around the corner from her apartment. It was a quiet stretch of road, a few houses at the end, with woods on one side and a large cemetery on the other. I immediately saw the yellow tape on the chain link fence, and then noticed the paint markings on the road in several places. I pulled safely off the road and parked my car. I tried to collect my thoughts and gather strength. "I need to do this for Jenna," I told myself. She needs me to watch out for her best interests right now and that means finding out exactly what happened here on Saturday. I tried to steel myself for what I was about to do.

Slowly, deliberately, I got out of my car and walked over to some markings on the road. I followed the tire marks in the dirt from the point where they left the road. "This is where Jenna saw the car coming at her," I thought to myself. I noticed the yellow tape on the fence and another painted mark. "This is where she was hit," I thought. This was where the police found strands of her clothing and hair and flesh on the wire barbs of the fence. I put my hand on top of the fence to feel the sharpness of the barbs. The fence was a full four or five feet from the edge of the pavement. "He was totally off the road when he hit her," I was now recording the scene in my brain, although I had no idea why. "My poor baby," I thought. "My poor baby girl." I'm sure I was crying at this point, reliving the accident in my head.

I followed the tape down the fence about one hundred feet. There were more markings here. "This must be where she landed," I thought. I looked at the headstones nearby in the cemetery. "How weird is that – to land in a cemetery." But it wasn't her time, I reassured myself. It wasn't her time.

Out of the corner of my eye, near the cemetery gate, I saw some flowers, yellow roses actually, that seemed oddly out of place. Some mysterious force inexplicably drew me to walk over to them. "Did someone leave them there for Jenna?" I wondered. The dozen roses were placed in a glass vase and they were starting to wilt. There was an empty plastic cardholder sticking out of them - no way to identify who the roses were from or for whom they were intended. "Odd," I thought.

Several feet away on the still-brown April grass lay a small green envelope. Again I felt fate pulling me toward it. Inside I found a card. The handwriting looked like that of a small child.

> There arnt any words in the humen language that could exsplain how sorry i am for putting you throw this. I hope u get Better realy soon and nothing series happens I don't know what to say to show Im so sorry for this if I can do anything to help please let me no.
>
> *-Anderson*

I could not believe what I was holding in my hand. The person who hit Jenna now had a name. I felt surrounded and swept up by the immense powers of fate and destiny that had somehow led me to this place and this moment in time. Everything in my universe seemed connected in that exact moment – Jenna, me, Anderson, our family, the road, the fence, the roses, the card, the day – even the weather. It was supposed to rain later that day and the card would have been ruined and illegible had I not found it just now. "I was meant to be here" I said to myself. "At some point when she is ready, Jenna will need this card – she will need to know he was truly sorry."

Despite the immense sadness that was smothering our whole family, I was glad I had come to this awful place. I looked up and down the road with new eyes now. There were forces much stronger than me that were working to help Jenna heal. Again, I wondered who had been walking on this quiet stretch of road to call 911? Who was the angel that had quickly gotten Jenna the help she so desperately needed. I walked down the road toward the first house at the bottom of the hill. A young woman had just come out from the house and was getting into a car parked in the driveway.

"Excuse me," I called to her. I explained who I was and told her I was trying to find out who had made the 911 call so I could thank them.

"Oh my God!" she exclaimed. "You're Jenna's dad?"

"Uh, yeah, you know my daughter Jenna?" I said, somewhat confused by her response.

"Of course!" she said. "I'm Abby. I went to college with Jenna. My dad was the first police officer on the scene when Jenna was hit."

I had goose bumps, again sensing that I was merely playing a small role in a much bigger series of events. "You live here, and your dad was the first cop on the scene?" The coincidence was incomprehensible. I shuddered to think of what that scene must have been like for her father.

She told me that her father thought it might be Jenna who had been hit because of the college tee shirt she was wearing. He was off-duty, heard the report and immediately ran up the hill to help out. I gave her an update on how Jenna was doing and I wrote down their phone number so I could call her dad and thank him personally. I asked if she knew who had called 911.

Abby did not know who had made the call either. I wondered if I would ever know. Our family would remain eternally grateful to whoever it was that made that call, and to all the first responders who saved my daughter's life. Perhaps someday I will find out. Someone might come upon this story, recognize their role and contact me to identify themselves. I would like that. But just as likely, it may never happen. I suppose it all depends on whether or not it is part of the master plan. All we can do is play our part.

59

IN THE ROUNDEST OF PLACES

I was back at the hospital by midday. Jenna was still in the recovery room and Carol and I were allowed to see her shortly after my arrival. She was pretty out of it, but we were able to hold her hand and let her know we were there by her side. The drugs were working their magic, so she was not in a lot of pain. There were more medical decisions to be made, and Carol and I found ourselves asking questions of the doctors, learning about medical procedures we never knew existed.

The doctors wanted to schedule Jenna's next surgery for Wednesday, two days later. It turned out her 'good' leg was not so good, according to the CAT scans. Her knee was totally blown out – the doctor had never seen one so bad. He wanted to reconstruct the ligaments and muscles using a series of grafts and cadaver tissue. He explained the options to us, but it really boiled down to trying to fix her knee to regain some degree of movement, or Jenna being permanently disabled. So ultimately, there was no decision but to proceed with the surgery.

Next came the decision to insert a PIK line into Jenna. A PIK line is like an intravenous tube, only it lasts longer and is more versatile. Medicine can go directly into the veins, nutrients can be supplied directly, and blood can be drawn – all through the same source. No more poking and pinching every time the nurses needed to draw blood or inject medicine. It was strongly recommended and apparently a routine procedure at the hospital. The PIK line seemed advantageous considering Jenna's condition and the likelihood that she was going to remain in the hospital for quite some time. So we took a deep breath and went along with it, overcoming yet another level of fear.

Jenna needed to have some post-surgical scans done on her broken leg and she also needed more scans on her other leg before her next surgery.

The hospital staff wanted to get them done as soon as possible. Carol and I left Jenna in the recovery room and went ahead to her room to wait for her return from the CAT scan department.

When we entered her room, we saw that several beautiful flower arrangements had arrived, along with some cards. A little later, after Jenna had returned to the room, another delivery was made with a few more arrangements, one of which had balloons tied to it. Carol and I tried to spread out the flowers around the small room, lining them along the windowsill. We opened the cards and read them to Jenna and then started taping the cards up on the wall opposite her bed where she could see them.

As the days and weeks passed, flowers and cards continued to arrive on a regular basis. The wall with cards was now covered and started to spread onto other walls. The flowers were everywhere – we started putting some out on the nurses' station to spread them out. There were 9 x 12 envelopes stuffed full of cards from the various classes where Jenna had been teaching. There were even cards from my students at the ALT school, kids who had never met her. As visitors began to arrive, so did boxes of assorted cookies and candy, magazines, books, and stuffed animals. Space was beginning to become an issue. The clutter almost began to make us feel like we were 'home' again.

Carol and I got to know the floor nurses who were taking care of Jenna very well, but once in a while somebody new would show up. "I like what you've done to the place," one of them remarked. Another one told us he could judge a person's character by the number of cards and flowers a patient received. Never in his fifteen years of nursing had he ever seen anything like the show of support that was evident in Jenna's room. "She must be quite a young lady!" he told us.

"Yes, she is," we agreed.

And the show of support wasn't just in Jenna's room, either. Casseroles and pizza delivery boys were showing up at our house for my son and his family who were taking care of the home front. (I told you how fate had worked things out so they would be close when we needed them. Somebody had to hold down the fort, answer the phone, bring in the mail, take care of the dog, etc.) Gas cards, gift cards, restaurant certificates were arriving from countless friends and acquaintances. The answering machine was full of messages of support. We received phone calls from relatives and friends we hadn't heard from in years. Collections were taken up at work to help defray our unexpected living expenses while we stayed at the hospital. The outpouring of support for Jenna and our whole family touched us deeply. We had never experienced anything like it. An unbearable experience became a little more bearable.

Meanwhile, Jenna endured more procedures, constant pain, complications from medications and several subsequent surgeries. The surgery on her knee took several hours longer than expected, but the doctor assured us the operation went as well as could be expected. It would take time and many months of physical therapy to know the final outcome. She might need more surgery in the future depending on how well she healed. She would never play soccer again, but she should be able to walk on her own if things went well. In the general scheme of things, that was good news – walking was good. Jenna should be able to walk again.

This was difficult enough for Carol and me to accept, but I knew it had to be life shattering for Jenna to hear. Jenna loved soccer – she had been playing since she was four years old. She had more soccer trophies than she could display. She had recently coached the middle school team where she was teaching and the kids loved her. Carol and I truly enjoyed watching her games too. From travelling premier teams to Olympic Development teams to high school and college championships, we rarely missed a game. We were suddenly faced with the realization that soccer was all over for us now, another adjustment we would all have to make in our new life together.

It was obvious we were going to need all the support we could get. Jenna's beautiful body and her entire future lay tragically shattered in a hospital bed because a young drug addict had driven his old car off the road one sunny Saturday afternoon on a quiet road. Jenna just happened to be jogging in the wrong place at the wrong time.

In the back of my mind, the phrase I had read in the Wally Lamb novel kept floating to the surface. "The evidence of God can be found in the roundness of things." Surely, in this hospital room, we were in the roundest of places. Our edges had been entirely worn off by the sudden and dramatic turn of events. God must be nearby, I thought as I surveyed Jenna's hospital room.

One could say there was evidence of God in the colorful flowers on the windowsill, or in the cute stuffed animal that was supposed to look like a golden retriever. Surely, God must have helped author the kind words scribbled in the cards and notes taped to the wall. God was there, of course, it was true. And God was certainly with us when we walked to the cafeteria to buy a meal with money that had arrived in a 'thinking of you' card.

But the greatest evidence of God could be found in the stories that people told us. We never realized how much tragedy and adversity ordinary people were able to overcome until people started sharing their stories with us. It seemed that tragedy had struck many, many times before Jenna's unfortunate accident, but we had somehow been sheltered from it. Now we listened with new ears about accidents and illnesses, people living with chronic pain, loss of life – even the incredible heartbreak of losing a child. People told us about years of rehabilitation and physical therapy they had undergone. Ordinary people, people you would pass in the supermarket, felt our pain and offered us a bit of comfort and support. It was as if we were walking along an endless beach, stooping down and picking up these stories of support scattered all around, each one a small round stone you could grasp in your hand and hold onto for a little while for comfort.

I was still sleeping on the floor of the hospital lounge when one of the hospital staff put me in touch with a local hostel. It was affiliated with the hospital, and I could sleep in a bed for a mere fifteen dollars a night. Many of the people staying there had travelled quite a distance to be treated at the hospital for a variety of conditions. Several were undergoing a series of chemotherapy or radiation or both. The people staying at the hostel were as sick as a human being can get. But as we shared a cup of coffee and a piece of pastry in the morning, they listened to my story and offered me their prayers and best wishes for Jenna's recovery. Surely God was with us too, in that round place.

I came to the realization that everyone gets tested at some point in their life, we just never know when it is going to be our turn or what the test will look like. The only certain thing is that it will require major pain and sacrifice by everyone involved.

This was our test – our life-altering readjustment. It was going to be tough. Our test was going to try to wear us down, make us question our most basic beliefs. It would round us out and we would have to see beyond the tragedy if we hoped to find evidence of God. Once again, I reminded myself that, somehow, we would get through this. We had support to help us on this part of our journey, for sure, an incredible amount of support. In the prophetic words of Wally Lamb, that much I knew was true.

60

RECOVERY

Grief washed over me like the waves on a beach. One minute I would be fine, the next minute, I couldn't stop crying. At times I could talk about the accident, the medical procedures, or the long road ahead of Jenna as if I was discussing the weather forecast. Other times, I shut down and locked myself away from everybody – even Carol. I just couldn't face the agony in their eyes; I couldn't bring myself to talk about the pain we were all feeling. It was more than I could bear.

The swelling in Jenna's face had started to subside a bit and we were getting used to the routines of the medications, bedpans and shift changes in hospital staff. She was starting to look and feel better. There were days when we definitely felt we were on the road to recovery. Her pain levels would range from fours or fives when the meds were wearing off to a comfortable level of two or three. The drugs were taking their toll, though.

One day I was sitting by Jenna's bed and she asked me who the little children were.

"What little children?" I asked.

"The ones sitting on the end of the bed," she answered.

"Jenna, there are no little children sitting on your bed." I said.

"Yes there are, they're right over there," she insisted, gesturing with her arm.

"No, Jenna, I think you're just overtired from not getting any sleep." In fact, she had hardly slept at all since the accident several days earlier. "You're brain is trying to dream while you are still awake," I told her. That seemed to appease her and she drifted off for a while.

Another time I looked over at her to see her crying.

"What's the matter, honey? Are you in pain?" I asked.

"I know about Matt and Meghan," she told me.

"What about them?" I asked. Matt and Meghan had visited on the weekend but had not been back up since. They were at our house with their two children.

"I know that they were in an accident and died," Jenna blurted out, tears running from her eyes.

"Oh, Jenna, no, no. They're fine," I assured her. "Nothing has happened to Matt or Meghan. The drugs are making you think these things. Just relax. Everything is going to work out."

I went down the hall to the lounge where I could cry without her seeing me. A lot of people seemed to use that lounge for crying and for making telephone calls out of earshot of the patient. It was very handy. I still slept there some nights when I wanted to speak with the doctors during their morning rounds at 6am. Other nights I slept at the hostel up the road a couple of miles.

Jenna was getting good at using the suction hose to remove spit and mucus from her mouth. She was not eating or drinking much of anything so I wasn't sure why her mouth needed to be suctioned. It gave her something to do, though, a small act that she had total control over. She was still getting all her nourishment through pouches of a milky substance that was being put directly into her veins through the PIK line. But Jenna kept suctioning her mouth every few minutes.

At some point I noticed she seemed very determined to get something out of her mouth. She was poking the suction tube around her mouth, covering every square inch of her gums and teeth. I told her she should give it a rest.

"I've got to get it all out," she told me. "I feel like I'm choking." She continued working feverishly on her gums.

"It's OK Jenna, let me have the suction tube," I said gently.

"No!" she cried. "I've got to do this. The doctor told me!"

I tried to take the tube away from her. By this time, I could see blood coming from her mouth into the suction tube. She held on tight, working the end of the tube around her teeth. She was not letting go of that tube.

I reached behind her bed where the suction tube came out from the apparatus on the wall. I turned a nozzle there, hoping it would cut off the vacuum for the suction. It worked.

Jenna cried, "No, no, don't turn it off! I need it."

"It's OK, honey. We're going to give your gums a rest now."

In a little while, she was dozing and the battle was over, for now at least. Until the next wave hit, that is. Carol and I had to keep preparing for the next unpredictable phase of her recovery.

Jenna's third surgery was by far the most serious and the most frightening for us as parents. The plastic surgeons wanted to insert some metal plates into her shattered cheekbone, and align her fractured skull and jaw bone. The optimal time window for such a procedure was rapidly closing. If they waited too long, the bones would begin to heal incorrectly and fixing it would be more difficult, if even possible. They were concerned that Jenna's eyeball was collapsing into the shattered eye socket and she might start to have complications beyond mere disfigurement. They were confident of their ability to help her despite the gruesome nature of the operation. The alternative was to do nothing and hope for the best. If they did not operate, her face would be unbalanced and her eye would always droop, but at least she would be alive.

Carol and I put our hearts and our daughter into the surgeon's hands. Jenna went in for surgery again the following Monday, nine days after the accident. Carol and I took a walk outside the hospital to try to keep our minds off of what was happening to our daughter in the operating room. We were told it might be five or six hours of surgery. It was a beautiful spring day, sunny and warm, and even the mountains of snow in the parking lot had dwindled over the course of the past week.

In the afternoon, we settled down in the crowded waiting room along with everybody else that had a friend or relative being operated on that day. Mondays were always busy days in the operating room, we learned. Mid-afternoon, we were becoming concerned and asked if we could get a status update. Word came out from the operating room that everything was fine, but it was taking longer than expected. Several more hours passed. I grabbed some sandwiches to eat from the cafeteria and brought them back to the waiting room. Carol just picked at hers; I ate mine in two bites. This was followed by more waiting.

The crowded waiting room had emptied out and there were now only a few families left. Carol and I were beside ourselves with worry at this point. Jenna was twelve hours into the surgery and we were counting every second. A nurse came out to tell us they were closing the waiting room for the night, and she would lead us to another waiting room which was used for overnight surgeries. When we got to the new waiting room, I insisted on getting an update immediately on what was happening with my daughter. I guess the hospital staff person recognized that panic was taking over because she got on the phone immediately. We were informed that the surgery had just been completed. Jenna would be kept overnight in the recovery room as a precaution. They would be out to speak with us shortly.

After another short but painful wait, one of the surgical nurses led us out into a hallway that led to the recovery room. There she told us that they were going to keep Jenna sedated for the night. She was out of surgery and the surgeons were pleased with the way things went, but they felt it best if she remained in an induced coma for the next eight hours or so. It was not unusual in this type of case, we were told.

"We can't see her tonight?" I spat out. The word *coma* kept reverberating in my brain. Carol had started to cry.

"No, she is not conscious, she needs total rest tonight," the nurse calmly told us as she clutched her clipboard.

"It was only supposed to be six hours!" Carol said between tears.

"I know, these things just take time," the nurse tried to reassure us.

Carol and I staggered like zombies back up to Jenna's empty room. We wondered if our nightmare would ever end. The flowers and cards, the balloons and stuffed animals offered us no solace that night. We clung together tightly on the little cot in her room and maybe dozed off for a few minutes here or there. We were just waiting – waiting to get our daughter back.

In the morning we were told that we could go back down to the recovery room, that Jenna was just regaining consciousness. Her head was bandaged and tubes were coming out all over but she was once again aware that we were there by her side. Her jaw was wired shut to keep the bones from moving so she couldn't say anything. Her eyes peered out from the bandages, imploring us for reassurance.

"That's the worst of it," Carol told her. "Everything is going to get better from here on in."

The surgeon eventually made an appearance and he told us he was able to do everything he wanted to do. The skull fracture had aligned nicely, and he had inserted metal plates in her cheekbone that should help support her eye socket. Her jaw will have to remain wired shut for a few weeks. "She looks like hell right now, I know, "he told us, "but it went very well."

We stayed with her for a little while in the recovery room. I did not pass out this time. I guess people can get used to anything. Eventually they told us she could go back up to her room, but they would be doing another CAT scan on the way so we should meet her up at the room. Carol and I once more made our way through the hospital labyrinth to her room. I picked up some coffee and bagels for Carol and me to eat while we waited.

The scheduled surgeries were over for now, as far as we knew. Sure, there might be some more in the future, but for now, the worst was over. It was another tough day for Jenna and a tough day for Carol and me. But once again, we pulled through.

As the anesthesia drugs continued to wear off and Jenna's spirit started to improve later that day, so did ours. We were all in this together. We slept a little better that night thinking we were finally on the road to recovery, wherever it might lead.

61

LIGHT AT THE END OF THE TUNNEL

Jenna spent two more weeks at Dartmouth Hitchcock Medical Center with Carol and me at her side. Each day was marked by her progress or her setbacks, sometimes both in the same day. Physical therapy started in earnest. Cards and flowers continued to pour in. Friends and family traveled very long distances for incredibly short visits. We were getting accustomed to life after the accident.

We had all decided not to spend any more of our precious energy thinking about 'what might have been' or 'why did this have to happen to Jenna?' We knew the kid who hit her was eventually going to have to pay a price, and we prayed that it would be a steep one. The County Attorney's office told us it was doing everything in its power to see that he would be brought to justice. Our ultimate hope was that he would use these unfortunate circumstances to turn his life around, get help, and never be a menace to anyone else ever again. If he could do that, we would be satisfied. That was our hope.

The reality, however, was that in the meantime, the kid was not even in jail, and he was arrested again shortly after the accident for possession of marijuana and hypodermic needles. We were angry and upset to hear this, but it was all out of our hands. As far as we were concerned, the damage was done. All our energy would be devoted to healing, to getting on with living, not dwelling on the past.

One day the director of patient services brought in some brochures about rehabilitation hospitals for us to consider. Jenna would soon be out of medical danger and ready to be moved for her next phase of recovery.

Once she could eat on her own without the feeding tube and move her bowels, she could be discharged from the hospital. We needed to choose which rehab hospital we wanted her in, preferably one closer to home. Carol and I were proud of how far Jenna had come, but we were also petrified she would no longer have access to the expert care that had been such a crucial part of her recovery. We had heard horror stories about conditions and care at some rehab hospitals and we were determined to see that Jenna continued to get the best care possible.

It turned out that the rehab unit at a hospital near our home was affiliated with the Spaulding Rehabilitation Center, famous worldwide for its medical expertise. There was a bed ready for Jenna and they were anticipating her arrival. Most of their patients were elderly and they were looking forward to the challenges a young, female, former-athlete would bring. Best of all, the hospital was only five minutes from the school where I was teaching, so I would be able to visit her during my plan periods and be there right after school.

Before we knew it, we found ourselves saying goodbye to the nurses and doctors who had saved Jenna's life, feeling like we had lived a lifetime in three and a half weeks. Some doctors and nurses received hugs, others only handshakes and our tearful thanks. I composed a letter to the hospital's president, which attempted to express our gratitude and admiration for the entire staff at Dartmouth Hitchcock. They were, and I'm sure still are, the finest trauma team that Jenna could have stumbled upon. They gave us our daughter back.

The day before Jenna was scheduled to be moved to the rehab hospital, there happened to be a small craft fair in the main lobby of the hospital. A number of small kiosks were set up displaying ceramics, quilting, hand-made scarves and hats – the usual assortment of local crafts. I began browsing through the selections, partly to kill time, partly thinking I might pick up a small souvenir for Jenna to mark the occasion of her departure.

I was admiring some hand-made, beaded necklaces, thinking that perhaps Jenna might like one. Her taste in clothing and jewelry had always been simple and down-to-earth. She had always been a pretty girl who did not require much jewelry or make-up.

As I browsed, my eyes were drawn to a beautiful small necklace made up entirely of small round stones – the exact same stones I had been collecting on the beach and giving to some of my students. I could not believe what I was seeing. It was perfect for Jenna, for the situation, for the message I was trying to send her. I was convinced it had been displayed there by the unseen force for me to find. It was too much of a coincidence.

Excited about my purchase, I hurried back to Jenna's room to find her battling yet another bout of nausea. One of her medications was causing it but a substitute medication had not yet been found that wouldn't irritate her stomach. A nurse was by her side performing some procedure, I can't remember what.

I couldn't wait to show Jenna what I bought for her.

"Jenna, honey, you know all about the kids I teach and how rough their lives are," I began. "They have to overcome incredible obstacles, a lot like you now, and sometimes it's really tough. It can wear anybody down." She looked out at me as the nurse was pushing some fluids into the PIK line that ran into her shoulder. "So sometimes I give them these little round beach stones that are just beautiful and I tell them how the stones were formed. Water and wind and sand pushing them around, day after day, grinding them and grinding them and trying to wear them down." Jenna and the nurse were both watching me intently now.

"Would you like me to leave?" the nurse asked thoughtfully.

"No, that's OK, you're welcome to stay," I replied. They both studied me as I pulled the small necklace from the bag.

"I never thought I would have to give some stones to one of my own kids," I said, half to myself. "I always thought I could protect you and spare you any real hardship. But now I guess we all know that's impossible. I just bought this necklace down in the lobby and I thought it was the perfect gift to mark your courageous battle and your move into the next phase of your recovery. You're going to win this battle", I told her. "You're as beautiful as ever and nothing is ever going to wear you down so much that you won't be strong and beautiful, just like the stones on this necklace."

Jenna was quiet, studying the necklace that I had placed in her only available hand. The nurse had looked away; she appeared to be wiping something from her eye.

62

PET THERAPY

The hospital that Jenna was moved to for her rehabilitation had another great feature besides being close to home and my school. It allowed dogs. Yes, dogs. Visitors could bring dogs right into the patients' rooms whenever they wanted.

About two weeks after the accident, we had brought our old golden retriever up to visit Jenna while she was at Dartmouth, but it was against the rules to bring him inside the hospital. I considered covering him under baby blankets and smuggling him in; we were so desperate for Jenna to have something positive in her life. But we were not the type to cause any problems. Instead, we maneuvered Jenna into a wheelchair (no small feat) and wheeled her down to one of the hospital entrances where Bailey greeted her as best he could under the circumstances. She had always loved animals of all denominations, but Bailey was her special baby and he knew it. The awkward meeting in the hospital entranceway did not have quite the therapeutic effect we all hoped for. Jenna was still struggling under the weight of all she had been through.

Now, at the rehabilitation hospital, things were different. Once Jenna was settled into her new surroundings, Bailey followed us up to Jenna's room just like he was any other member of the family. The hospital believed in the recuperative power of pets and encouraged people to bring them in. They even brought in their own therapy dogs on a regular basis. Jenna was so excited to be able to see and pet her baby regularly.

During the first visit, as soon as Bailey realized who it was in the bed, he jumped up on the bed before Carol or I could stop him. Of course he landed right on Jenna's injured legs and she let out a yelp. Carol and I were petrified he would crush what was left of her legs. In minutes though, we were all laughing as she snuggled him safely by her side, clear of any damaged body parts.

There was another reason why the hospital's pet policy was so important to us – actually two more reasons. Their names were Fenway and RemDawg. (Did I mention that Jenna was a big Red Sox fan?) Bailey enjoyed a couple of weeks of Jenna's undivided attention, but then the puppies arrived.

Bailey's brother, Bear, sired the puppies up in Maine. Bear belonged to Carol's brother, the doctor. Long before the accident, we had planned to take one of the puppies from the expected litter for Carol because Bailey was getting on in years. Carol was very attached to Bailey and didn't know what she was going to do without him when his time came. Our house was crazy as it was anyway, so I had agreed that Carol could have a puppy. What difference would a little puppy make?

Well, Carol's brother decided that Jenna should also have a puppy and offered her the pick of the litter. He told us it would be great for her motivation and recuperation. Everyone agreed. So now we were going to have two puppies.

There was no way I could walk through the main entrance to the hospital with a golden retriever puppy under each arm and not attract a bit of attention. But that is what I did almost every day. The puppies visited Jenna, but also the nurses on her floor, other patients, the therapists, children visiting other patients in the hospital, strangers in the parking lot – you get the picture. God bless those two little puppies because they really worked. They accomplished more than we ever could have imagined.

Jenna's spirits began to lift. Our conversations shifted from medications and how far she walked in therapy to laughter and playing and plans for the future. How long were they sleeping? Were they having a lot of accidents? They constantly wrestled on the floor of her hospital room and tugged at each other and a variety of dog toys providing hours of entertainment. Those puppies were signs of life moving on and we were grateful for the joy and motivation they brought with them. They were therapy for us all, and just what the doctor ordered.

63

WELCOME BACK

And so Jenna began her long road of physical rehabilitation while Carol and I tried to ease back into our own former lives. It was now early May and Carol was thrust into the end-of-the-year activities and kindergarten graduation. I headed back to school not quite sure what I was going back to. I had no idea what had been happening in my classroom. I felt like I was an alien; I was returning from a distant planet.

Everyone at my school was very gentle with me, both staff and students. I tried to express my appreciation for all the support, but it was difficult because expressing it always brought on more tears. My colleagues understood and we shared many unspoken hugs. I tried to spare my students from the gory details, but some wanted to know exactly what happened. I told them, as best I could, knowing full well that they expected nothing less than the truth from me.

I found myself looking at my students with new eyes after the accident. The kid who hit Jenna was driving a shitbox for a car. He had a drug problem and a dysfunctional family life. At nineteen years old, he could barely compose a sentence. I surveyed my students. They could all fit that description a few years from now. Which of these kids in my classroom were going to make a similar mistake and seriously injure or kill an innocent victim? I looked around the room, desperately studying their faces for clues that might tell me who it was. There was no doubt it could be any one of them in his shoes five or six years from now. And here I stood before them: powerless to prevent it.

The kids were surprisingly adorable, though, very sensitive - asking about Jenna and telling me about things that happened while I was out. They let me know exactly who had been taking care of Buddy, and who had not. They showed me work they had done with the substitute. In a way it was a bit weird, having them be so nice and thoughtful to me. I wasn't used to it. Nobody shouted "Hey, old man, where the fuck you been?" I should enjoy this while I can, I thought.

The second day of my return, an unexpected visitor showed up in my classroom near the end of the day. It was Nando, the kid who had hitchhiked to my house to rake my leaves, brainstormed the latex-balloon piñata fiasco, and nearly ran me over with a toboggan at the farm.

I was always happy to see former students, but to see Nando – with all our history – I was ecstatic. I hadn't seen him in quite some time. He was now in high school. He told me he was doing well, thinking about becoming a fireman. High school had gotten out early for the day and he just thought he'd stop by to see me. He had this sheepish look on his face, and I knew there was something on his mind.

"How you doin'?" he asked.

"Well," I began, "do you know anything about what has been going on in my life the past few weeks?" The accident had been reported in the newspaper, but I didn't know who really knew about it.

Nando looked at the floor, then at me, then back at the floor and nodded his head. "Are you alright?" he asked. "How's your daughter?"

Oh my God! All of a sudden it struck me. I realized he'd come here to check up on me, to see how I was doing! This young, tough, Latino gang-member wannabe, a budding street thug, had come back to his see his former schoolteacher. He was here to see *ME*, to make sure that *I* was all right. He had gotten word on the street that I was back in school, and he needed to see me for himself, to make sure I was OK.

I put my hand on his shoulder, composed myself and said, "She's alright, and she's getting better. Thanks for asking. We're all getting better. It's been a tough time, and it's gonna take a while, but we're all getting better."

Nando nodded. I saw something in his eyes as he looked back at me – though I'm not sure what it was, some sort of connectedness. We chatted for a while, mostly small talk, and then bid each other good-bye, promising to keep in touch.

There have been many, many times since I became a teacher for troubled youth when people have come up to me and said, "I don't know how you do it! How can you stand working with those tough kids? They're rude. They won't learn. They don't appreciate you. They don't appreciate anything."

If there were words to describe how I felt during Nando's visit, to describe the look in his eyes, the power that connects us, then people would understand why I work with at-risk kids. But there are no words, only emotions, connections.

Shit happens to people, even good people. Nobody knew that better than Nando. He had experienced more than his share of heartache in his young life. But somehow he has been managing to pull himself through. Nando instinctively knew that sometimes, in order to survive, you need to lean on people, especially the people you care about most. And he stopped by my classroom for me to lean on him a little. It was simple as that; no rocket science here.

So I leaned on Nando for a while that afternoon, and it really helped. I *was* getting better, too.

64

REHAB

Jenna spent the next five weeks at the rehab hospital working hard to regain the use of her legs. Carol and I visited her every day, sometimes more than once a day. Once the puppies arrived, they became daily visitors too. But I can't really say that we marked that period of time in the number of days or even weeks. Time, as we usually measured it, actually seemed to be suspended.

Instead, time was marked by how many degrees Jenna was able to bend her reconstructed knee. Or how many steps she was able to take around the hallway using her walker. We measured time by who had come to visit her that day or how long her physical therapy session lasted. We joyfully marked time by how much the puppies weighed – they were growing fast. When Jenna was finally able to take her first shower on her own, we knew that time must be passing. Another milestone was marked when they unwired her jaw and she was able to eat real food again.

As Jenna's condition continued to improve, so did mine and Carol's. We both managed to function well enough to get through the end of the school year. This happened to coincide with Jenna's release from the hospital. Finally, after eight incredibly long weeks at two hospitals, our daughter was able to return to our home.

Her brothers had moved her stuff out of her old apartment and put most of it into storage. We set up our computer room to become Jenna's new bedroom. It was downstairs so she would not have to negotiate steps and it was right next to the bathroom. We made a few minor alterations to the bathroom so a seat would fit into the bathtub for Jenna to use in the shower.

Carol and I drove her to physical therapy four, five, six times a week – sometimes even on weekends. We took her to follow-up appointments with the various doctors. We brought her to our water aerobics class where she quickly became a popular member of the group. We tried to get her to talk to a therapist so she could deal with the trauma and move on, but she was not ready. She told us she was doing fine. The dogs were therapy enough.

Eventually, she was able to walk up the street with us using crutches while we walked the dogs. Life continued to get back to normal, but Jenna was working hard every step of the way. At night she would stretch out her leg with a special brace while she watched the Red Sox. She would have us put weights on top of her knee to keep the pressure on. It was the old athlete in her, pushing herself to be her best. Getting her life back was her new sport now.

By August, Jenna was walking on her own, although with a pronounced limp because she could not yet straighten her bad leg. She was excited about a deal she had worked out with her grandma. If she could get herself on an airplane, Carol's mom would pay Jenna's expenses so she could attend her cousin's wedding in Puerto Rico. A lot of the family would be attending and we were all so grateful to have some happiness to celebrate. Jenna wasn't exactly dancing at the wedding, but she was pretty close to it, just happy to be there with everyone.

While we were down in Puerto Rico, Jenna had asked if we could go snorkeling; she thought she should be able to handle it. I found a place that led snorkeling tours to the various tropical reefs, but unfortunately the ship's captain had taken ill and was not going out again until after we were scheduled to leave the island. I was very disappointed and I briefly told the kind lady on the phone why.

"I'll tell you what you do," she said, sounding a lot like a grandma herself. "You go to this little marina on Beach Street and you rent snorkels and fins. It'll cost you six dollars a person. Then you drive to the state beach, you take the trail at the end of the beach and walk about a half mile." I started jotting down notes as she continued talking.

"When you come to a fork in the trail, go left and it will bring you out to a gorgeous beach. The reef is just out about 25 yards, you can't miss it."

Well, we carefully followed her directions and, sure enough, we enjoyed a whole afternoon of snorkeling among the most incredible fish we had ever seen. All this and it only cost eighteen dollars for the three of us. Exploring the reef, floating in the water, lying in the sun, I was beginning to relax and feel like the nightmare was finally over.

And yet, there was always an unsettled feeling lingering within every small pleasure. "Don't get used to this," my mind kept telling me. "There could be danger lurking just beyond the reef in the dark, murky water where you can't see clearly. Everything can change in the blink of an eye." I guess trauma does that to people. All kinds of trauma. All kinds of people.

65

COURT

When we returned from Puerto Rico, the air was full of promise and new beginnings. I dove into the back-to-school rituals with a vigor I had not felt in quite some time. There were workshops to attend and school materials to prepare. I would have a number of new students this year and a brand new classroom that boasted its very own utility sink. It sounds silly, I know, but small things like a utility sink in a classroom make a science teacher happy.

The location of the ALT school had been moved and the staff was all excited about a fresh new start– it was like having our own *do-over.* Plus, we were finally getting out of the basement! The school district had leased space for us in a commercial office building. There were upgrades, reconfigurations and accommodations required, but the work was progressing smoothly. The layout and location of the building held great promise for us and our little troop of delinquents. There would even be an intercom system to communicate with the office in case of an emergency.

Jenna's life began to settle into a routine as well. She began working at Carol's kindergarten as the 'closer', working from 3pm to 6pm each day taking care of the kids whose parents worked full-time. It was perfect for her since the hours were not too long and she was still able to have physical therapy every day. She was not yet ready to apply for a full-time teaching position, but at least she was working in the field of education.

Along with the expected chill of autumn arrived the equally expected but unsettling correspondence from the County Attorney's office and various lawyers. The case against the kid who had run down Jenna had been proceeding behind the scenes, following the slow but diligent pace of the criminal justice system.

A grand jury had been convened and an indictment was issued. A court date was slated for early December. Jenna would be expected to attend the court hearing and she should have a prepared victim's impact statement ready to be presented to the court. It was unclear exactly what the court would decide, but serious jail time was looming for the young defendant.

Jenna struggled to express in words the new reality that had become her life. Where should she begin? The physical scar tissue that permanently disfigured her young body would be a powerful opening. Or should she start with her inability to work or live on her own? What could she say to Anderson that would have any impact at all, let alone one that could even begin to compare with the actual impact his actions had on her?

Valiantly, Jenna composed her statement. She even agreed to read the statement out loud in court in the hope that Anderson would be finally forced to confront the consequences of his actions and perhaps, turn his life around for good. Carol and I had never been prouder of her courage and dignity. In the end, the victim's advocate offered to read her statement to the court knowing how difficult it would be for Jenna and for us. We were grateful.

"No sense putting you through any more pain. You've all been through enough," she told us.

On the morning of the court case, we quietly made the long drive to the Keene courthouse through a small snowstorm. It was the first time Jenna had been back near the scene of the accident. Carol and I sat with Jenna in court, as any parent would. Across the courtroom we watched as a young man was led in – a boy really – Anderson. He was remarkable only in his plain-ness; he could have been anybody. Nine months after the accident, the monster that nearly killed our daughter, now had a face to go with his name. I studied this face, looking for, what – remorse? Several times the anger and hatred in my gut rose up and I found myself listening to my breathing as I attempted to retain control of my body.

We were told to rise as the judge entered and the proceedings began, following some pre-ordained script that seemed only to be known to the judge, the court officials and the lawyers. Anderson had agreed to plead guilty and had been accepted into a substance abuse program. In fact he had already begun serving time at the county jail in advance of the expected sentence. We were spared the ordeal of a trial, which would have presented all the evidence of Jenna's shattered life. Papers were submitted and checked for the appropriate signatures. The judge asked questions and studied the paperwork. He seemed in no hurry. A sweaty, nervous Anderson occasionally stole furtive glances at us in the back of the courtroom.

I found myself, likewise, glancing over to *his* side of the room. Was that his father? No, it appeared to be someone from the newspaper. There were a few people sitting around, but none appeared to have any interest in the case. They must be next on the docket, I thought. "Where are his parents?" I found myself wondering. "Where is *his* family?" No one in the courthouse really seemed to care what happened to him.

Anderson was conferring with his lawyer, who had just been chastised by the judge for not following some protocol he should have known about. Anderson was all alone, I concluded. Abandoned by everyone who ever knew him or loved him. Facing jail time and whatever punishment the judge sought fit to render onto his young life, there was no one in the courtroom to offer him any support save a seemingly incompetent lawyer in a wrinkled grey suit. The sadness was inescapable.

When the appropriate time came, the judge allowed Anderson to stand and face Jenna to apologize for his actions. Though his grammar was poor and his words lacked eloquence, it was obvious that he truly regretted his actions on that fateful day in April and hoped that, in time, she would be able to recover and forgive him. Jenna, Carol and I, together, bit our quivering lips and our eyes glistened as we leaned on each other ever so softly for support, as any family would.

It was over now. We could get on with our lives. We drove back home through the quiet snow, each lost in our own thoughts.

66

JUST A HOCKEY GAME

A couple of days later, the guidance counselor at our school scored four free tickets for an upcoming Monarchs hockey game. The Monarchs were a semi-pro team who played locally and their games were a lot of fun, so I had heard. I had never been to see a game myself, not being a huge hockey fan. The counselor offered them up as a give-away for a behavior incentive at school. Stevie, the kid with the egg at the farm, happened to win the tickets and could invite a few friends to go with him to the game. There was just one problem: he needed someone to drive them.

"Pleeeeese, Rick? Can you please take us to the game?" Stevie pleaded.

Having no plans that night, I agreed. It felt like another step toward normalcy after the accident. I found out where to pick the boys up and told them to be ready at 6. It would cost me some gas and parking, and I knew I'd better have some cash on hand to buy them something to eat, but it was nice to be invited. One of the other guidance counselors agreed to meet us at the arena since he lived nearby and thought I might appreciate the help, which I did.

Walking into the arena with the game crowd, I realized this was a new and exciting experience for the boys. They were bouncing all over and chatting and taking it all in. We got settled in to our seats (which were located about as high as a person could sit in the huge ice arena) and in about five minutes, the boys were ready to go find something to eat.

I walked down to the concession stands with them, not wanting to let them out of my sight – they *were* my responsibility. The boys quickly noticed how the vendors had their wares displayed for customers to help themselves, especially bottles of beer and wine coolers. Kiddingly (I think) they pretended to purchase various items including beer, but ended up settling on some slushies. I watched them like a hawk as I paid for the drinks. They were darting around the various stands, touching everything, and asking how much things were. While I was monitoring them, I heard someone calling my name.

"Hey, Rick, how are you doing?" It was Rachel, our water aerobics instructor, who also happened to teach at another school in my district. "I didn't know you were a Monarchs fan." Rachel noticed how I seemed to be watching a small swarm of boys running between the vendors. "Are these your children? I thought your kids were older."

"Oh, they're not my kids, they're my students." I explained. "I brought them to the game. One of them won free tickets."

Rachel knew about my students. Everyone in the school district knew about my students. She looked at me like I was crazy. "Wow, you're brave," she gave the expected response as she observed them darting from vendor to vendor. I just smiled and gave her the obligatory raised eyebrows. What could I say?

Back up in our seats, we enjoyed a great game. The boys were especially psyched when a fight broke out on the ice between the two teams. "That was AWESOME!" declared Stevie. Most of the game was uneventful except for a little popcorn throwing among the boys and other kids sitting nearby.

I noticed that there seemed to be an unusually large number of young people in the audience and eventually the announcer told us why. The huge loudspeakers boomed as he welcomed students from a number of schools and organizations: Auburn Christian Academy, Saint Christopher's School, Bishop Brady High School, Manchester Bible School, Infant Jesus School, Saint Joseph's, Saint Mark's, School of Our Savior – on and on, dozens of schools and organizations affiliated with one religious group or another. I half-expected the announcer to welcome the small group of heathens from the Holy Shit Not-So-Immaculate Conception School. The boys could not understand why I was laughing so hard and couldn't stop.

On the way home, it was obvious that the boys had a fine time and did not want the night to end. Robbie called his mom and got her to agree they could all sleep over at his house. I told the other boys they would have to go home first and get permission from their parents before I would take them to Robbie's house for the sleepover. An interesting discussion followed.

"My dad won't care," Stevie announced. "He's always drunk. I'm sure he's shit-faced by now."

"Yeah? My dad is a drunk, too," chimed in Jason. "Sometimes he doesn't even know when I'm home."

At this point, Robbie joined in. "My dad used to smoke a lot of pot, but now he mostly just drinks. He buys these huge jugs of wine," he told them, gesturing with his hands.

I continued to drive in silence, just listening as the boys compared notes about their parent's substance abuse problems. When we got to Stevie's house, I told him his dad would have to come out and tell me if it was OK for me to bring him to Robbie's house for the sleepover. After a short time inside, Stevie burst back out through the front door carrying a pillow. A short, stocky man appeared behind him, a cigarette hanging from his mouth.

From inside the car, I greeted him and asked if he had agreed to let Stevie sleep over Robbie's house. He shrugged his shoulders and nodded his head slightly.

"I don't know the kid," he mumbled, "but I guess it's OK."

Slipping silently into parent mode, I said, "If you'd like, you can speak to Robbie's parents and make sure everything is OK." Robbie happened to be talking to his dad on his cell phone in the back seat.

"Yeah, yeah, maybe I should." His words were slurred but intelligible. Robbie handed him his cellphone.

What happened next must have been a strained, if not strange, conversation that ensued between the two drunken fathers. I could not really make out the specifics of what they were discussing there on the sidewalk, but some form of communication took place. I was satisfied I had done my part facilitating and modeling what a concerned parent should do in such a situation.

I dropped the boys off at Robbie's house, admonished them to stay out of trouble and get some sleep, and waited to make sure they got in the front door safely.

Back in school on Monday, all the boys seemed safe and happy and eager to tell everyone about the fight at the hockey game. And of course, all the other boys gathered around to listen. One of the older boys, Andrew, grew tired of listening to their stories.

He wandered over to me and said, "Yo, Rick, I just won some tickets to a hockey game too. When can you take me?"

"Let me get back to you on that, Andrew," I told him, not quite ready for yet another night on the town. "These fatherless boys are going to kill me," I thought to myself. "There's no end to them!"

67

NANDO'S TURN

The tiny white ceramic casket looked oddly like a frosted wedding cake with the blue flowers arranged on top of it. It rested solemnly at the front of the church on a small cart draped with silky white fabric. There were two more floral arrangements on the floor directly in front of it to complete the illusion of happier times.

Nando sat up front with his mother and sisters. He had somehow purchased a new suit for the occasion. From behind he appeared strong and tall and handsome. He kept his left arm wrapped around his mother who was struggling to keep her composure, while his stiff right arm clutched the top of the pew to hold them both up as everyone waited for the service to begin.

It was just two weeks earlier when Nando had showed up to visit me at school. His nephew Sidro, a student in my science class, had relayed the message that Nando wanted to stop by for a visit. Of course, I told him to come by anytime; former students of mine were always welcome. I hadn't seen Nando since he stopped by to see me after Jenna's accident. Besides, I was having a hard time getting Sidro to do his schoolwork, so I thought it might be a good idea to see if Nando held any leverage with him. Maybe he could give Sidro a good talking to and bring him to his senses. Lord knows, nothing I was doing was working with Sidro.

The actual timing of Nando's visit was ideal. I had just turned my class over to a guidance counselor for a class intervention: they were all yelling at each other, calling each other nasty things, and the entire class was about to erupt into an all-out brawl. My students were in no condition to learn science that particular day and I needed someone objective to intercede and restore calm. Even I needed to call for help sometimes.

As I left my classroom, I found Nando coming up the front stairs. "Nando!" I called, holding my arms out wide to greet him. I hugged him, surprised at how tall he had grown, and he gave me that silly grin he could never hold back. "Your timing is perfect!" I told him as I ushered him into a small conference room where we could visit.

He looked great: hair freshly gelled, tight jeans, silk shirt, a cheap, heavy silver chain draped around his collar. His pants were held up by a fancy, patterned belt and he wore the pointiest black leather shoes I had ever seen on a guy. Style had always been important to Nando and so, for today's visit, despite his impoverished finances, he was dressed to kill.

He was smiling and telling me he was back at the high school, determined to get his diploma. His plan was to attend the state fire academy next year after graduation. He was working at a coffee shop, living with his mother, but hoping to get a place of his own real soon.

We reminisced about the trip to the farm, sledding in the moonlight, and the time he and Toby hid in the back of my van so they wouldn't have to ride on the bus. We laughed as we recalled his idea to make piñatas in class. After a while, I struggled to keep composure as I asked him if he remembered the time he came to see me after Jenna's accident. My voice quivered as I told him how much that visit had meant to me. And just like that day, in that moment, in that room, we were again connected.

He asked how Jenna was doing and listened intently as I gave him a brief update. I told him she was doing well, still living with us at home, still recovering, occasionally substitute teaching in an elementary school. Nando nervously reached into his shirt pocket and pulled out a photo of a newborn baby. "This is my son, Antonio Immanuel," he declared. The baby's eyes were unmistakable; this was indeed Nando's son. I was surprised and congratulated him.

"He's beautiful!" I told him. "How old is he?"

"About two months. He was born premature. He lives with his mother in Greenville," Nando explained as he proudly gazed at the picture. He sat up a little taller in the chair as if to say, "I may only be eighteen, but I'm a father now. "

I had heard through the grapevine that Nando was in a serious relationship with someone. Sidro had told me that Nando took a bunch of pills one night and ended up in the hospital when he thought his girlfriend was cheating on him. Some of my students who knew Nando had made comments that he was totally crazy about this girl, but I had no idea they were expecting a baby. Not exactly sure what to say, I gently asked if he was still together with the mother, if he was going to be part of young Antonio's life.

He shrugged. He's not really with the mother anymore, he told me, but he's definitely going to do what he has to do for the baby. "I'm gonna be a father to him, that's for sure."

Nando spent the rest of the afternoon in my class. I introduced him as 'one of my favorite students of all time.' The kids asked him all sorts of questions and he tried to help out in the class as much as he could. At the end of the day he disappeared with Sidro at dismissal. I didn't even get a chance to say goodbye. I thought it was odd he could just leave like that, but social skills were never a strong point when you're working with at-risk kids. I guess sometimes it's easier to just walk away.

A week later, his nephew Sidro was having an awful day. He was in trouble in several classes and couldn't seem to focus on anything. Finally, he was sent to the assistant principal's office where he confessed that Nando's baby was very sick and might die. The baby was in Boston Children's Hospital. That was why he was having such a hard time concentrating. They were going to have to decide whether or not to pull the plug on the life-support machine that night.

The next day we received word that the baby had indeed died during the night. No one knew any details; we just felt awful for poor Nando and his family.

When arrangements for the funeral were made, I told the principal I would need to attend and she understood. She said the school secretary, also close to Nando, would be going to the church service as well.

Surprisingly, Sidro was in school the next day. I told him how sorry I was and that I would be going to the funeral. "Is there anything I could do?" I asked, knowing full well the foolishness of that question. "Do you have a lot of family coming in? Do you need any food?" I rambled on helplessly. Sidro didn't really respond, just nodded his head. He said Nando was doing OK, considering.

A few of Sidro's classmates asked if I would bring them to the funeral; they were friends of Nando also. "Sure, as long as you get permission from your parents," I told them.

On the morning of the funeral I was again surprised to see Sidro in school, sprouting a new haircut. "I thought you'd be needed at home today," I said to him. He just shook his head.

"Nando wants you to bring me to my aunt's house at 12:30," he informed me. I had been planning to go directly to the church for the service when my class was done. "He wants you to come over afterwards, too. My Grandma made a whole bunch of tamales. You gotta try em!"

I had Sidro call to see if it was all right if I just brought him with the other boys directly to the church, and that is what we did. Can you picture a middle-aged, Irish-looking man accompanying four large, tough Latino guys to the funeral for Nando's infant son? This was definitely never covered in any of my teacher preparation classes. When we entered the church, the boys immediately sat in the very back rows, each in their own pew. I guess they didn't want to be too close to each other, or to anybody else, in case they cried.

But we all cried some that day. How can anybody not cry at a baby's funeral?

From what I could see, baby Antonio's mother did not cry much though. She sat in the front of the church on the opposite side from Nando's family. Her colored hair, hoop earrings, makeup and black mini-skirt were unsettling. She's probably in shock, I rationalized. She, too, appeared to be about eighteen years old, although I had been told she also had a two-year-old daughter with another guy. Afterward, I was informed that she was sitting with her new boyfriend.

The priest and lay ministers did their best to comfort everyone during the service and the guitar music was hauntingly beautiful. But it was, after all, a baby's funeral, and there can be no comfort in that.

At the snow-covered cemetery, the wind was blowing hard and the temperature was probably in the upper teens. The small crowd huddled together, but there was no warmth on this winter day in the children's section of the cemetery. It overlooked the Salvation Army Thrift Store in the distance, adding to the sadness. After the priest led us in some prayers, cards with Antonio's picture and a short prayer were passed around as a memento of his short life. We were instructed to take one of the flowers to remind us of the life that had slipped away, and then the priest left us for the warmth of his car.

The sad group remained standing there around the casket, no one knowing what to do or say. After a few minutes Nando went over to the large SUV the family must have borrowed or rented for the day, opened all the doors, and turned on the stereo as loud as it would go. Reggaton music blared out over the somber gathering. It must be a cultural thing, I thought, never having experienced this before. Respectfully, everyone stood around the casket shivering quietly, listening to the music.

Nando's older sister stepped carefully through the snow over to the baby's mother and invited her to come over to their house afterwards for some food. "No, my family will not be coming over," I overheard the cold reply.

Eventually, after several songs, I went up to Nando who was standing next to the casket and put my hand on his shoulder. "This is the hard part, Nando," I softly told him. "You have to let him go now. It's OK; he's at peace. Say goodbye to him. You have to let him go." I squeezed his shoulder, walked by the casket taking a single white rose, and walked through the snow over to the line of cars. I did not look back, but I could hear others following my lead.

Back at the sparse apartment where Nando's sister lived, there were a bunch of little kids running around and the women were all gathered in the kitchen getting the food ready. I placed the boxes of pastry I brought onto the table and a little boy tried to grab one immediately. "Not so fast," Nando's mother said as she slapped his little hand. "You can have these later"' and she scooted her grandson away.

My students and I went into the living room and tried to think of things to talk about. Nando was outside smoking a cigarette. I had chatted with him briefly when we first got there, but it was obvious that he just wanted to be left alone. Nando's mother kept telling us to sit down but there was only one little couch for the five of us, so we just stood around chatting and watching the little kids.

The smell of tamales began to drift in from the kitchen and the women's voices rose as they argued about whether or not the baby's mother was actually laughing at the funeral. Two little boys jumped on plastic cars and squealed as they rode them like skateboards across the living room floor. This was Nando's family, I thought. This was whom he would be leaning on for support as he found his way through this, his roundest of places.

Eventually I made my way back into the kitchen and once again expressed my sorrow to the family for their loss. I hugged Nando's mother and wished them all happier times. The women placed some tamales in a plastic container for me to take home. "Don't eat the corn husk," they advised me.

Sitting behind my steering wheel, I contemplated the day's events as my car found its way safely home to my own family. It was the day before Christmas Eve. There was so much to be done. I looked forward to spending the holiday with my family and the taste of fresh tamales.

68

INVESTING IN THE FUTURE

The holidays finally over, the cold winds of New Hampshire provided a numbness that was both painful and comforting in its normalcy. All was as it should be in January: snow, ice, long nights. Just keep plodding along; the whole year lay ahead, despite the fact they none of us ever really know where our path will lead.

The day started out as just another routine day, blending in perfectly with the mid-winter doldrums that were upon us. I had arrived at school early as usual and was getting my classroom and lesson plans ready. I removed the chairs from on top of the tables and made a few minor adjustments in the placement of the tables. I logged into the computer to check for any pressing e-mails about meetings I was expected to attend.

I began typing some instructions for an assignment into the computer and, before long, one of my 6th grade students, Jermaine, arrived in my room, making small talk as he did almost every morning. His mom dropped him off on her way to work and so he was at school before most of the other kids.

I noticed almost immediately that Jermaine was very fidgety today; something seemed to be up. I asked if everything was OK, and he looked at me, startled, and insisted he was fine. "Why?" he asked. I knew Jermaine well enough to know there was something he wasn't telling me. After a little prodding, I finally got it out of him.

Jermaine pulled out a fairly large wad of bills from his pocket – mostly singles, but a couple of fives thrown in, too. He was always trying to show off, to appear important to the other kids, and to anyone who would give him the attention. This would certainly gain everyone's attention today; that was for sure.

"Jermaine! What are you doing with that?" I asked.

"I'm going to buy some stuff, that's all. Promise you won't say anything!" His eyes pleaded with me for complicity.

"What are you getting into?" I replied. "You know nothing good is going to come from this. Tell me what you're going to buy." I insisted.

"It's nothing," he assured me. "Forget I even showed it to you."

"Jermaine. You know that I can't forget it. It's going to get you in trouble." He knew I cared about him and I was not going to let this pass.

"Alright." He sat down on a stool and gave a loud sigh. "I'm going to buy a bunch of tech-decks from some of the kids."

"Tech-decks?" I repeated, incredulous. "All that money for tech-decks?" Tech-decks were the latest craze in the middle school. They were miniature skateboards in various designs that the boys skated all over with their fingers. Some of the kids could do all sorts of fancy tricks – flips, twists, whatever – the tricks all had weird skateboard names. Teachers found them to be a major nuisance and distraction. Besides, they were often stolen and the cause of many fights and arguments.

Jermaine was smiling at me with his sheepish grin.

"You know that someone is going to try to steal your money from you and it's going to be a problem, right?" I tried to use logic to get some sense into his adolescent brain. He studied his sneakers, a sure sign that I had gotten through to him.

"Give me the money," I said softly. " I'll hold onto it until the end of the day and give it back to you before you get on the bus. That way it will be safe." I held out my hand. Surprisingly, Jermaine placed the wad of bills right into my hand without an argument. I counted it out, twenty-four dollars in all, and placed it in my wallet, telling him it would be safe there. He was doing the right thing. I told him to come and see me at the end of the day and I would return it, safe and sound.

The school day proceeded as usual. I had some good classes and some not-so-good classes, but overall, it was a pretty good day. During my last period, I was working with a group of eighth-graders. We were gathering data about paper airplanes using an electric paper plane launcher. The lesson was really about the process of using data to draw conclusions, but many of the kids were caught up in the excitement of launching their creations in the electric launcher.

Jermaine came into the room. "I'm here for my . . . you know," he stammered, giving me a look with his eyes. I had totally forgotten about the bills in my wallet until his presence reminded me.

"Oh, yeah, right!" I said taking out my wallet. This got the attention of some of the eighth-graders. "Here you go," I said giving him a dollar bill, while the kids near me looked on. Jermaine stood his ground. He just looked at me and smiled, his hand remained outstretched.

"You're right," I said suddenly. "You *were* good today. I think you should get more than a dollar." Now I had the attention of the entire class. I put another dollar into his hand. Still Jermaine held his hand out and smiled.

"More? You think you deserve more?" I could tell Jermaine was happily going along with the joke. "You're right. You were REALLY good today, Jermaine. I tell you what," I said to him, "I'm going to keep putting money into your hand until you tell me to stop. That's how good you were today!" I started pulling out bills and piling them into his hand, one at a time. Mouths were literally dropping open among the eighth-graders. The only sound in the room was one of money being pulled from my wallet and slapped into Jermaine's outstretched hand.

"OK, we're into the fives now. Tell me when to stop." The speechless eighth-graders continued to watch in silent amazement.

When I reached twenty-four dollars in Jermaine's hand, he said, "That's enough, I'm OK with this." He stuffed the bills into his pocket and shot me a smile as he quickly darted out of the room.

"Are you crazy?" someone asked.

"Crazy?" I replied. "That was an opportunity, an investment in our future. That kid is going to be good for me now for the rest of the year, maybe even his whole life! It was worth every dollar." I pretended to get back to what I was doing, acting as if it was just another ordinary day.

"I was good today," said Josh from across the room, sitting up very straight at his desk. He was studying me for my reaction.

"Me too!" chimed in Lisa.

All the kids in the room were studying me now, waiting for my reaction.

"Yeah, you guys *were* good today, that's true." I responded smiling and nodding. "But not *that* good. Maybe tomorrow."

Secretly, I wished I did have access to just a tiny bit of the venture capital I helped to raise in my former life. I wanted to invest in *all* of their futures. Every one of them. I wondered if I could make a difference in their outcomes. Could anyone?

69

MAKING THE CONNECTION

Almost a year after Jenna's fateful accident, I found myself tossing and turning in bed. The numbers on the clock changed – 3am, 4am, 5am – but I was unable to sleep and unaware of what was keeping me up. I told myself that this recent pattern was nothing unusual, that lots of people have trouble sleeping as they grew older.

My mind rambled between what was scheduled for the day, my family, my students and lesson plans, the bills I was struggling to pay, my former life with its big, fat paycheck, the accident. People and events were all swirling together in a crazy pattern that was somehow connected through me in a strange and mysterious way. My life was getting back to normal, but it was a *different* normal now. There always seemed to be an uneasiness floating around me, a restlessness I could not describe, something unfinished that needed to be done.

As Carol lay sleeping by my side, I struggled to find a comfortable position and a few more desperate minutes of sleep. My mind would not, could not, shut itself off. In a blinding flash of insight, I suddenly realized what needed to be done, why I couldn't sleep. There was no question about it: I needed to tell my story, the whole thing. That's it; it's all connected! *We're* all connected! All of us! It was the only thing that made any sense. Why did it take me so long to figure it out?

And so I began to write. There were so many stories I needed to tell. It seemed overwhelming at first, but if I wrote a little each night, it was possible. I could do this; I could tell this crazy story. One step at a time - that's the only way anything ever gets accomplished in this mixed up world we live in. One day at a time, one story at a time, one kid at a time.

There were specific people who needed to hear this story, not the least of which was my family. Carol had been with me every step of the way. In many ways it was her story too. But my kids really needed to know why I walked away from the big paycheck, why I work with those awful, pathetic, incredible children. My kids need to know who their father really is.

My own parents needed to hear this story as well. They needed to know exactly who their son had become. They deserved more than a fifteen-minute conversation when we got together for the holidays or a superficial phone call. In fact, I realized that they could still play a major role in helping me piece this whole mess that had become my life together.

At eighty-years-old, my mom was not doing so well down in Florida. She was lonely, depressed and her health seemed to be failing. I decided to write a chapter each night and e-mail it to my mom. My e-mails would give her something to look forward to each day and something to talk about with my dad and with me. And selfishly, the commitment to e-mail her a chapter each day would provide me with the discipline needed to get the story written.

And of course, there were others, including you, who needed to hear this story as well.

A couple of months into the writing, I was feeling focused and confident. The stories were spilling out of my memory in vivid detail, each one leading to new landmarks along my journey. I began to realize just how far I had come, how far we all have to travel sometimes to find out who we really are and what we can become. There was just one small problem: I had no idea how my story was going to end. In fact, *was* it ever going to end?

Once again, Jenna's fate and my own became intertwined. It was now June, fourteen months since the accident, and Jenna had made remarkable progress. She was even applying for full-time teaching positions for the following school year. She had interviewed at a few schools and remained optimistic about landing a teaching job, but as yet, there were no job offers. One of her eyes began bothering her – it had been tearing constantly ever since her facial surgery. Her plastic surgeon had passed it off as a minor annoyance, just another thing she would have to live with.

Jenna's eye continued to swell and, after a couple of days, she went to the doctor thinking she had contracted conjunctivitis. After a few more days on antibiotics, she looked and felt worse than ever.

It just so happened that my son, Scott, and his girlfriend Amy had recently become engaged and were having a party that weekend at their house to celebrate. Jenna wanted to go with us, despite her swollen face. Her accident had brought our whole family closer together. She was especially appreciative of the fact that Scott and Amy were still making her car payments for her since she could not yet afford them on her own. Her presence at the party was partly to show her appreciation for all they had done for her.

Lots of young people showed up at the party – friends of our kids from when they grew up, college friends, acquaintances from work. Single people, fun people, vibrant people in the prime of their lives. Jenna spent most of the day sitting uncomfortably next to her grandmother and great aunts, in obvious pain, her eye red and swollen. But as always, Jenna was trying to make the best of an awkward situation.

Carol and I shared her pain that day. Not just the physical pain that was surely throbbing against her eye, but her emotional pain as well. We were acutely reminded of her loneliness and isolation, the youth and vitality that she had been robbed of during one fateful afternoon jog. Her life was not at all like those of the other young, happy, carefree partygoers. No, this nightmare would never end for her.

At home the next day, we took Jenna to the local emergency room because her eye was now swollen shut and she was in agony. She was put on an immediate intravenous dosage of antibiotics and we were told she needed to go directly to the hospital for a CAT scan to see what was going on. Here we go again, we thought.

After the scan at the hospital, it was decided Jenna needed to travel the two hours up to Dartmouth to see her plastic surgeon. Her tear duct was apparently being blocked by a small piece of titanium that had been placed there to support the eye socket. Once at Dartmouth, the ophthalmologist who had come in on a Sunday afternoon just to see Jenna decided she would probably need surgery. He recommended we take her immediately to Massachusetts Eye and Ear Infirmary in Boston, three hours away. This is an absolute nightmare, we thought as we drove through the never ending darkness, arriving around midnight.

After hours in the waiting room and the usual questions that we had grown so accustomed to, date of birth, on a scale of one to ten . . . Jenna was admitted to a hospital room around 4am. Carol and I found ourselves sleeping once more on the floor of a small hospital lounge down the hall from her room. We needed to be nearby when the doctors made their rounds at 6am. This nightmare knew nothing of sleep.

To make a long story short, she spent another week in the hospital, another surgery was scheduled and completed, the infection was drained and began to subside. We drove hours for follow-up visits, received more medical bills, and knew one thing with absolute certainty: this nightmare will never end. It may subside for a while, like the infection in Jenna's face, but it will not end. This nightmare has become our past, present and future. We are all going to have to learn to live with it.

At the end of June, with Jenna once again on the mend and school out for the summer, Carol and I decided to take a small, but badly needed, vacation. We drove down to Washington, DC, pulling our old camper. I had purchased tickets to see the Red Sox play in Baltimore for Carol's birthday. We desperately needed a break and some time together, just the two of us, and we had never before visited our nation's capitol.

We were thoroughly enjoying our time together, taking in all the usual sites and monuments. We found time to talk, to relax, to enjoy each other's company – things we had not really allowed ourselves to do in a long, long time. We were perfectly anonymous among all the crowds herding around Washington's national monuments for the 4th of July. After all we had been through, it felt oddly intoxicating.

One morning, we rose early and took the Metro into the city to visit the Holocaust Museum. We heard you had to get there early if you wanted tickets. Standing in line, we were asked if we were members of the military – we could go to the front of the line if we were, a nice gesture for the troops serving our country.

"No, we're just teachers. I don't suppose that qualifies us for anything, does it?" I responded in good humor.

The woman standing in line in front of us turned around and her mouth dropped open.

"Oh my God," she practically screamed. "I overheard you say something about being teachers, and for some strange reason I thought about Jenna! I can't believe this!" Now she was hugging Carol and me. We were all in disbelief that this was happening.

Christine, the teacher Jenna had done her student teaching with in New Hampshire, was bubbling over with excitement. It seemed like eons ago when Carol, never having met her in person, had spoken to her on the phone after the accident. Carol had broken down and sobbed uncontrollably in the middle of their first conversation providing an update on Jenna's condition. Christine had been one of the first to visit Jenna in the hospital after the accident. She was a sweetheart, a fabulous teacher, and Jenna had loved the time spent in her classroom. Christine had since moved to Virginia, and now here she was, at the Holocaust Museum, hundreds of miles from our home, asking us, "How is Jenna doing?"

With the throngs of tourists visiting DC for the holiday, and the vast number of museums and sites for visitors to see, I was convinced that this could be no coincidence. There was definitely some higher power working here behind the scenes, a power over which we had no control. The lives of certain people were undeniably tied together in unexpected and inexplicable ways. Some people were meant to be connected. There was no other way to explain it, and there was certainly no escaping it. It was one more piece of mounting evidence that we are all connected on this planet, every one of us.

70

DENZEL'S STONE

Two weeks later I was once again walking along a beach on Cape Cod with Carol, but this time I was purposefully searching for stones to add to my collection. As we strolled along the serene stretch of deserted beach, a light rain blew down from the clouds. I must have stepped over millions of well-worn beach stones. Every so often I would spot one worth picking up and place it securely in my pocket.

Carol tried to help pick out stones as she looked for fragments of sea glass, but she finally confessed, "I'm not quite sure what you're looking for."

"I'm not quite sure myself," I told her. "Somehow I just seem to know one when I see it."

My pockets were quickly filling and I found myself becoming increasingly selective about which stones to pick up and which to leave in the sand.

"No, not you," I would say to a stone as I put it back down. "I'm sorry," I apologized. There were so many stones, and so many truly beautiful ones. But I could not save them all. I could only bring a few with me to their new life. I thought about Andrew and my hedging about taking him to the hockey game. I suppose he was one of the rejected stones, one I had to leave on the beach.

The last stone I had given out had occurred just a few weeks earlier, on one of the last days of school before summer vacation. The kids were outside playing basketball and throwing a football around during recess. I was assigned to help monitor them and I noticed some friction between Denzel and the other kids. Denzel kept instigating fights with some of the smaller kids. I spoke to him once about keeping his cool and then found I had to speak to him several more times to diffuse the tension.

I had developed a good relationship with Denzel over the course of the school year. He was often hungry and knew he could usually count on me to give him some peanut butter crackers or some juice to keep his voracious appetite at bay. He was a hard-working student and I could always depend on him to help me with just about anything I needed help with. I had even written him a letter of recommendation for a job as a bagger at the local supermarket.

So that day I finally had to pull him aside, away from the other basketball players, to find out what was going on. I asked him why he was having such a hard time controlling himself and getting along with everybody.

"They're pushing me around," he told me, his defenses all up.

"Well, that's not exactly what I was seeing on the basketball court," I tried to sound factual.

"They were!" he insisted. "They were all pushing me around. Everybody's always pushing me around," he claimed. "I'm tired of everybody always pushing me around!"

"Denzel," I spoke to him calmly. "You're a big, strong kid. Everybody likes you. I never see anybody pushing you around. Exactly *who* is pushing you around?"

"Everybody!" he was getting excited now. "The kids! My mother! Everybody!"

"Your *mother* is pushing you around?" I asked. A big, strong Jamaican woman, I knew she *could* be intimidating if she chose to be.

"All the time!" he said. "Do this! Do that! And now I'm grounded for I don't know how long! This whole summer is really gonna suck!" OK, now we're getting to it. So *this* is what it's all about, I thought.

"Denzel, come with me. There is something I want to give you," I told him as I led the way inside the school building and upstairs to my classroom.

"You got something to eat?" he asked as he obediently followed me.

"I've got something better than that," I told him.

In my classroom, Denzel watched expectantly as I pulled down the green plastic alien head from its watchful perch on top of my cabinet. I pulled out some of my beach stones and placed them on the desk examining them closely until finally choosing one he would like. With a permanent marker I wrote my phone number on one side of it. I held it tightly in my hand for a moment, and then placed it into Denzel's hand.

"Squeeze it hard," I told him. "It feels good, doesn't it? Strong, solid, smooth?"

Denzel nodded, his eyes sharply focused on mine.

"The only way that this stone could get this way is by being pushed around, pushed around a lot. The wind, the sand and water, they were constantly pushing this stone around," I spoke slowly, calmly, purposefully. I could see in his eyes that he was beginning to *get it.* "But this stone is strong," I continued, "It's solid and it's beautiful the way it's been polished so smooth."

His head continued to nod as he grasped both the stone and the full meaning of what I was telling him.

"Your Mom loves you. She cares about you more than anything in the whole world," I told him. "That's what parents do. That's why she's pushing you around. She's making sure you're strong, solid, polished. She's doing her best to make you the person she knows you can become. I want you to keep this stone and hold onto it whenever things get tough."

We were both quiet for a few minutes as I gathered the other stones and placed them back in the plastic alien head.

"I'm think I'm ready to back outside now," Denzel finally said.

"I think you are too," I replied.

About ten o'clock that night my phone beeped with a text message: "Hey, Rick! U there? It's me Denzel."

"Wazzup," I texted back.

"U got anything to eat?" flashed the message on the cell phone.

71

WRAPPING IT UP

It is time for me to wrap up my story, or my stories, as it were. I know it is time, just as surely as a wave knows when it is time to crash upon the beach. Another summer has come and is almost gone. The rhythm of a new school year looms ahead of me and there are a million things that need to be done to get ready for my next wave of students. I am finally ready to send my story off on it's own journey.

It seems fitting that I write this last chapter as I sit in a hospital cafeteria with an undetermined amount of time to ponder the wonder of it all. A year and a half after Jenna's fateful accident finds me once again waiting for the word she is back in the recovery room where I will be allowed to see her. This latest surgery is to insert a small tube or stent into her blocked tear duct so that it will not become infected again. In the general scheme of things, it is a minor surgery, and she is just one of hundreds of patients who will have some sort of surgical procedure here today at the bustling hospital.

But for me, my presence here at the hospital represents part of a much larger cycle - one of adversity, determination and hope. I am surrounded by the cycle of *becoming*. Undoubtedly, Jenna will have more surgeries and challenges as she struggles to overcome the life-altering events of that routine afternoon jog. A positive energy deep in my gut assures me she will recover again, another step along her journey to become the amazing young lady she is destined to become. She has triumphs and joys yet to be experienced that cannot even be imagined at this point in her young life. She swims in the current of her own becoming.

Waiting for the phone call that will inform me that she is out of surgery, I find myself reflecting on how far I, too, have travelled and who I have become over the course of the past seven years. No one could have predicted the difficult challenges I would have to face, or precisely what forces would be there to help pull me through. Some of it was determined by accident, some by my own stubborn determination, and some was a result of sheer dumb luck. But I can't help feeling that all of it was *meant* to be, although I'm not going to begin to speculate why.

What began years ago as a dream for personal and financial success –

my version of the American Dream - eventually turned into a nightmare of corporate despair. That, in turn, gave birth to new dreams, each with their own nightmares and more dreams interwoven into them. Dreams and nightmares, nightmares and dreams – are we *ever* truly awake, truly aware of our own potential?

In a few hours, when I hold Jenna's hand in the recovery room and get her to smile, I will be awake. When I bring her home and watch Carol hug her, I know I will be awake. When I walk the dogs, or cook some food, or make phone calls to my family to touch base, I am wide awake. And of course, I am very much awake in my classroom. Awake is what we *do* in between the dreams and the nightmares. It's the only thing that's real, the only thing we really have any sort of control over.

This brings me to the reason I felt compelled to tell you my story. For one thing, it gave me something to *do,* some sense of control over the unpredictable current of events surrounding me. It roused me from my fitful insomnia and brought reality into focus. And of all people, it was *you* who woke me up. *You.*

So it is time to wrap up my story, literally. I am going to wrap it up and seal it inside a large manila envelope – several envelopes, actually. If you are reading this, it means that at least one of my packages successfully arrived at its destination.

Most of the envelopes will be addressed to a publisher or literary agent. I have never been published before so I have no idea when, or *if,* my story will ever be published. That chapter of my story will be out of my hands. My part was to write it – the rest is all up to fate, or chance or luck – or maybe a combination thereof.

I hope it does get published though, because this world can never have too many stories about hope and determination. People need to hear about the connections we all share. Along my journey I have come across people facing incredible pain, frustration and hardships of every nature. From time to time, we all find ourselves in the roundest of places, and we just need a little encouragement to get through, someone to lean on, someone to give us a stone we can hold onto.

One of my packages, however, is destined for something – no *someone* - special. It has an entirely different destination and purpose. It may also provide some hope and a bit of encouragement in a very round place and, if it does, I am just as glad as if it had reached millions through a national publisher. But make no mistake; my intention for this particular package is entirely selfish. I need something in return. It's going to cost you.

I need *you* to hear my story. I need you to *know* my family and me. I need you to make the connection. I work with kids like you every day, trying to bring some sunshine into their dark little lives, maybe even providing some light at the end of their tunnels. But unfortunately, many of them can't see it. And don't think for a minute that I am the only person who does this. We are all over the place, working every day to change outcomes, your outcome, even though you might not realize it, and we may never know how it turns out.

I want you to understand how our lives are now inextricably woven together. The choices you make affect me, and others around us. Everything you do makes a difference to me, for now, and for the unforeseeable future. We are all connected on this planet, every one of us, and we can't escape it no matter how fast we run or how we try to hide.

The stories I have told are all true. A small part is about me, and how I was able to change my whole life around. But most of it is actually about how *other people* have struggled to turn their lives around. The real story is about *them*. And of course, there is a huge chapter that as yet remains unwritten. It will be up to you to write it.

You too have had your share of hardship and nightmares. The police reports and depositions have painted an ominous picture of your young life. I can only imagine what it was like to be abandoned by drug-addicted parents in a day care center, to be smoking pot regularly at ten years old, to be lost in the bureaucracy of the social system, craving your next fix. I know you have spent time in the roundest of places.

But now it is time for you to dream. In fact, I need you to dream, not about who you are or who you were, but about who you would like to be – the person you *can* be. And I need you to stay awake while you do so, staying on the road to your own recovery without veering off, without causing any more collateral damage. I need you to become the person you were meant to become. It's the only way either one of us can ever fully recover from the events that have connected us.

I am enclosing a small stone in your envelope, a little symbol you can hold onto from time to time. I hope the prison guards will let it pass through security. It is surprising how harmless and yet how powerful such a small beach stone can become, all at the same time. As you can see, I am not yet able to write my phone number on the back of it. The wearing down of the past eighteen months has surely helped me become stronger, but I am not yet that strong, the pain still too raw. You are going to have to do this on your own, without my help or support. But you can do it. You can write the next chapter.

We cannot change the past, Anderson; that much is true. But we can change ourselves, one step at a time. We can actually become people we could not even imagine.

I did it. I know you can do it too. I have a sense about these things. And I'm usually pretty much right on target. You see, I am one of those rare people who truly recognize the power and inner strength you possess from being so worn down. I *get* you.

And so, Anderson, I give you my story, along with a small round stone. It is all I have to give. I hope it will be enough.

72

EPILOGUE OR PROLOGUE?

The day after completing the last chapter of my story, I was painting the room in our house that was for many years our old bedroom. More recently it had been serving as our computer room. Jenna has been living in it for over a year now and she is ready for a new look. The room had not been painted since she was a baby and the carpet smelled faintly of dogs and mildew. Jenna and her brother had finally ripped out the carpet and stripped off the wallpaper while Carol and I were on vacation in Washington. I was now painting the walls a color Jenna had carefully selected. It was a happy project, a labor of love. We had no idea how long Jenna would be living with us and we wanted her to feel comfortable, to feel at home.

Jenna lay on the couch in the living room with a frozen bag of peas on her eye, still swollen from the surgery of the previous day. The phone rang and Carol answered it, nodding occasionally and asking few questions.

The victim's advocate informed her of Anderson's release from jail. He had been a model inmate at the county correctional facility and it was not unusual to have a sentence reduced for good behavior. He had served eight months instead of the twelve he was sentenced to. It had nothing to do with us, she told Carol. It was how the system worked. She just thought we should know.

It was difficult news to swallow for all of us, especially Jenna, whose sentence would never be commuted. I thought it an odd coincidence that Anderson should begin his new life just as I completed writing my story. Again, it was almost as if it were meant to be, unseen powers at work.

"No matter," I thought to myself. "I'm still sending him the story, and the stone too. He'll need it more than ever now."

Some stories never really end. They just keep winding themselves into new stories.

ABOUT THE AUTHOR

In the Roundest of Places is Rick Lydon's debut novel. He hesitates to label it as a novel since the events described in it are essentially all true to the best of his recollection.

Rick Lydon lives with his wife Carol and their two golden retrievers in New Hampshire. He teaches middle school science in Nashua, New Hampshire, where he continues to work with at-risk youth. In his spare time he enjoys outdoors activities, including hiking, biking and strolling along the beach. His daughter Jenna continues to make remarkable progress in her recovery.

27867701R00131

Made in the USA
Charleston, SC
21 March 2014